# Ask the Master

## Also by Harold Klemp

Ask the Master, Book 1
Be the HU
The Book of ECK Parables, Volume 1
The Book of ECK Parables, Volume 2
The Book of ECK Parables, Volume 3
The Book of ECK Parables, Volume 4
Child in the Wilderness
The Living Word
Soul Travelers of the Far Country
The Spiritual Exercises of ECK
The Temple of ECK
The Wind of Change

The Mahanta Transcripts Series
Journey of Soul, Book 1
How to Find God, Book 2
The Secret Teachings, Book 3
The Golden Heart, Book 4
Cloak of Consciousness, Book 5
Unlocking the Puzzle Box, Book 6
The Eternal Dreamer, Book 7
The Dream Master, Book 8
We Come as Eagles, Book 9

MAHANTA

This book has been authored by and published under the supervision of the Living ECK Master, Sri Harold Klemp. It is the Word of ECK.

# Ask the Master

## Book 2

### Harold Klemp

ECKANKAR
Minneapolis, MN

**Ask the Master,** Book 2

Compiled by Sharon Douse and Mary Carroll Moore
Edited by Joan Klemp and Anthony Moore

Cover photo by Luanne Lawton
Cover photo hand-colored by Peg Bonner
Text illustrations by Ron Wennekes

**Library of Congress Cataloging-in-Publication Data**

Klemp, Harold.
    Ask the master / Harold Klemp.
      p.  cm.
    ISBN 1-57043-013-6 (v. 2) : $11.00
    1. Eckankar (Organization)—Doctrines.  2. Spiritual life—
Eckankar (Organization)  I. Title.
BP605.E3K54   1993
299'.93—dc20                          93-70681
                                            CIP

*When one is an infant, he is often a self-centered, selfish person. Because he is helpless, he is used to the world catering to his whims. All the baby has to do is cry or whine to get attention. Of course, sometime between infancy and adulthood, the individual learns that he's got the workings of the world backward: He is to serve life; life does not serve him. Until this lesson hits home, he is not understanding the purpose of Soul's reincarnation, which is to become a Co-worker with God.*

—Sri Harold Klemp

# Contents

vii

viii

ix

# Introduction

When you're traveling the road to God, you venture into uncharted territory. Sometimes a crossroads appears: Which direction do you turn? Decisions made in the smallest parts of your life can affect your journey. How do you make those decisions? Is there anyone who has been there before and can answer a seeker's questions?

The sincere seeker of truth often finds his deepest questions unanswered and his inner experiences with the Light and Sound unexplained. Where can he find a modern Master who has successfully traveled the road to God—and come back to tell about it?

Sri Harold Klemp is one such Master. He is the Mahanta, the Living ECK Master. As the spiritual leader of ECKANKAR, he receives thousands of letters from seekers of truth around the world. All want direct and helpful answers about traveling the road to God. Sri Harold responds to many of these letters personally, sharing insights and advice from his experience. In this book questions and answers from over two hundred of his letters are compiled.

Topics covered are diverse. Among them are the

value of spiritual exercises, self-discipline, planning versus surrender, how to avoid creating karma, divine love and human love, what we learn from our children and our pets, how spiritual healing really works, and how to love God more. *Ask the Master,* Book 2, is the second volume of this valuable guide to living a life of joy and service.

Contemplating on these topics will benefit the spiritual seeker at any stage in his journey home to God.

If you are successful with the spiritual exercises, you ought to become aware of either the Light or Sound. You may also meet the Inner Master, who always awaits the individual who is sincere in seeking truth.

# 1

## Spiritual Exercises

*What is the purpose of ECKANKAR and the spiritual exercises? Will they take me where I want to go spiritually?*

The whole focus of ECKANKAR is direct experience of the Light and Sound of God. This can come through practice of the Spiritual Exercises of ECK.

Different spiritual exercises are given in the ECK books. Look especially in *The Spiritual Exercises of ECK*. Simply try them, and see if they work. Don't push yourself, though. There's no reason to.

If you are successful with the spiritual exercises, you ought to become aware of either the Light or Sound. You may also meet the Inner Master, who always awaits the individual who is sincere in seeking truth.

Some people have quite an active inner life and travel widely in the inner worlds; others are quite content to let Divine Spirit guide them indirectly in their daily lives. Let any teaching you are studying fit you instead of trying to adapt to something that is not comfortable.

Take your whole lifetime to make up your mind if you want. After all, it is your life.

# Experimenting

*How can I get the most out of my spiritual exercises? What should I be learning from them?*

If you eat the same food every day for two weeks, it can get pretty dull. You may enjoy it the first day, and the second day is all right. But by the second week, you're tired of it. So you experiment; you experiment with something new.

It's the same with the spiritual exercises. You experiment with them; you try new things. You're in your own God Worlds. I've gone to different extremes with the exercises, trying very complicated ones I developed for myself, dropping them when they didn't work anymore.

It's like a vein of gold running through a mountain. You're on it for a while, then the vein runs out and you have to scout around and find another one.

Are we learning something new every day from what we're doing? Are we getting insight and help from the inner? This is what we ought to be working for.

How can we face life as we find it? The key is always through the Spiritual Exercises of ECK.


# Two Techniques

*I have tried diligently to do my spiritual exercises but have not made the progress I hoped for. When I mentioned to a High Initiate that my exercises last from two to two and a half hours with spotty results, she advised me to write you.*

Two and a half hours is too long for the Spiritual Exercises of ECK. It is understandable to try harder when there is no apparent success, but the door of Soul opens inwardly. No amount of pushing from the wrong side will open it. Twenty minutes to half an hour is the limit of time to spend with the spiritual exercises during one sitting.

Alternate these two techniques for experience with either the Light and Sound or the Inner Master.

1. Count backward slowly from ten to one, then picture yourself standing alongside your resting physical body. Do this for a few weeks. You may also recite the alphabet backward from *J* to *A*.

2. The second method is done when you've finished contemplation and are getting ready for bed. Say inwardly to the Dream Master, the Mahanta, "I give you permission to take me into the Far Country, to the place that is right for me now." Then go to sleep without giving the thought command another bit of attention. The command unlocks the unconscious so the experiences of Soul can be retained by the human mind.

Practice these two methods for a month, with a notebook within easy reach to make notes.

## Hearing the Sound Current

*I am having a problem hearing the ECK Sound. Most of the time It is very faint. Am I trying too hard?*

When Soul reaches into the lofty God planes, the Sound rises to a high, almost inaudible pitch. The Mahanta lifts Soul into these sublime worlds of bliss long before It gets the initiation there.

You adjust gradually to a new state of being before getting the outer initiation, which may be years hence.

Then Soul takes Its rightful place as a true citizen of that region. Paul's experience in *The Tiger's Fang* happened about 1957. Only in 1965, eight years later, did he first become the spiritual leader of ECKANKAR.

## Experiences of the Higher Planes

*Sometimes the Sound and Light come to me before I can even start a spiritual exercise. The Light comes in huge waves, the Sound is loud and in the distance. Why does this happen?*

The experiences are often very vivid when we first get on the path of ECK. As we go into the subtler regions beyond the Causal Plane, they become less and less vivid. That's when you find the experiences with the Sound and Light are fewer and farther between.

When that happens, what keeps a person going? That's when they must work toward self-mastery and begin carrying this Sound and Light, that they may no longer hear or see, out into the world.

Self-mastery is what this path is all about. Up to the Soul Plane, I walk in front to show the way. After that point, you can ask the Inner Master to walk side by side with you.

## Out of the Body

*A few minutes after I start to contemplate, with my attention fixed on my Spiritual Eye, I feel a slight pressure inside my forehead. Is this a step toward an out-of-body experience, or Soul Travel?*

It's Soul getting ready to go out of the body through the Third Eye.

4

## Seeing an Inner Eye

*I have been visited several times by an eye which appears on my inner screen. It always brings a feeling of love. What is it?*

The single eye you see means your final destiny is complete service and devotion to God. Soul is actually chosen by God before It becomes aware that It is one of the chosen ones.

Usually, people who see the eye miss the desertlike world upon which they stand while viewing it. This means that all substance and life for Soul is beyond the sandy wastes of the lower worlds. The only goal for such a one as you is the Ocean of Love and Mercy.

## Beings on the Other Planes

*Whenever I closed my eyes while you spoke at the ECK Worldwide Seminar, a white desert scene appeared. A man on a beautiful horse led a brigade of soldiers, also on horseback, to hear your talk. The last day it changed—the leader was seated on a throne, while the men sat on the white sand. Why was I privileged to see this?*

I am happy that you gained a realization at the seminar. Beings on many planes can hear the eternal message of ECK while it is being given on the physical plane, because it reaches into all the worlds of God. You could see this because you were ready. The secret lies with the Spiritual Exercises of ECK.

## Changing the Way You Contemplate

*Are there times when it is best* not *to do a spiritual exercise? When the negative energies in my life become*

5

*overwhelming, I try to stop what I am doing and do
a short spiritual exercise.*

*But I wonder whether there are times when it would
be better to just wait out the period of difficulty.*

Keep doing the spiritual exercises, but do them in
a different way.

People often get more intense with their spiritual
exercises when things appear to go wrong. Why?
Perhaps because they want to force something in their
life to go where *they* feel it ought to go. Or, the going
is tougher than they expected.

Do a spiritual exercise anyway when all goes wrong.
However, do it with a new thought in mind. Say to the
Mahanta, "What is thy will?" Then chant HU and put
your full attention on the problem, for the Master will
show you how you can grow spiritually by meeting the
problem.

HU opens your heart to the SUGMAD, the ECK,
and the Mahanta. In other words, it opens you to God's
sweet love.

## Three Inner Sounds

*I am intrigued by, but don't quite understand, the
significance of this: I constantly hear three separate
sounds of ECK anytime I give my attention to them
when in a quiet place.*

You are operating in the higher planes where Soul
can listen to melodies from several sources at once.

Examples of the higher sounds that one might hear
include the high whistle that is like a teakettle in the
kitchen signaling that the water is boiling. Another
sound, similar to it but still higher in pitch, is a series
of intermittent beeps, rather than the steady, continuous whistle of the former. A third sound is sometimes

heard in conjunction with the first two: running water.

Of course, these are only examples of the various combinations that can be heard. Any combination of the Audible Life Stream melodies may come to one who does the Spiritual Exercises of ECK with love for the Mahanta.

The sound of running water in the example above is the anchor for the other two sounds, the whistle and the beep. One of the three sounds you hear is likewise the anchor which tethers Soul close enough to the body for the mind to recall the music from the upper planes.

Soul, in the higher viewpoint, has the advantage of simultaneously looking at several of the planes at once, to collect the knowledge and wisdom that is available to It. Keep up the spiritual exercises, for they are the door to the Ocean of Love and Mercy.

## Challenging Inner Sounds

*I've heard that to hear a sound in the right ear means that it is the ECK and to hear a sound in the left ear means that it is the Kal, the negative force. I would like to ask you if it is true, and if it is, why? How could I recognize if it is a sound of the ECK when I hear it in the left ear?*

Challenge it with your word. There is not an absolute rule that the left ear equals the Kal and the right ear equals the ECK. The important thing is to challenge it, no matter whether it comes from the left or the right.

## Curtain of Memory

*I often lose conscious awareness during the spiritual exercises. One moment I am chanting, and the next thing I know, twenty minutes have passed. What has happened during this time?*

This is not at all unusual. The Inner Master has simply pulled the curtain on your memory. The ECK takes us into full consciousness at our own pace. That's why ECKANKAR is an individual path to God.

As you develop spiritual stamina, your memory will retain bits and pieces of your inner Satsang with the Mahanta. What is important, however, is to continue faithfully with the Spiritual Exercises of ECK.

## Spiritual Names

*I've received a very strong impression of a spiritual name for myself. I know the Living ECK Master has an inner name, Wah Z. Do I?*

The true spiritual name is given to the initiate of the Ninth Circle, which is an inner initiation. The Ninth Initiation, however, is always preceded by the first eight outer ones. These initiations are given by the Mahanta or his representative, usually in succession and stretched out over a number of years. This allows time for the lower bodies of man to adjust gradually to the changes in spiritual consciousness, and avoids unnecessary upheavals in the life of the ECKist.

Experiment with chanting the name you were given during your daily spiritual exercises. You will soon know if it is suitable for your use.

## Spiritual Vitamins

*I don't feel anything when I chant my secret word. Could I be doing something wrong? How does Soul link up with the ECK through mantras?*

The personal mantra has no power but by the Mahanta. The secret word fits the individual's rate of vibration and is the tuning fork that puts him in tune. The ECK is one and the same, but each Soul is at a different level of consciousness. The word attunes one to the ECK.

Please do not become discouraged by your apparent inability to have any experiences during contemplation. The secret word is like a spiritual vitamin that builds one's inner strength over a certain length of time. Deep changes occur in you when you chant your word. Karma is dissolved from the lower bodies until the weight on Soul is lightened. Then, when you are most relaxed in the serenity of the Mahanta's abiding presence, he will take you into the Sound and Light of God—which is your main goal at this time.

Within twelve months, you should find yourself suddenly in a new and joyful inner state that will prove to you once and for all that you are Soul, a spark of the SUGMAD.

## Big Ball of Karma

*Is your secret word used for working off karma? If you don't use your secret word in your Second, Third, or Fourth Initiations, will you have a big ball of karma to work off as a Fifth Initiate?*

Your secret word is indeed for working off karma.

Now what about the "big ball of karma" theory? Some initiates are lazy. They shortchange their own unfoldment by not using their secret word or doing the Spiritual Exercises of ECK. Yet they appear to move ahead through the initiations like everyone else.

But how are they different?

First, they have serious problems with others in the ECK community. Second, often they refuse to support the Mahanta, the Living ECK Master. Third, they are unhappy.

What's it all about?

Their lazy past has caught up with them, and suddenly they are out of harmony with ECK. Like an untuned violin. Although some reach the Fifth Circle, they begin to have more and more problems in ECK. They believe they have fooled the ECK, the Mahanta, and others, but it all catches up with them.

A Fifth Initiate has worked off fate and reserve karma, but a lack of spiritual discipline during the earlier ECK initiations will begin to show up on the Fifth Level as bad habits. These make too much daily karma. Some Higher Initiates create so much of it that they won't work it out in this lifetime, so it spills over into their file of reserve karma.

In short, they have slid backward in their spiritual life. Some will lose outer initiations, and a few even try to leave ECK.

You win heaven daily with your secret word.


## How's Your Desire for God?

*I'm not an ECKist, but I am sincerely endeavoring to have some of the experiences via spiritual exercises that most followers of ECKANKAR seem to have. Is it possible that my failures are due to Soul simply being not yet ready to receive the ECK? Am I wasting my time?*

Desire for God must become an all-consuming fire for Soul, and not just an avocation. Only a single-minded effort to reach the Light and Sound of ECK will bring success. You must want to learn the ways of Divine Spirit as much as a drowning man craves air. Yet this must be an inner drive that gives purpose and balance to the outer life. Avoid austerities and love the Spirit of God within you.

## Ignoring Guidance

*If someone slacks off on their spiritual exercises for a period of time, is he or she still under the guidance of the Mahanta? Can one still be in touch with the ECK at this time?*

Let me answer you like this: One day in late spring I took a walk near a pond. The sun was very hot. On the edge of the grass by the water stood a duck. Under her were three ducklings using her for a sunscreen.

A chela who neglects the spiritual exercises is like a duckling who leaves the protection of its mother. He is ignoring the guidance of the Master. His contact with the ECK will only be a small part of what it was before.

When the sun of karma gets too hot for comfort, the chela, like the duckling, can run back to his sunscreen—the Mahanta. The run back is the spiritual exercise.

## Universal Mahanta

*How can one man, as the Living ECK Master, be everywhere and talk with everyone at the same time?*

This is one of the miracles of ECK, to be sure. The fact is that behind the face of every ruler of every plane of God is really the Mahanta, the Living ECK Master. The Mahanta is the ECK and is therefore

11

everywhere at once. This is why every Living ECK Master in history can make the statement "I am always with you." He speaks with the Voice of the SUGMAD, the Word of God, because that fills all space in every plane of creation.

You must learn to trust the Inner Master, but always be aware that the Kal Niranjan can play tricks on you and come in the disguise of the real Master. How do you tell the real one from a fake? Judge him by what he tells you to do. If the directions you get are those which build harmony and good actions, then listen to the voice of the Master within. Otherwise chant your word and tell the impostor to get out of your world at once!

## Always More to Learn

*In contemplation I began to think of myself as part of the body of the Mahanta. I decided to let the Sound Current go out from myself into the vast nothingness around me. It felt good, but I soon grew tired. There was nothing but myself; all else was merely my own creations returning to me. I became very sad and lonely. I realize that everything you send out always returns to you, but is that all there is to life?*

You have realized something important through this experience. Some never understand that every thought and action sent out must return to the sender. There is also a point about the ECK that is not understood. When the ECK comes in, we find the experience exhilarating. After a little while we wonder what can be done with this uplifting Force now?

As an experiment, we try to direct It. Yet a close study of the laws of Divine Spirit shows that one cannot direct the ECK. If this is done it becomes a use of the psychic power.

When this experience is given within the circle of our own worlds, then there is really no harm done. It is when we find ourselves in the outer consciousness again and we try it in our everyday life that we've slipped right into the role of the unknowing black magician.

There is a lot to learn, of course, but the lessons get much more subtle as Soul approaches the first of the true spiritual planes.

Continue with the Spiritual Exercises of ECK. It is only an illusion from one of the mental passions that convinces us we have learned all there is to know. When we give up and let go, then we slip into the dawn of a new spiritual day. As surely as the night, the dawn appears. That is true in all things. There is always one more step that you can take.

## Direct Information

*In my spiritual exercises, I get direct information about what's needed in the moment. But these aren't grand inner experiences. Is this just a passing phase? Is there a technique I could do to be a more conscious explorer of the Far Country?*

There is a way to be more aware of your travels in the higher worlds of ECK. You must train your mind to recall details. This means developing the power of your imagination, which is a lot harder than it sounds, but there is an enjoyable way to go about it.

Do you play golf? Let's say you have trouble with a slice when you tee off. You can work out that problem both here in the physical world and on the inner planes.

Get a book by a golf pro that shows ways to correct a slice. Study the exact methods given. Then, when you lie down for the night or while at rest some other time, imagine yourself on a golf course. Now practice the expert's advice—all in your imagination. Address the ball, hit it in the proper way, and watch it fly straight down the fairway. Do this again and again. Pay attention to your grip, your stance, and the position of your arms and head.

If you are a golfer, you'll like this exercise. It works with any sport.

Your game will improve, but more important, you'll soon find it easier to recall your journeys into the higher worlds of God.

## Living Spiritual Exercise

*At a recent seminar, you talked about being a living spiritual exercise. Does that mean I don't have to do my spiritual exercises for thirty minutes a day?*

A few ECK leaders who are very busy in ECK may have little time for a twenty-minute spiritual exercise each day. But they do it when they can.

The daily exercise of twenty or thirty minutes gives a better focus and a deeper strength to your life. It is what lets you be a living spiritual exercise the whole day long.

## Falling Asleep

*Why can't I stay awake during the spiritual exercises? I always seem to fall asleep, and I feel like I'm missing something.*

Do not be overly concerned by falling asleep during

the spiritual exercises. Sometimes this is the only way Divine Spirit can work with us at first. This is also true when we don't remember our dream state.

You can finish the Spiritual Exercises of ECK in the evening before bedtime, then carry a light sort of contemplation to bed with you. This is done simply by lying down at night to go to sleep and saying something like this: "Please, Mahanta, take me to the place in the heavenly worlds that is suitable for me tonight. I place all my love and confidence in your decision."

Then erase the entire resolution from your mind. Go to sleep in a normal manner without concern whether or not anything will happen. Take your time and don't hurry.

## Free Spirit

*I don't know the purpose of the spiritual exercises. Now in ECK, I have a hard time feeling like I fit in. Growing up, my father believed I could find my own religion when I was ready. He never explained anything in terms of God; it was always in terms of nature. Mahanta, where am I?*

I much appreciate your letter asking for help to understand your spiritual place in life. By upbringing and training you are a "free child." Your methods of contemplation are simple and direct, and should be upon some aspect of nature. The mental route is not for you, because you instinctively feel the pulse of life by just being who you are.

There is room for you to express how you'd like to live in ECK, and it may be quite different from what other ECKists find comfortable.

15

The spiritual exercises are to open you to divine love. You are able to design your own exercises through your love and respect for the things of nature. Your path to love, wisdom, and power is unique, but under the surface, so is everyone's.

## Charged Words

*Can spiritually charged words such as* HU, SUGMAD, *or* Mahanta *be overused, as were* God *and* abracadabra? *And, is it OK to change the inflection, tone, or meaning of such words in songs, jokes, or conversation?*

*God* and *abracadabra* lost their meaning when people lost the Living Word. The Sound Current was beyond their reach, and the priests could not lead them to It. Perhaps it was frustration with a dead religion that first led people to take the holy names of God in vain.

One who communicates daily with the Word of God, the ECK, can only speak words of joy and reverence. The Sound and Light are his heartbeat and breath, his golden love. How can he then but love the SUGMAD—and himself? Pure and holy songs spring from a pure and golden heart.

This also answers your second question.

## Black Dot

*When I received my new discourse lesson, I tried the exercise for visualizing the globe of golden light. But all I could see was a black ball floating past me. I was so upset I cried.*

The black ball you saw floating past when you were

trying to see a globe of golden light was to focus your attention. It's like the black dot on the ceiling that Paul Twitchell used to talk about. The black ball and the black dot have the same purpose.

Next time you see it, try to imagine yourself inside the ball. Then look back at your physical body. In the meantime, think of a flower during contemplation. And always fill yourself with love, because I am always with you.

## Taking a Break

*This seems to me to be one of the most difficult years in my life, not only physically but spiritually. I had a dream about a young girl from India who had thin slats for legs. I was trying to teach her to dance. I asked our dream class to help me interpret this, and someone said legs could be the foundation in ECK—shaky to say the least. Maybe I should start over again?*

The dream was to confirm for you that the approach of the Eastern religions (the young Indian girl) is stilted (she had thin slats for legs). It's much more difficult to learn the rhythm of dancing on such legs. The dream implies the need to learn the rhythm of life, because that's living ECK.

For a month, just forget about doing the formal ECK spiritual exercises. You will still have my protection. Use that month to see how the ECK is revealing Itself to you through the words and actions of other people.

Watch both for things that are harmonious to you but also things that upset you. Try to be very honest now. After each experience, ask yourself, Am I changed even a little? If so, how?

## On Your Own

*I'm the only ECKist in my family of three children, my husband, and me. I've been studying ECK for eight years, but recently my mind has been filled with worries. Is it all right to study ECK on my own? I don't seem to feel the need for other ECKists. I live out in the country and simply can't afford to come to town that often. But lately I've been feeling guilty about not wanting to attend classes. I also wondered if I'm doing the contemplations in the right way.*

It's OK to study ECK on your own at home. You do not have to run into town at night or on weekends and neglect your family. The teachings of ECK are to fit you and your life. It's not the other way around, where you try to bend yourself into a pretzel trying to fit ECKANKAR.

The teachings must fit your spiritual needs. Other people have different needs, so their inner guidance for living does not necessarily apply to you.

You asked about the right way to do a contemplation. If you're having a hard time with the spiritual exercises, just don't do them for a while. For some people, it's also a spiritual exercise to serve their family and enjoy the happiness that their attention and love gives to their loved ones.

There are as many ways to communicate with ECK (meaning, to do the spiritual exercises) as there are people. Do what seems natural and good to you. Listen to your inner guidance in this regard and don't let anyone make you feel guilty about the way you choose to return to God, the SUGMAD.

Also, if you feel that ECKANKAR is not going in your direction anymore, please feel free to leave it with my blessings. You, and everyone, have the right to choose your own direction in life. That is your spiritual right.

## Getting Experience

*The writings of ECKANKAR talk about proving ECK to yourself. But I have yet to see you on the inner. Where are you? Am I doing something wrong?*

I greatly appreciate your letter about the apparent lack of experience with the Spiritual Exercises of ECK. *The Shariyat-Ki-Sugmad,* Book Two, pp. 211–12, gives reasons for failure in ECK.

The ECK is present. It is real and working in some manner or form in our daily lives, but the individual must develop the self-recognition of Its action.

Start a daily journal of little insights that come gently to the forefront of your attention. These are the ECK opening your awareness at a rate you can handle. While the Inner Master sees that one chela requires a Soul Travel experience, another gets a healing. Another, an overwhelming flood of love. Each gets what he can handle without throwing him into imbalance.

Keep a daily journal for several months, please, and let me know the results.

## Meditation

*My husband began meditation a short time ago and has changed considerably. He used to be a good doctor but has stopped that. He is so silent now. He's decided that money is no good; but how can we survive without it? We have four children. What can I do?*

I am not able to interfere in family matters. But

19

I can give you an understanding into meditation, which induces lethargy.

Many do not know the act of leaving their loved ones to follow God is not necessary. We must accept responsibility first for the obligations that we have taken on in this life. Even family men have become saints in that they found the source of all life—the Sound and Light of Divine Spirit through the Spiritual Exercises of ECK.

I also have a wife and daughter to care for. Although it would be much simpler to run away from my duties, I know that the Divine Essence is working through my daily life and family to give me what I need to unfold spiritually.

The monks who hide from life are mistaken that God loves them more for giving up their duties. There is nothing evil about money nor the ability to pay one's way in this world. The spiritual law is that everything must be paid for in the true coin. ECKANKAR is not a spiritual welfare program.

You may turn the matter over to Divine Spirit for It to handle however It may choose, and in Its own time. The love of the Holy Spirit is always with you.

## Testing a Secret Word

*I am puzzled that I am not able to penetrate through to the inner planes during my spiritual exercises. I also have not gotten a secret word during either my Third or Fourth Initiations.*

The Spiritual Exercises of ECK are creative techniques. You may have to cast about for the secret word by studying *The Shariyat-Ki-Sugmad*. Find a word in the ECK writings that seems worthy of your highest spiritual aspirations. Or use one of the words found on the God Worlds of ECK chart, which is also in *The Spiritual Notebook*.

Test a word for several weeks. Watch for either subtle changes in attitude brought by the word, or else for direct experiences in the Light and Sound of ECK. They will work, for they have worked for others.

## Am I Doing Something Wrong?

*I've been in ECK for twelve years and haven't been able to recognize any spiritual experiences. Am I doing something wrong?*

The first natural question one has when memory of the spiritual exercises is not forthcoming is that perhaps there is something wrong. Please be assured that the Master is always with you. The meetings with the Mahanta are constant, whether one remembers them or not. The Light and Sound that come to one on the inner translate to service of love to others on the outer during waking hours.

The whole key to the works of ECK is the spiritual exercises. What is often missing during the practice of these exercises, if they are done daily, is love or good feeling in the heart center. The contemplative exercises will not work unless one practices them with love and goodwill.

Often it helps to think of something happy from years ago, or someone today who has brought you a feeling of warmth. Then if you can carry this feeling of upliftment with you into contemplation, you stand a better chance of success.

Not all ECKists are aware of Divine Spirit coming to them through the Light and Sound, but they see Its influence in their daily lives. This help comes only after we have tried to solve a problem ourselves, as if the solution depended completely upon us. Then we often get a little help for the problem to come into resolution.

For most who find some assurance of the presence of the Master, it generally comes within a month or so through several years of self-discipline in the ECK works. Occasionally it does happen that someone has waited eight or more years to get some proof that what he is studying is truth for him. Each individual must decide this question for himself.

Just before dropping off to sleep at night, after completing twenty to thirty minutes of the spiritual exercises, you can make a gentle thought command to the Inner Master for help traveling to some location in the inner worlds. For example, say, "I give the Mahanta permission to take me to that place I have earned on the inner planes, to study the Shariyat-Ki-Sugmad." Try that for several weeks, then rephrase it for the benefit of the mind. Drop off to sleep after making this statement and do not give another thought to it.

## Dry Spells

*After my Fifth Initiation, my spiritual exercises brought many thoughts and awarenesses. Now they are dry. Is there a way you can help me open my awareness? Perhaps I am missing something.*

I've put a lot of attention on the Soul Travel end of unfoldment because it was needed by many. Soul Travel is often missed by a person who is not aware of a rushing movement out of the body; therefore, he is satisfied to call his experience a vivid dream, when it was really Soul Travel.

The ECK actually fills all our nooks and crannies with Itself. We feel so comfortable with life as it is—and rightfully so—that we must be reminded to review what uncertainty life was before ECK. ECK is indeed in our innermost being. Therefore, we are instruments of love. This is what attracts people to us and makes us natural leaders. So even if you are not yet aware of Soul Travel, or the Sound and Light, the ECK is coming through you all the time. You are serving It by your very being.

## Colorful Contemplations

*I once saw your shape in a circle of purple and blue, like an aura. I mostly see a purple ball of light in my Spiritual Eye, and I hear the ECK in both ears, but I don't know what to do to get a Soul Travel experience. I long for it so badly.*

The colors you see in contemplation are also the colors in your aura. They show that you have it in you to become aware of life on the Etheric Plane, and later the Soul Plane.

You have the Sound and Light of ECK. They are more important to you now than Soul Travel, for they can lift you into the Soul region on the Fifth Plane, where Soul Travel is left behind in the lower worlds of space, matter, and time.

## Do We Have Inner Protection?

*I am disturbed by a figure I see in contemplation that seems to be attacking me.*

Conflicts take place on the inner and outer planes, but the people who are the main characters in the play

23

never suspect that the whole world of ECK is watching every gesture with great interest.

The actors think they are performing in their attics, judging by some of the things they say and do. But it's all done on stage, never behind the scenes as they imagine.

The pain is always greatest when we find that the person who is trying to harm us is someone we entrust our lives to. The person you saw during contemplation thinks he is the actor hidden in his own attic where nobody can see him. But we all know his lines.

It depends on whether he is going the way of love or power. This choice is his, the free will that is the whole measure of ECK.

Your inner travels will mostly be what they appear to be, but it pays to be skeptical if someone claims to be even the Master. Does his visit leave you feeling up or on edge? The "up" feeling is the Mahanta.

## Who Is This Master?

*While doing a spiritual exercise, a picture flashed before my Spiritual Eye. It was a man in a white robe, with a healthy head of black, curly hair and a long beard. Who is this Master?*

Zadok, who served as the Living ECK Master during the time of Jesus, is often seen like this. (Sometimes differently, though.)

## A Being of Light

*For me the path of ECKANKAR began consciously when I was five years old. I was awakened by a being of light that came down the hall and through the open door to my room. It remained as a vortex of whirling colors of near-blinding intensity. I felt very old at that moment, not a child.*

Your story of the being of light that appeared to you at age five is a treasure. It's proof in a spiritual way of Soul coming into this life for greater understanding of the invisible things.

An experience such as yours lingers at the back of the mind for years, until one day the Mahanta, the Living ECK Master reaches out his hand from the Light and Sound, and says, "You are now ready for the path of ECK."

Life then takes on a whole new meaning.

## Let's Meet and Talk

*I've been reading the ECK books for eight years and recently began studying the discourses. My life has been going at such an uneven pace! Can we meet in the dream state and talk?*

The initiate meets with the Inner Master when he begins a study of the ECK discourses. Be assured that this is so. If one is very interested, he may develop the self-discipline to remember the dream state, although frequently memory is blotted out for protection of the emotional body.

The spiritual exercises can be done for twenty to thirty minutes before bedtime, upon arising, or anytime during the day that fits your schedule. There is another method, the effortless way, that often works before another technique. Before retiring for the night, make a brief thought command to the Inner Master, like this: I give you permission to take me where I've earned the right to study the Shariyat-Ki-Sugmad in the other worlds.

Then go to sleep without another thought. Vary the statement every few weeks for the benefit of the mind.

## Sound All the Time

*Why do I hear the Sound Current constantly in Its many aspects? I talked to an H.I. recently who said she'd never met anyone who heard It except in contemplation.*

I wish everyone had your ability to hear the ECK so clearly, but Soul, the higher being, realizes that for some the Sound would be a distraction.

There are cases of people in business who simply could not function at their jobs because the Holy Music of God drowned out conversations needed to carry out their duties. So the Mahanta shut down the Sound Current (just the audible aspect of It).

You hear the Sound all the time because of your ability to incorporate It into the activities of your daily life. You are most fortunate.

## The Inner Master

*Will I ever get to know the Inner Master? I am discouraged because I have no proof that he exists.*

It is indeed a distressing thing not to have the storybook experiences of other initiates in ECK. Sometimes—always, in fact—the ECK withholds from us what we are not yet ready to meet.

It wants to ground an individual in the spiritual principles before he is allowed to go further on the path in the hoped-for direction. The idea is to keep one in safe territory inwardly until such time that he is actually able to fend for himself to some degree, beginning first with life on the physical plane. Don't measure your stride by another's. There's no hurry to this journey to God, because you are the journey. You are the beginning and end of it.

Your spiritual concerns are certainly known by the Mahanta. Please remember that nothing may happen to you except what you allow. This may not always seem to be so, but you are obtaining the spiritual insight that should within a year put you in better control of your personal situations.

Please watch for the ECK in your daily life, because you must first build a solid foundation there before you will be at ease inwardly.

### Enhancing Our Own Efforts

*I've been doing the spiritual exercises for a few months, but my spouse says I'm not any easier to get along with. Why aren't they working better? Should I be doing them longer or more often?*

The Spiritual Exercises of ECK open us to be a vehicle for Divine Spirit. We develop harmony and common sense in our dealings with others. The greatest challenge for us to learn is how to work with the spiritual insight and incorporate it into our daily lives.

The path of ECK merely enhances our own efforts toward Self- and God-Realization as we come to trust the guidance that comes from the inner planes. We keep on living our lives, paying our own way. Outwardly, an observer may see no change in us. The difference is that now we begin to reflect the subtle nudges of ECK in our decisions and plans.

If one takes his time with the ECK works and does not let them unbalance his personal life, a spiritual

27

stamina comes that helps us through the ups and downs of daily living.

The spiritual exercises are like physical exercises. Don't run a mile the first time out jogging. Go slowly. Build up stamina. Otherwise you burn out and cause a lot of needless personal stress. Find the balance. You have common sense about this.

## What's the Cause?

*Anytime I start doing the contemplative exercises, I always begin to have a lot of personal problems. The problems make me afraid to resume the exercises. I have gone through a divorce, I filed for bankruptcy, and I've lost my job and can't get a new one. I feel like I need to do the ECK contemplation techniques but fear the consequences.*

I can understand your reluctance to do the contemplative exercises when on the surface they appear to be the cause of your rash of troubles. So you feel yourself torn in two directions at once: to do the Spiritual Exercises of ECK, or not.

You must remember that life can only return to us what we've sent out previously. When so many things go wrong in our lives, we sure don't like to think ourselves responsible. But life returns our former deeds to us. It is the most difficult thing on earth to own up to our responsibility. Perhaps that's why so few people do.

The spiritual exercises, as you can see from your own experiences, have a definite power to set things into motion. All we're ever doing is facing ourselves. And each person has his unique experiences in ECK, for It will only try to clear away the problems that an individual has been carrying along with him, like unpaid bank charges. For once one's individual karmic debt begins to clear up, he suddenly finds that life becomes easier, more forgiving, and a greater pleasure to live.

So should you start up with the spiritual exercises again? You'll have to go into contemplation, perhaps each day over a period of several weeks or months, and decide for yourself with the help of the Inner Master. At all times, in all ways, I am with you spiritually.

## Getting a New Secret Word

*While I was sewing the other day, I suddenly remembered a dream I'd had where someone told me a new word I'd never heard before. Is it the name of an ECK Master or a new secret word to chant?*

The secret name you received is a good one and may be used in your spiritual exercises with either HU or *seva* (see-VAH). It means a service of love. Any of these three words may be used together or individually.

It's often helpful to begin a contemplation session with HU, chanting the word aloud or silently for about three minutes. Then pause for a minute or two before beginning to sing the second word, which may be chanted letter by letter (S-E-V-A) or as a whole word at once.

During the fifteen to thirty minutes of the second part of the spiritual exercise, it helps to fill yourself with fullhearted love and goodwill. Use this method for three months. Please tell me whether you need more assistance.

## What's in Your Heart?

*I often find myself using a kind of prayer to talk with the Mahanta. I speak of what's in my heart at the time, but I don't have the experiences that others have with the spiritual exercises. Am I missing the true experience of the Light and Sound?*

By now you should be more aware of the love of the Mahanta in your spiritual life. Though the outer things we love are put to the trial, the Master is with us at all times. Please know that your concerns are in the hands of the ECK, which is always working in behalf of your greatest good.

A spiritual exercise that may help you to open up to the Mahanta is a simple one. Every morning upon awakening, say to the Master, "I am a child of the ECK, and I move and have my being in the arms of Its love." Then go about your day in sweet confidence, for the presence of the Master will be with you everywhere, even in the most troubling of times.

You will be a shining light to all who need help, for you are then a clear and open channel for the Sound and Light of ECK. It will gently reach out through you to bring comfort or healing of spirit to those near you who need it.

A spiritual exercise for bedtime that may be useful to you is the following: Sing quietly to the Mahanta, "I love you with all my heart. Take me home to the SUGMAD."

Then, with your eyes still shut, look at the screen in your inner mind and imagine it to be white. Have a movie projector set up in front of the screen and run a film across it of a meeting with the Master. Talk with me in contemplation as you would if we were in the same room physically. Talk about those things which are a sorrow to your heart, but remember to speak also of the blessings which the ECK is giving you every day, but which are easily forgotten.

# Relaxing Images

*Yesterday morning right after waking up, there suddenly came into clear inner view a picture of a person sitting in a rocking chair, like the one in the painting of Whistler's mother. The picture remained clear for about ten seconds, a little longer than usual, then it faded. While I am not aware of this picture's significance, it certainly reminded me that the Master is with me.*

The significance of the picture with a person in the rocker is simply this: the Inner Master puts a familiar, nonthreatening image up on the screen so that you could become confident in the naturalness of contact with the inner planes.

Even as the picture stayed longer than those in the past, even so is the ECK in your consciousness for increasing periods of time. You must continue the spiritual exercises and the greater truths will be shown you in time.

# Creative Principles

*I've been gaining some insight recently into the reality and power of the creative imagination. There are two material things I would like to bring into my life, so I have been using those situations as test projects to focus my attention on. There is, however, another direction I want to focus on with the imaginative techniques—a more spiritual direction. I want to visit the inner planes and establish an inner life there, which I can be aware of and move about in consciously.*

It was good to see that you're working on the principle of the creative imagination. All the worlds and planes do indeed lie behind the thinnest of veils. Reality is what the imagination can see as a picture fulfilled. Words are too awkward to tell of the simplicity of how this principle works.

Know that the worlds described in *The Tiger's Fang* do exist. Humbly ask the Mahanta before sleep to take you to one of them. Put either the ⊄ symbol in mind or chant HU or Z, which is my true spiritual name. Relax your anxieties and know that the Mahanta, the Inner Master, will suddenly put you into one of the locations in the Far Country when all preparations have been made.

## Facing Your Doubts

*I have been studying ECKANKAR for nine years. Despite all that time, I still have difficulty believing that this is the right path for me. I have trouble doing my spiritual exercises; part of me doubts that I am getting anywhere. Can you give me a sign that I am on the right path?*

Words are such a poor way to convey truth, so I hesitate to use them, but sometimes there is no better way. The experiences of life are simply to open us to the love of God. However, without meaning to, we often take a roundabout route to it.

The reason is mainly due to our unconscious memories of past betrayals of our affections. When we finally meet the Mahanta, we're not sure about him. We hold back, not wanting to suffer pain and disillusionment again.

Our fears become so ingrained that we actually begin to draw pain and disillusionment toward us outwardly. Fear drives away love. Without love, there is no surrender of all our inner cares and worries to the Mahanta.

So you see, we enter a vicious cycle that seems to have no way out. I don't like to advocate blind faith to anyone, but in some cases the blind leap of faith is the only way to outrun fear and find love.

All the problems you have are really with one cause: Soul (you, in the Higher Self, of course) wants to find divine love and serve God. A short contemplation to try in order to bring love into your life is this: "I come to thee, Mahanta, and open my heart to love."

There is no force greater than love. It will begin to enter you and make those changes which are spiritually good for you.

Life is trying to teach us one thing: to see the ECK in the eyes of all we meet.

# 2

# Help in Daily Life

*Why can't I get and keep a job? It's been a real problem for me. Please shed some spiritual light on what I am doing wrong.*

Millions of people hold jobs; there certainly is one out there for you too. The question is, Where are you looking and what are your skills? Line up your potential with your previous training. Everything builds upon what we've done so far.

Life is trying to teach us one thing: to see the ECK in the eyes of all we meet. The Mahanta is every ruler of every plane, and every man, woman, and child you meet on the street. This means that those who have the enlightenment, or work themselves into it, have the ability to know that the Master is always with them. From then on they find peace and contentment, and accept themselves without apology.

Try to straighten out your physical-world affairs first. The Mahanta has been trying to give you a direction that is for your own good. The message is given in quiet ways, through the words of your friends, in the heartfelt nudges that come to you in moments of silence.

Take one step at a time, little ones. The little ones will lead you to where you belong right now. There is too much straining and pushing, and this is responsible for shutting out the words you so need to hear now from the Inner Master.

## Taking Care of Yourself

*How much of an active role should one take as a spiritual student in taking care of daily affairs?*

Too many on the spiritual path have a misconception that the ECK will do all good things for us if we just *believe* in It, and also give a token nod to the spiritual exercises.

But under the surface, such people are actually passive and introverted individuals who never connect the need for material self-sufficiency with the path of ECK.

The individual is responsible for carrying his own weight in society in this lifetime. Earth is a training ground to learn the self-disciplines of Soul, which then lead It to the state of grace known as God-Realization.

Some ECKists will overreact to this direction and become full-fledged materialists. But there are lessons in that too.

## A More Spiritual Individual

*How can I become a more spiritual individual? I must struggle hard in my business to have enough money to get married this year. As a result, most of my time is spent thinking about making money, thereby neglecting my spiritual needs.*

You are living the spiritual life when you conduct yourself and your business in the name of ECK. The ECKist touches many Souls during the course of the business day. Although he may never say one word openly to his customers, nevertheless Divine Spirit touches all whom he meets, in some manner or another.

This life is for Soul to get the experience It needs to open Its consciousness so that the ECK can flow through It as a vehicle. The ECKist always lives the spiritual life when all his acts and deeds are done in the name of the Mahanta.

## Planning versus Surrender

*How important are plans and planning? I wonder about this in relation to administration of an office. How does the ECKANKAR Spiritual Center handle planning and projects?*

The ECKANKAR Spiritual Center operates administratively. Every time a problem comes up, it is studied to see whether it is the result of not having some essential administrative principle in motion. Generally, that is the heart of a problem in any office.

But the heart of our direction is in making plans before using even an ounce of energy to carry out a project. Plans developed by the gathering of pertinent information and reflecting upon it are the keys to getting things done according to the will of ECK.

You know how to surrender to the ECK to handle your life. A person is obligated to do all he can for himself, but then, when his best efforts fail, he turns the whole bundle over to Divine Spirit to see how it can be done the right way.

## Sharing Goals

*I have just finished school and am beginning to pursue a career. How can I know when to apply the Law of Silence and when to share my goals with others?*

First, who do you mean by others?

To use the Law of Silence the right way, you must first know when to apply the Law of Discrimination. Be sure of the people you would entrust with the dreams of your heart.

Heed the old saying: Never lend more than you can stand to lose.

A sad note about human nature is that the average person will try to discourage a dream that tries to reach beyond the ordinary. I call this attitude the great social leveler. It is afraid of excellence.

So if a goal is very important to you, keep quiet about it—or only share it with one or two close friends. Be sure they have given support to your past dreams and goals. Such encouragement can help.

## Getting Things Done

*It's amazing how little I am able to get accomplished lately. I have always been able to go through mountains of work, but now many little things interrupt my day. Can you help me understand the reason for this?*

You showed concern about how little work you set out to do in the morning actually got done by nightfall. More important details push your daily "to do" plans out the window. Don't be overly concerned.

Give your best effort each day, *and leave the rest to ECK.*

Outsiders will not believe it, but there is a tremendous resistance to the spiritual works of ECK. That resistance makes it an overwhelming job just to complete the simplest task.

When this happened to me, I put all my efforts behind the job highest on my priority list for that day. I did all possible to stay on track and complete it. *The principle: Do one job at a time, then hand-carry it to the next station.*

Of course, you can't always do that, but if you try to use the principle above, you will begin to gain momentum over the resistance that has dug in against you. Once you gain momentum, things will go your way again for a while.

Concentration is the key.

## Inertia

*I have a physical/spiritual affliction that the doctors are unable to diagnose. It's sort of a nervous disorder. All of the vitality within me seems to close off, suddenly, with no apparent reason. I am still able to walk around and ostensibly function, but with no animation whatever—a "dead man." I have had this condition for so long that I have developed techniques for survival. But I am always in fear that it will jump up out of nowhere and immobilize me.*

The cause of the feeling of deadness you described came to me almost immediately: You are in a line of work you don't like.

Of course, the solution is not to drop out. As Soul, you chose the conditions of this lifetime as a chance to grow out of the mental shell that you've put around yourself for protection from things that hurt or threaten.

39

You need to do two things urgently: do something you enjoy that's restful and quiet, and do something special for someone else every day.

Something else to consider is "light starvation." Some people with a finely tuned nervous system feel the lack of sunlight greatly during the winter. There are light products on the market that supplement light intake.

Such a product can make a world of difference in restoring a feeling of goodwill.

When the inner life seems to come to a halt, some initiates find it helpful to write and send a monthly report as a discipline. These reports must be made a regular project for at least six months. Along with the Friday fasts and imaginative daily spiritual exercises, they are a direct way to work off karma.

## Snowball Technique

*I've read about the Snowball technique. In your mind's eye you roll all your problems into a big snowball, throw it into the ECK Stream, and watch it dissolve. What is the purpose of this exercise? Is it a step down from direct experience with the Light and Sound?*

The Snowball technique is for those times when you don't have conscious awareness of the Light and Sound, when problems are a burden and you don't know how to get rid of them.

The spiritual exercises are tried and true methods that Soul can use in Its spiritual development. When the work is routine and everything is running without problems, you may not think you need them. But when something goes wrong, the first thing you do is reach into your bag of tools.

You can't outgrow the spiritual exercises.

40

## Self-Supporting

*My husband has to retire because of his age, and we will receive a government pension. This is really bothering me. It is said in the works of ECK that one must be self-supporting. I am not finding it easy to come to terms with this. Can you help?*

In regard to your husband's retirement and having to accept a government pension: Accept it without guilt. You've been paying into the system, and now it is returning the money you put into it as a kind of savings for retirement.

That's how our life is today. It is in perfect agreement with the ECK teachings.

## Finding Success in Work

*Since the seventies, my work record has been bad. There have been very few jobs and long gaps in between them. Although I have filled out over three hundred job applications in seven years, it is an exercise in futility. Out of the three hundred applications, I got two jobs. Can you help me understand this?*

Does your job record tie in at all to your experiences in the Vietnam War? The war tore a lot of G.I.'s up inside because they feel they could have won the war but were held back because of political factors. In the meantime, they were helpless to stop the deaths and mutilations of their buddies.

My brother was in the First Air Cavalry and got hit by a mortar. He came out of it OK, but quiet. People are now beginning to make studies of the impact of the war on G.I.'s.

Maybe there's a VA hospital you can call; tell them your problem—that it's hard to hold a job. Do they

41

have ideas to help you? Feel it out on the phone first—
don't go in unless you feel that the people care.

## Adjusting to a New Life

*About four years ago I moved from my hometown
to a foreign country. Newly wed, my heart full of love,
I thought all obstacles would be leveled by time and
love. I was wrong. I still cannot adapt to this new
country and language, and I feel lonely. I need to find
peace of mind and get rid of this feeling of being a bird
without wings.*

Often the Holy Spirit has reasons for putting us
where we are until we've learned certain spiritual
lessons. It is true that most of us feel more comfortable
around our friends and loved ones. In a way, you are
homesick. This experience is making you very much
aware that you, as Soul, are also separated from your
true spiritual home.

In you is awakened the desire to return to God.
This spiritual side has a physical counterpart: your
desire to someday return to your country. If that is the
only way you feel you can ever be happy again, let
Divine Spirit work out this problem for you. It may
take time, for Spirit works in Its own way and in Its
own time to bring relief to those who ask.

A way to let the ECK, or Holy Spirit, guide your
life is to say inwardly (and often): "Thy will be done."
Let me know in four months how you see your situation.

## Presence of Love

*I live in a war-torn country that is nevertheless
making great strides forward toward an equality of*

*races. How can I help this in a spiritual sense? I work as a nurse.*

The world you describe is the kind of world that the ECKist finds himself in: The unending play that swings back and forth between one kind of power structure and another. We do the best we can in sorting out our personal lives and making things better for others.

We don't do this out of a desire to improve the social conditions of society, but rather as an act of benevolence done out of love for God, the SUGMAD. This is the difference between the ECKist and the social reformer.

Your presence is of utmost importance in your country during these potentially volatile times. We are a spiritual group that wants to realize the experience of God and are not given to making ECK an excuse for militancy.

You are in the nursing profession and respect life in all forms, which is a good background for any initiate.

We in ECK know that there is never an absolute, perfect equality of any kind as long as Soul is in the lower worlds. This does not mean, however, that we stop working for whatever can be done to make it easier for the next person.

## Joyful Translation

*Recently two Higher Initiates in ECK died in plane crashes. Can you help me understand why this happened? Can I say anything to help the families of these ECKists?*

While it is difficult for the survivors to understand the reasons for such unexpected deaths, the ones who have gone to the higher planes are delighted with the change, for they have earned it. This is especially true of the Higher Initiates.

We can show compassion to the family and give help to them if it is wanted. It is a time when we appreciate the caring of others who have suffered in a like way, and that includes most of us.

As an outer teaching, ECKANKAR is young. Time will develop for us a comfortable way to actually cope with the barrenness left by a loved one's translation.

Some cultures, it is said, celebrate the passing of an individual from this life. Our attitude about death is therefore culturally derived. But if the conditions have been set up around us like that, the pain of separation is real. No amount of detachment and letting go gives us any comfort at all. A quiet positive statement to the family about the departed one is best, along with an offer to help them get over the hurdle of errands in the first hectic days.

## House Hunting

*I am looking for a new home. Is it all right to turn over materialistic matters like this to the ECK? Should I expect the ECK to find a buyer for my old house? Am I being silly?*

How does one use the help of the ECK in daily living? The first thing is to act as if receiving the longed-for goal is wholly dependent upon our own ingenuity.

Then we must be willing to surrender the matter completely to Divine Spirit. It may not work out according to our wishes, because Spirit may see a good reason down the road why it would be a step backward to let our plan reach its goal.

# Business Advice

*I am considering opening a new business with a man I met. Can you tell me if this is a good idea?*

As the Living ECK Master, my function is primarily to find those Souls that are ready to return to the Divine Source. As such, I am not able to give advice in personal business affairs.

May I suggest that you take your question to the inner worlds through the Spiritual Exercises of ECK? It is more important to learn how to work with the Inner Master than getting an answer through the mail.

As with any business matter, one must proceed with great caution. A talk with the banker you plan to get the loan from can give valuable information to make a sound decision. He will have seen your situation before, in one form or another. If possible, get two additional opinions from successful business people you trust.

# A New Age

*I remember past times when the teachings of ECK had to be couched in poetic prose that only initiates could understand. It's great to be able to say the charged words aloud. I have the feeling that this is a special time—is that right?*

This is an exciting time. ECKists have a chance to develop their talents in ways that will be spiritually beneficial to many people.

New people, those just coming into ECKANKAR, will often catch the vision of the Golden Age before a lot of Higher Initiates do. It's like what happened in the 1960s. Few knew then that they were living in a special decade. It was the old problem of not seeing the forest for the trees, which is what confounds the ECKists who today cannot see what is so clear to you.

An emerging area of development is the increase in visits by space visitors. Not all are friendly. As predicted by many science fiction writers, some of earth's wars in the future will be to fend off space intruders rather than neighboring countries on earth.

All Souls—earth and space—will be stretched in their spiritual unfoldment. I see the future as one of opportunity. It will be an exciting age, and we're on the threshold now.

## Mankind's Purpose

*We live in northern Europe and were very conscious of the effects of the Chernobyl accident. How can we help with this? Can you give some perspective?*

The spiritual need in Europe is far greater since the accident with the nuclear reactor. Not many people know the enormous capacity of the ECK to change the consciousness of man, but when mankind forgets his purpose for existence, a calamity occurs which reminds people that earth is only a temporary school.

Only that done in the name of God, the SUGMAD, for spiritual unfoldment will mean anything at all when it's time to enter the Far Country. So the ECK initiates keep their attention on the high and holy things of Divine Spirit.

## Spiritual Overlap

*I have created a prosperity seminar which introduces people to some important spiritual principles. It is not linked to any particular path or teaching. Is this a way people can be gently introduced to the golden wisdom of ECK or does it conflict with the ECK teachings?*

Thank you for the information on your prosperity workshop.

As long as you keep a personal project completely separate from the ECK program there would be no spiritual or legal objection. There is a need for many to learn how to bring a more spiritual element into their lives. If they do not actually become more wealthy in material goods, at least they might reach such a goal spiritually.

If your publicity for the prosperity workshop is done through public or professional circles, and not the ECK circle, then there's no cause for concern if ECK initiates read these public notices and attend your presentation. Caution any who might bring it up for discussion at an ECK class that the prosperity program is apart from the ECK activities.

## Misplaced Trust

*It would appear that everything I have touched has turned to ashes. My business has been one gigantic disappointment. I have boxes in my garage full of books that contain deals that never happened. After ten years of intensive effort, why has not one transaction been successful for me?*

In time, I think you'll find yourself able to piece together an honest living for yourself again. Even though times are extremely hard now, you will look back upon them as the most spiritually productive in your whole life. This alone will give a sense of worth that no one will be able to take from you.

It may not seem so, but a divine chain of events does trace its way through the conditions of our life. This is especially hard to understand in times of difficulty. As you've noted, misplaced trust has been your downfall. There is a way to love others and still be able to see behind their motives and act accordingly. I think your experience of late has taught you more about yourself and other people than you have learned in all the rest of your life.

Life, in some way, requires that we surrender to it all the things most dear to us—if we would have its secrets. Your past loss has been a necessary loss, if only for you to realize why it is no longer necessary. Be aware, for the ECK is opening doors for your advantage.

## Giving Back

*I'm involved in working with the aged in my community, but a training I want to take conflicts with my ECK responsibilities. As a Fourth Initiate, I want to be sure to give back to ECK what I have gotten. Am I being selfish to want to continue with my work in the Bhakti Marg and give up my work at the local ECK Center?*

By now I think you know what to do about your concern of a month ago. Do what you feel most comfortable doing, which is to expand your skills to serve the aged better. In doing that, you are giving back to ECK what It has given you.

Your job training will require you to get as much rest as possible. Ask to have someone else help with your Arahata duties at the ECK Center. At least until your training ends in eighteen months, don't take on any more ECK responsibilities.

You are working in the Bhakti Marg. You are one of the leaders in the field. It is one way an ECK initiate learns to become a Co-worker with the Mahanta. That is the reason for spiritual existence.

So in the future, let yourself be the one to say what's to be done in your life. Let other people make their own mistakes, without involving you.

## Your Niche in Life

*I am newly discharged from the Army, without a job. My marriage broke up recently, and my wife got everything. Can you help me figure out why my life's so bad?*

First, you'll have to find a way to live. You need information. Call the library, and ask for the reference librarian. In a sentence or two, explain that you're newly discharged from service and can't find a job. Rent is due at the end of the month, and you can't pay. Can the reference librarian think of someone you may call for temporary help?

The reference librarian may be able to get you the number of a public agency that helps people in trouble. Call the number the librarian gives you, and tell this person the same story. After a few phone calls, you should be able to find help to get you by.

Let's say that works and you find help for the moment—what about the real problem? You're a bright man, yet your life is a wreck. Have you ever sat down to figure out why?

It's time to take an inventory of your life. Make a list of all the jobs you've held in the past twenty years, including the service, and give the reason you quit. One rule: Don't blame someone else for why the job washed out. Maybe it was somebody else's fault, but let's say the finger points at you. What did you do or not do in each job that caused you to move on? You've got to be honest with yourself in this personal inventory. Do the same with your marriages and relationships.

About work: Have you applied at fast-food restaurants? Regular restaurants also need good kitchen help. Be open to the ECK. It has a place for you, but you've got to have the love and humility to accept it. It never abandons Its own.

Another place to call for help is the Veterans Administration. They may have ideas or give you a referral to perhaps get food stamps. Public agencies are there to help people who need a boost.

Do the steps I've given you. Please let me know in a month or so what door opened and how you are doing.

### What Would I Really Like to Do?

*How does one use the all-knowingness of Divine Spirit to make a decision about a career move or a new job?*

The way to work with Divine Spirit in our daily decisions is to consider quite honestly: What would I really like to do?

One must put aside thoughts of asceticism, thinking that God loves us more if we are poor. A business decision must be made using all input that's available. What's good for me, my family? It must allow one to grow.

Any decision is not without setbacks, for that's the nature of life. What sets the ECKist apart is that he

50

gives it his best effort and more, staying open to the subtle nudges of Divine Spirit through the Spiritual Exercises of ECK.

These are decisions I am not able to make for you, but the ability to do so yourself is well within your grasp.

## Money and Spirituality

*I have feelings of guilt about my job. It is a good one, but I keep feeling I should quit. Is there anything wrong spiritually with earning money?*

There is a misunderstanding about God's will for his children. God loves both those Souls that are rich and those that are poor, because God loves Soul. It is a divine spark of God.

It's all right to earn a respectable livelihood, if that's your wish. The ECK wants to bring the fullness of life to us, but we must set aside the fear and guilt that blocks our success.

There is usually somewhat of a struggle when we move into a higher state of awareness and that is natural. The problems in life can be dreaded with fear, or they can be seen as opportunities for growth—and a challenge.

You must make up your own mind as to what you want to do. Consider all parts of your life, the financial and emotional included, and do what seems to be common sense. Then plan and work carefully.

## Looking at a Problem

*I have a damaged back muscle and work in a job that strains it every day. It's been there ever since my tour of duty in Vietnam. I quietly suffer until the time clock says I can stop causing pain to my body. Isn't there anything I can do in this physical world that won't hurt me so much?*

*I am also having trouble remembering my dreams. What does this mean?*

Let's start from the beginning—with the spiritual side. Some people don't remember their dreams because of fear that a nightmare will come instead. You've been in Vietnam. These things are being hidden for your own sake. When the heavy memories have finally dissolved from the emotional and mental bodies, then your dream memory will come back.

If you don't remember dreams, don't be too impatient, for you will when you are able to handle them. In the meantime, look for some help from Divine Spirit in daily things. Do you have any idea why you are having all this trouble?

Regarding work: Creation is finished. Therefore there is a way already established for you to make a living. Two of my friends here wash windows for businesses. They charge so much per window; they've found financial independence and security.

Have you seen doctors about your back? The first doctor doesn't always have the answer, and it looks as if the trip was not worth the trouble. But this visit helps narrow the search for the next doctor. We have to look into every source of healing that makes sense. The ECK is behind all healing.

To get help on earth, the surest way I've found is to go to doctors, go to personnel offices, and do everything I can. Life has been hard for me also at times, so much so that I know there is always the straw that can break the camel's back. But I also know from hard experience that there is always a way out.

52

## Careers in Other Paths

*I volunteer for the Salvation Army at Christmas and recently I was asked to begin working for them full-time. This would help my finances greatly but since it is an official job, I would be required to join their church. I explained to the lieutenant that I already have a spiritual path. He is willing anyway. What should I do?*

The Mahanta brings an individual the opportunity to care for himself in the most unexpected ways. Above all, a way is provided for you to survive in daily life. Therefore, take whatever job with the Salvation Army that you are comfortable with. To work for them will in no way slow your spiritual growth. You have my blessings.

This is a new time in ECK: a time of moving out among people under all conditions, and serving as a channel for the SUGMAD. Do what you can to be such a channel, without offending the people in the Salvation Army group, if possible.

It will be a mighty challenge to learn to do this, but it can be an enjoyable exercise of your creative imagination. If you have other questions in this regard, feel free to write again. An answer will come to you by either the inner or outer channels.

## Times of Need

*I've recently been informed that I will soon be out of a job. My career and future job possibilities here are ruined. I would be grateful to know what brought all this on.*

The moment you drop your letter of request in the mailbox, the ECK begins to work to bring the spiritual upliftment that you need in times of trouble. Its first concern is that you have the purification needed to take you into the high spiritual planes.

Crises and troubles push us against the small self within us. The conflict between what we think our life should be and what the ECK has in store for us is quickly resolved in favor of the individual's spiritual growth.

The greater spiritual advances are made in times of extreme stress. When there's no place else to go, true surrender of our cares and worries to the Mahanta occurs. The ECK provides a way out of the darkest, most threatening circumstances.

Chant HU inwardly every time you are in the presence of anyone who is determined to destroy your peace of mind. The word sets up a circle of protection around you such as few could believe.

## Spiritual Payment Plans

*Should I ask to have my karma speeded up in the dream state to give me more space in my day?*

Speeding up your karma will make it worse. If you speed it up, all the things that you've created from breaking spiritual laws in lifetimes before come due. It's as if you have a lot of bills out there on payment plans and you try to pay them all off at once.

The Dream Master will take you along at a rate that's right for you. It may seem a little fast at times, but there's always a way to carve out a little area around yourself of peace and serenity.

*I am eight years old. I think the ECK knew I was going to do something wrong before I did it. So I got sick to pay for my future karma. Can this happen?*

Yes, it can. If you know that thoughts are real, it should make you think twice before even thinking of doing wrong.

Most of our illnesses, though, are from something we've done in the past—such as eating too much of a certain food that our body cannot digest. At your age, I ate as much candy, cake, or pie as possible, because I never truly believed they would hurt me. They did.

You'll do better all around if you take it a little easy in everything. Enjoy yourself, but also understand that the responsibility to help or harm yourself, either physically or spiritually, rests mainly in your hands.

So first ask the Mahanta inwardly about the right way to act. Your life can then become easier and far richer in more ways than you could ever imagine.

## Imagining

*I know that if I imagine what I want and see it inside myself as real, then those things will actually happen. But how do I balance what I want and still leave other people their freedom? Especially when my desires involve others?*

Let's say a person wanted companionship. He might put the request to Divine Spirit, then do those things out here that he had to do to get ready—shave, dress nicely, whatever. Then he would leave the results to Spirit.

But if the person directs his request, saying, "That is the person I would like to share my life with," maybe his desire is not part of that other person's life scheme. He'll probably find what he imagines won't come true. It gets into the freedom of another individual.

When you don't put a definite shape to what you imagine, Divine Spirit can have unlimited freedom to fill that mold. But if you put a limit to it, you often strike out because you've allowed for only one possible outcome.

## Getting an Education

*I am trying to decide about a future career and an outer goal that is right for me. I was wondering how important a college education is today. Will attaining all of that mental knowledge affect my spiritual unfoldment? Also, does God care what one does in regard to a career, or is that up to the individual Soul? Is there some way I can tap into what God wants me to do?*

How important is college today? It depends upon where you live and your cultural background. Pockets of golden opportunities dot the earth. Everything is of the ECK. We live where we do because of what there is to learn there.

Allow yourself a lot of breathing room when picking a career. If you lock on to a certain profession too soon, you will miss many chances to grow spiritually. Yet in the meantime learn all you can, no matter where you live. Learn for the joy of it. If your goal is purely to get rich, you will box yourself into a dull life.

Times and conditions change for each generation. A secret I've found that always helped for promotion was to do as well as I could in everything. Success has a way of finding those who always do their best.

SUGMAD just wants you to become a Co-worker. You can be that anytime and in any place.

## Creating Karma

*I have recently enrolled to be a professional deaberrator for Scientology. I feel this is a science of*

*the mind and ECK is much beyond that, but not ev-
eryone is ready for ECK. Will this create more karma
for me or hurt me in any way?*

I received your letter asking whether you'd create
unnecessary karma as a professional deaberrator for
Scientology. You won't as long as you're an instrument
of ECK to help people up the spiritual ladder instead
of down it.

In other words, if Scientologists are inspired by the
Light and Sound of ECK that comes through you and
want to know about ECKANKAR, that's fine. To reverse the order, however, would create karma. For
example, let's say an ECKist recruited ECK members
to join Scientology.

So I give you my blessings. We can be channels for
ECK in groups outside ECKANKAR. Thank you for
asking about the spiritual concerns in your plans.

## Karma Speedup

*I have noticed that my karma has speeded up lately,
ever since my husband and I ran into you in a restaurant during an ECK seminar.*

Karma is not at all what it seems to most of us;
it is a love-gift to help Soul reach the heights of
SUGMAD. It is opportunity.

The most joyous existence is the life lived in the
Light and Sound of God. I encourage the practice of
the Spiritual Exercises of ECK—done with love.

## Serving God through Love

*Since I was very young, I've known that when I
leave this life I will have the choice of whether I go to*

*another place or come back here. But someone has just told me that when I translate I'm going to be judged, and if I lie or steal or do anything wrong, I'll have to come back. This has made me very confused.*

Is an ECKist judged when he translates? Not by the Lords of Karma, who deal out justice according to the old principle of "an eye for an eye."

The Mahanta will continue to guide your spiritual efforts toward God Consciousness, whether in your present or following lifetime on the other planes. He is the ECK, and the ECK is love. Therefore, fear does not enter the relationship between the Mahanta and the chela.

The path of ECK is purposely made so broad that practically anyone can find his own way to God on it and be comfortable. Some live ECK and go to Satsang classes, but again, others live their spiritual lives in private, through contemplation. You get out of ECK what you put into it, and everybody does it his own way.

To give you a perspective on what heaven is really like in comparison to what some people on earth think it is, read Mark Twain's short story *Captain Stormfield's Visit to Heaven.* Twain touched on the vastness of the Astral heavens, and he didn't even know about the grander ones above them.

Love the ECK in all you do, and you are serving the SUGMAD.

## Standing Up

*How can I be an ECKist and still stand up for what I believe in, such as the abortion issue?*

The abortion issue is an emotional one. If you believe in something, do what you can through community groups already established. This is how the ECK initiate becomes a vehicle in a quiet way, standing behind issues that he feels strongly about, issues that threaten to rob him of basic freedoms of choice. Then if you can find other ways to blend in an ECK viewpoint, this gives added impetus. Let people do what is comfortable for them, because that is where their talents will shine. The fight to preserve our freedoms is unending and will change faces again and again. The ultimate purpose is for the negative power to enslave Soul in the clutches of the materialistic world. It is that simple.

These are perhaps the most trying, yet most significant times ever encountered by people in their search for truth. In truth, the path of the Master is his own path. Although we can learn from his experiences, our unfoldment depends entirely upon our own encounters with the nitty-gritty of life.

The old song applies: "You have to walk that lonesome valley, you have to walk it by yourself." The difference is that the initiates of ECK walk in the Light and Sound of God and are the only seekers with any assurance at all of being on the direct path to God, and gaining ITS attributes of wisdom, power, and freedom.

## Master's Protection

*A chela committed suicide. Chelas in the area asked, "Where was the Master's protection?" I didn't know what to say. Can you give me any insight on this?*

In ECK, we learn that a person always has free will. The Master cannot give anyone protection unless that person allows him to do so, because that is the spiritual law.

In dealing with people who are out of balance, you must remind yourself they are human beings who need love, compassion, and understanding now more than ever.

## Being Clear

*You have made several comments about how important it is to be clear. What does "being clear" look like from the Mahanta's viewpoint? What are some of the subtleties of "being clear"?*

Being clear means to be an open channel between the ECK and the work you do on Its behalf.

What are some of the subtleties of that? Perhaps the most important one is humility, the flip side of vanity. It is the ability to say to someone, "Go on, I'm listening" or "Excuse me, my error."

Being clear means to be free of illusion most of the time. It lets you see a situation, and especially your own self, in a true light.

How do you do that?

When a problem comes up, you can slip into a higher state of consciousness at a moment's notice. A technique that works is to say inwardly, "Wah Z, let me see and hear with the wisdom of ECK."

## The Opportunity of This Life

*I am new to the path of ECK, and a crisis at work brought up this question: If I were to save someone's life by CPR or other emergency means, would I take on the other person's karma by interfering? Or do I create karma by not taking action?*

*I thought I did not care about death; if my time came, I felt I was ready. But now I realize I do have*

60

*that fear, and during the recent incident at work, I could not face it in someone else.*

ECK is an active path. We recognize that each experience that comes our way is spiritually instructive. If someone needs our help, we do what we can to the best of our ability.

An ECK rescuer takes on none of the victim's karma, because the initiate does everything in the name of the Mahanta. A crisis such as you faced may be the Mahanta's way to kindle a new respect for the opportunity of this life. At the same time, the experience makes one dip into the well of reflection, to broaden his compassion for an individual in trouble.

As you realized, fear of death has hidden itself in you. Now think about it: if there's room for fear of death, there is also room for its counterpart—a fear of living. In ECK, you will find that fear will diminish its hold on your life. There is the beginning of love.

Keep up with the all-important Spiritual Exercises of ECK. They're your key to freedom.

## Rich but Poor?

*Before ECK, I was a very shy person. Over the next twenty years, I developed into a motivated leader more interested in giving out my newly found treasures than trying to get any for myself.*

*Yet my life is rich. I realize that the Living ECK Master is teaching me how to love life more than ever and how to live the present moment to its fullest.*

*But I had more experiences on the inner planes in my first fifteen years as an ECKist than I've had within the past five. I find this puzzling. Am I cut off from the spiritual worlds? Is everything OK?*

Many who first come to ECKANKAR lean toward the side of introspection. That's why they remember so many inner experiences. But these people often serve no useful spiritual purpose, since all their attention is upon themselves.

It apes an old attitude from Christianity. Many feel that a person who spends his time soul-searching is more holy than a merchant who hawks his goods at the market. A highly spiritual person is actually one who has found the comfort zone that exists somewhere between the two extremes.

People who first come to ECK often have the habit of putting most of their attention on the inside. So it's natural for them to remember so many inner experiences, because they think that's what the spiritual life is all about. However, they've got it wrong.

Their point of view is a simple illusion.

If they allow the Mahanta to help them grow spiritually, he will begin to open their hearts. They will start to think of serving others first. The Mahanta is now bending the tree strongly away from self-interest toward compassion for others. Though an ECK chela may not recall many of his inner experiences, they are still going on anyway. In fact, he is living more richly than ever—in both his inner and outer lives.

In time, you will again remember more of your inner life. Don't measure your spiritual unfoldment with a short ruler, because there is much more at stake here: spiritual freedom. You are already finding more freedom, both at work and in your ECK duties.

## Living in a Fast World

*I've been in ECK for many years, and I've watched my friends come and go. It makes me sad. Do you have any help for this?*

It's hard to stay on the path of ECK for someone in your shoes. Especially when good friends are no longer on the outer path. But it's good to have you along.

It's like the seasons changing. Autumn has come to Minnesota with a snap, putting my beautiful geraniums to sleep. That was yesterday morning. The plastic bags I put over them did not work, as they had the first two times. This summer I also bought a bird feeder and have the plumpest sparrows and cardinals and blue jays. The birds are very particular about the brand of bird seed I buy. Apparently, some of it is not fit to eat. Our robins don't eat bird seed but do like the earthworms that come when I water the lawn. A happy little world. And now, winter. Actually, the snow thrower is fun.

It's a fast world. The karmic speed is set on high, and ECKANKAR must keep up with what the chelas want to help them in their lives. The ECK, or Divine Spirit, begins to change a person's whole outlook on life once he commits himself to this unique approach to God Consciousness.

The "pocket philosophies" leave one with a sense of emptiness because they feed the superficial mind, but not the heart. Outer teachers speak to the superficial part of an individual, but the Inner Master in ECK adds the five-dimensional element to the outer ECK works.

This is the reason Soul is drawn to the teachings of ECK. It gets spiritual satisfaction that is beyond mental or emotional satisfaction.

Therefore, keep your face to the Mahanta. He is the true teacher.

On the outside, divine and emotional love may look the same, but divine love is joyful, thankful. It gives itself fully.

# 3

# Divine Love and Human Love

*What is the difference between the love one has for one's mate and the love Soul has for God? Is one sort of love better than the other? And is it still possible to fall in love with someone after you reach God Consciousness?*

The highest love is a pure love for God.

A pure love for one's mate is the same as a pure love for God. There is no difference. But, frankly, pure love is a rarity—whether for God or for mate.

"Falling in love" usually means falling into karma. Karma—good, bad, or neutral—sets the tone for a relationship. For example, some couples love to fight.

The attraction between people of a high state of consciousness is a mutual desire to serve God and life. Such a couple join forces to help each other reach even higher states of being.

A high, pure love is sweet indeed.

## An Understanding of True Love

*What does the ECK Master Rebazar Tarzs mean when he says in* Stranger by the River *that a woman's heart is the throne of God on earth?*

Read this chapter, "The Great Tree of Life," very carefully again, from beginning to end. Rebazar is comparing a life full of love to one without it.

Look especially at the paragraph before that, where he speaks of beauty. It is the harmony between joy and pain that begins in the body but ends beyond the mind. Beauty is "the power which leads man's heart to that of a woman, which is, on this earth, the throne of God."

*Throne* here means the source of divine love.

But Rebazar goes on, and what he says now is highly important, for it explains where true love begins and what conditions the lover must meet.

Love, says Rebazar, is "that holy liquor which God has wrung from His great heart and poured into the lover's heart for his beloved." Notice also the hint that not everyone can drink of this holy love, because the lover must meet a set condition: purity of heart. "He who can drink this liquor is pure and divine, and his heart has been cleansed of all but pure love!" That means, among other things, a lack of selfishness.

Next, he speaks of the power of love in very powerful language: "Thus I say that the lover whose heart is drunk with love is drunk with God."

But Rebazar goes a step further. Love does not begin and end with one's love for his beloved, but it will of its own accord flow out to embrace all life. So his message is this: Open your heart to love, for it can help you reach the fullest satisfaction in life, with all its joy and pain.

"Let this be thy understanding in ECKANKAR," he adds. "Share thy cup with thy beloved, and never fail to help thine own in pain and suffering. This should be thy law unto thyself, my son."

A final word: When Rebazar here speaks of man and woman, he doesn't only mean male and female, but the plus and minus sides of a human being. His message is about the power of love. This divine power can touch the heart in many ways, and love between a man and a woman is simply one of them.

## The Key to Love

*I have been very lonely for many years, and I don't understand how to bring love into my life. Can you help me?*

We all experience loneliness at one time or another. But we each differ in the ability to adjust our attitudes to bring light and divine love into our lives.

Some make a great mistake in thinking that the way of ECK, Divine Spirit, is to withdraw from life. This is not so. It enhances our interests and activities, for we gain insights into ourselves through experiencing a wide assortment of activities, thoughts, and feelings.

The key to bringing divine love to us is to first give selflessly of ourselves in some way. It can be a small service for the ECK, although it can also be visiting the elderly or helping with some community project. But we must give of ourselves without any thought of reward.

First, do one small thing, like help with an ECK talk or put out a book. Something small but important to us.

Loneliness is Soul's desire to find God. The spiritual exercises bring the Light and Sound of ECK. Read *Stranger by the River.*

*How can I learn the nature of love? I feel so afraid of it. Recently I had a dream where a monster was chasing me, and I shone a flashlight on it. I think the monster is fear.*

Your question gets to the crux of the problem in spiritual growth: Fear is a poison that paralyzes a person, and the only remedy is love.

You've asked to learn the nature of love, and so it will be done in ways that are suited for you. Quite frankly, love scars the heart, but it is the only way to get purification.

You got a clear picture of the dream's meaning, that the monster is fear. The flashlight's beam is the blinding light of Soul that pierces the blackness of not understanding. A change can begin to come gradually into your life in regard to love, because you had the courage to face fear.

The heart of the ECK teachings is indeed love. For example, a businessman in his early forties got married recently, and the couple has a baby girl. All of a sudden he knows something about love and giving that had eluded him. A new world opened itself to him in a way that suited him.

He'd seen parents and children everyday, but until he had a child to care for and love, he was seeing in black and white. Please do not misread that I'm suggesting marriage. It is the power of love, however it comes, that makes you a new creature in ECK. And you will have it.

## Deciding If Love Is Real

*How does one know if a relationship is based on love and is worth developing?*

No one has the final word on love, but consider the following points in deciding if you really love someone: (1) Does he bring joy to your heart when you think of him? (2) Do you want to make him happy? (3) Will you love him for what he is and not try to change him? Will you let him be as he is and not what you want him to be? (4) Young people tend to fall in love with their ideal of love. This means that one has the ideal of a Prince Charming who is really a toad. Not all Prince Charmings are toads, and not all toads are Prince Charmings. (5) Don't forget your self-worth. How does he treat you—like a treasure or someone to be used?

Love is the expression of ECK, Divine Spirit, on earth, and these points should give you a fairly good opportunity to see what kind of relationship you are in.

## Common Sense

*A male ECKist who introduced me to ECK seemed to be a perfect match for me. Whenever we were together a tremendous flow of energy came through; he said being with me allowed him to travel to the Soul Plane. Now as I look back I wonder if he was using me. I trusted him so much that I looked beyond his lies and unsanitary lifestyle, thinking it was a test for me. How can I judge situations like this in the future?*

In matters of the heart, trust your common sense. Only you can decide whether any relationship is for your growth or not. I certainly do not endorse people who use the ECK teachings to get into bed with someone. Since that is a personal relationship between two consenting adults, it is outside the realm of my suggestions.

To give understanding in the future, the act of lovemaking does not raise anyone much beyond the astral, or emotional, level of consciousness, and certainly not to the Soul Plane. Thus ECKANKAR will never become a sex cult.

A rule of thumb is that a person's state of consciousness can be perceived somewhat by his cleanliness. Every clean person is not necessarily a highly unfolded being, but it certainly is true that no spiritually evolved individual is habitually dirty or slovenly.

Do not fall for the trap of guilt or self-condemnation, but rely on the common sense you used in relationships before stepping onto the path of ECK.

## No Strings Attached

*How can one have a healthy, loving relationship without getting too attached?*

*Not to get attached* is often taken to mean "not to get involved." It actually means not to let your idea of how things should be dictate the relationship. That kind of love has strings attached. It means always trying to have your partner do what you think is right.

Those with pure love do all they can to let their mates grow in every way.

So we come to the real meaning of detached love. It means to let others exist without forcing our will upon them. That is spiritual love.

## Higher Levels of Giving

*How can one remove ego when being a channel for the ECK and give and receive without the little self becoming involved?*

It's a battle that's never won as long as Soul lives in the physical world. We usually trip over ourselves when giving or receiving both human and divine love.

A friendship, for instance, may start on a high level. But once the two people begin to know each other better, the friendship is threatened when one gives a gift with strings attached. That's control, or power, trying to enter the relationship. See the ego at work?

Perhaps the hardest thing to learn as a Co-worker is to offer a gift, but then to let the other freely accept it or not. This is nonattachment. Our training to be a Co-worker with God occurs in the classroom of our daily life. The lessons are tedious at times, but always thorough.

## No Soul Mates

*In chapter six of* The Tiger's Fang, *Paul Twitchell mentioned the existence of Soul mates. Since then, other ECK writings have stated there are no Soul mates, but that Soul must reconcile the two halves of Itself. Why then did Paul write about the theory of Soul mates?*

Paul was in training for ECK Mastership when he wrote *The Tiger's Fang* in 1957. His spiritual knowledge was incomplete, if indeed anyone's can ever be complete.

Shamus-i-Tabriz says as much in chapter 9 of *The Tiger's Fang.* When Rebazar Tarzs and Paul met him, Shamus said, "He has become the Anami? . . . Then he should know all things, but I see by the light around him there are many things yet that he needs to know before being accepted into the ancient order of the Bourchakoun!"

Paul likened himself to a student who writes a thesis. Years later, after more experience, the individual may write on the same topic again, to correct earlier misunderstandings. Only now, few will accept his new findings.

Paul himself took back what he had said about Soul mates in *The Tiger's Fang*. Read chapter five of *The ECK-Vidya, Ancient Science of Prophecy,* "The ECK-Vidya Theory of Time-Twins."

Paul wrote that "Gotta, one of the first ECK Masters in this world was among the foremost of the Ancient Order of Vairagi to bring out the idea that the Time-Twins theory was not practical; that it is Soul Itself which becomes the one-in-one and finally faces the SUGMAD in ITS perfection of glory."

Soul cannot be split. But as you come into the lower worlds, Soul takes on two aspects, male and female, positive and negative. The positive and negative natures are both contained within each of us.

Some people think, If I only go out and find the perfect compliment of myself, then I will be whole. But the split is only the immaturity of Soul, and the balance comes within yourself. As you get greater experiences, greater understanding, there comes a point called Self-Realization where the two come together. Then you have the neutral state, the beginning steps of Vairag, detachment.

## Mixed-Races Relationships

*I have heard that one should not get involved in relationships of mixed races. If true, why is that?*

Everything depends upon the people, time, and place. If those three parts go against what a society accepts as normal, then members of that society will make life rough for the couple.

Let's draw a picture of an extreme case for you. Consider this: two people of the same sex *and* of mixed races who expect all the legal rights of a couple of opposite sexes. They would have a lot of problems in many parts of the world today. In a lesser way, a heterosexual couple of mixed races would have more problems in a lot of places than would a similar couple of the same race.

Weigh the odds, and do as you please. It all adds to your spiritual unfoldment if you love another.

## Sanctity of Personal Space

*A fellow ECKist visiting me disapproved of the non-ECK study materials on my coffee table at home. Was I wrong in feeling he was getting into my personal space?*

Whatever reading material we keep at home is our own business. The only thing of concern to me is how the ECK initiate gives the message of ECK to neighbors in the community. It is not to be mixed with any other path. As you know, the ECK will not allow any pollution within the stream of pure consciousness and moves to correct it in Its own sure ways.

The protection of our state of consciousness, however, depends upon us. We must tell somebody else to leave us alone if they do not know better. There is a tactful way to remind an initiate, who forgets, to give total beingness to other initiates.

## Surround Yourself with Love

*How can I feel the love of the Mahanta when surrounded by people with negative attitudes? It seems so difficult.*

It is difficult. There are two things you can do: (1) Be polite when these people are near you, but chant HU silently. Listen to them while you chant, rather than getting into a long conversation with them. Say as little as possible while still remaining cordial. (2) In your imagination, see the Mahanta near you.

The Kal Niranjan is using them as its channel to see whether you will agree with their opinions. And by the way, the Mahanta is also watching your response to the Kal. Each confrontation is a test.

## Problems in Marriage

*My husband has told me that as long as we stay in the higher states of consciousness, our marital relationship will be smooth. But I can't always hold this high viewpoint, and he blames our difficulties on my inability to keep a spiritual outlook.*

Generally speaking, marital difficulties among ECKists or non-ECKists stem mostly from these areas: (1) communication between the couple breaks down, (2) disagreement over finances (also communication), and (3) unfaithfulness.

The best way for any couple to address marital problems that have gone beyond their ability to handle is to seek marriage counseling. It's usually not any one person's fault that the marriage stumbles, although that is possible.

Initiates must avail themselves of responsible counseling whether the problem is marital, health, or economic. That's the way to live in this world. Divine Spirit provides a number of different ways for people to choose the most appropriate solution. It is for the people involved to make their own decisions.

## Communication Tools

*Can you help me with any advice on how to keep the love flowing in my marriage? It's been strained lately.*

Communication is a difficult thing to keep open in any marriage. One useful technique when things get strained is for one person to interview the other for twenty minutes, with notes.

The interviewer is free to ask whatever he wants. The only limitation is no question can be phrased so that it can be answered with a simple yes or no. That doesn't open communication.

The interviewer is not able to defend himself against any accusations but must sit there and take it. Of course, the roles change in twenty minutes.

The other spouse becomes the interviewer of hopes and dashed dreams. It is surprising what marriage partners learn about their companions that make them truly interesting people with goals too.

## Soul Is Unique

*Is there a difference between dating an ECKist and a non-ECKist?*

The best answer is a question: Are two different Souls the same?

Naturally, not. What, then, does an ECKist look for in a date? Can you respect her beliefs and feelings? Does she respect yours? Are you a better, happier person in her company?

A light friendship is fairly easy to deal with, but when a special woman brings thoughts of marriage or a lasting relationship, look carefully at her family, her education, her plans for a family, her housekeeping habits, her handling of money. Are they like yours?

New love overlooks a lot of shortcomings, like a partner who spends more than she earns. But what happens when the debts pile up and a baby is suddenly on the way? Where is the money for doctor bills? Problems like these can make for two very unhappy people.

No matter how great your love for each other, things will always tug at its seams. The song of love is sung through respect and thoughtfulness for each other. They are the best assurance of a gracious and loving bond for years to come.

## The ECK Wedding

*I'm married to an ECKist. We had a civil wedding two years ago before a justice of the peace. Now I'm just starting to care for my husband very much as Soul, a friend, and a husband; and I know he would like very much to have an ECK wedding. But does an ECK wedding imply inwardly that two Souls are condemned to wait for one another for the rest of eternity?*

You asked about the place of the ECK wedding in the life of an ECK couple. It is a spiritual bond, of course, but does not bind people to each other who find later that their unfoldment runs down two separate paths and they wish to divorce or separate.

The real marriage really happens anytime two people commit themselves to each other. Through the ages, the priests have gotten into the act to make themselves indispensable by sanctifying marriage. But marriage is holy from the moment the two people make a commitment to each other. Anything else is really something from the lower worlds, which has its place in our society. Today, marriage is needed in our culture if the children are to inherit the parents' property in the most direct way and gain welfare rights. Not essential, of course, but helpful in dealing with the bureaucracy.

What does the ECK wedding mean then for the ECK couple? It becomes a sacred commitment only because of the dedication of the couple. This commitment lasts only as long as they say it does. This is not for anyone else to tell them. The ECK wedding, if entered into with devotion for Divine Spirit, is one of the highest steps one can make in this life. But the wedding in no way limits one with fear or condemnation if the couple itself later decides that the marriage has run its course. You must make your own life together.

## Dream Advice

*I have been having recurring dreams which involve me, my boyfriend, and another woman. In all the dreams, my boyfriend treats me like extra baggage and ignores me while paying attention to her.*

*We have been having difficulties in our relationship, and for some reason, I don't trust him. How can I tell whether my dreams are intuitive or simply represent my insecurities?*

A relationship without trust won't last. What is the source of this mistrust? Does he look at other women when you are out together in public?

Dreams can prepare you for a relationship that may be coming to an end. They will tell you something is wrong. If your partner is showing less affection toward you, you must decide whether to try to patch up the relationship or let it go.

Think of your dreams as advisers. They may point

out problems and offer solutions, but consider all the facts before deciding on any important issue. Especially watch people's daily behavior toward you. Your dreams may suggest what behavior to look out for, but don't break up a relationship without some physical evidence to back up your suspicions.

No matter what happens with this relationship, try to be a greater channel for divine love. Love will overcome suspicion, which can destroy any relationship.

## Loving Self

*On the path to Self-Realization, how can Soul go about learning to love Itself?*

Love others more. Then, loving yourself just happens.

## Loneliness

*My wife and I separated a month ago and I am feeling pangs of loneliness and sadness. We could not work out our differences. I would like to know if I can ever find someone I can love in a warm, caring way.*

A marital separation is a painful experience. Both people in a relationship must approach the altar of love with gratitude, every day.

Our mate, above all, deserves the love that we can so easily show to others. Love means finding someone who can accept your outpouring of love.

## SUGMAD's Plan

*I am continually amazed at how hard life is for me. I am, frankly, questioning SUGMAD's system—it seems too difficult. I have gone to ECK Spiritual Aides, used all kinds of spiritual techniques, and I am still perplexed.*

*It centers on my personal relationships. I attract men who desire other women, even in the throes of the greatest love. No man seems to be able to love the way I am able to. What am I doing wrong to be so unhappy?*

If everybody had the deep problems you have, I'd be forced to say, "Yes, SUGMAD's plan for the unfoldment of Soul is impractical and unworkable." But very few ECK initiates have the ongoing life of misery that you report.

By all accounts, you are an attractive, desirable individual. Yet in your personal relationships, you continually find yourself in the most unhappy circumstances. Let's see if we can shed light on the reasons for this.

As a personal study, have you ever put the names of all the important men in your life on a single piece of paper, with two categories under each: *attractions* and *final weak points?* In other words, what about each man attracted you to him. Be both honest and fair.

Then look at each of the men to see what it was about them in particular that caused a parting. There is a gap between what you think you're getting and what you finally end up with. You want to close the gap between illusion and reality *before* you invest too much heartache in the relationship.

I've known people with the uncanny ability to choose three alcoholic mates in a row. Maybe it wasn't so surprising since they looked for their companions in drinking establishments. Not one of these people realized they were always fishing in the same water, using the same bait. No wonder they kept coming up with the same kind of fish.

If all the letters I got were as down as yours, I would shake up the ECK program from top to bottom to make it more responsive to people's real needs. Fortunately, there are few in ECK who so consistently ride on the underside of the wheel. Much—in fact, all—that comes to us is from choices we have made. Some people choose better than others.

To turn around a life that's so often upside down, the individual must first make an honest inventory of all the factors that have caused the trouble. It's too easy to blame something outside of us for our troubles, especially if we do not like what we see in ourselves. But fixing the blame elsewhere will not make the trouble go away.

First make the list of all the men in your life, with their qualities of initial attraction for you. In that should be a clue why your relationships always end up wrong. Don't forget *where* you met them. What mutual interests drew you together? Did those same interests later rebound on you to destroy the very relationship they helped create?

Please be objective in your analysis of the men in your life. Otherwise you're no better off than when you started. You are a loving, giving individual. Now you must learn to find someone who is worthy of that love.

When you finish the list of the men, take another sheet and write "Arguments" at the top of it. Again, list the same men. Try to put down the thing you and each man mostly argued about. Besides outside relationships, were any of the arguments about money? List all of the subjects of disagreement with each man. That list should tell you something about yourself.

If you like, write to me again with what answers

came up on your list and what you see as a next step in changing the conditions of your thought so that the old patterns of the past can be broken and give you a fresh promise of a better future. We'll go from there.

## Helping a Friend

*A friend wrote me recently with her problems. I know we should not intercede for someone else, but I feel this is not so easy for me to handle alone. She asked me to write you on her behalf. How can I help her?*

Write to her as planned and do the best that's possible. It's interesting how she tells of asking the Mahanta's help, "but nothing has changed except for some improvements in my physical and mental condition."

When the ECK does help, the little bit is overlooked, which prevents any further changes from occurring.

You'll never pick up karma from a friend's misfortune as long as you conduct yourself with true love. This is a pure love that does not try to change conditions. This same love is called charity. It simply loves those it loves and is willing to leave it at that. Any healing that might occur is up to the ECK.

## ECK and Other Paths

*Recently I have met and fallen in love with a devout Christian. He cannot follow ECK, and in order to maintain a harmonious home I made the choice to become a Christian. But in letting go of ECK and accepting Jesus, I feel such disloyalty and loss. How do I deal with these new feelings?*

In regard to your personal situation, love will overcome all. This does not mean we will be without problems, but that love is holy and must come before any other consideration.

Follow whom you will in your heart. It is the same Holy Spirit working through yet another of Its instruments. There are many ways to reach the kingdom of heaven, otherwise why would there be so many religious paths, even within Christianity (Baptists, Episcopals, Pentecostals, etc.)?

Life does not bring two people together without a reason. Our past lives get mixed up in this, and we find new friends in this life are actually old acquaintances from before. Love is what drew you to your Christian friend. The relationship, if followed through, will bring spiritual enrichment to the person who recognizes the hand of Divine Spirit as the motivating factor.

One's inner life may be in harmony with whatever Master is able to be there in joy and sorrow. No one else, no matter how close they are to us, actually ever knows what all is in our hearts.

## Encountering Prejudice

*I love serving the ECK, even though I've only been in ECK three years. Recently I was asked to sit the ECK Center, which I enjoy a lot. But I noticed one of the High Initiates didn't like me handling the money when someone selected a tape or a book. He would come to get the money from me. This made me feel really low. Is it because I'm black? I know some people don't trust blacks.*

I regret that your perceptions about the incident at the ECK Center are as you saw them. This is deeply disappointing—when Higher Initiates fall back on an excuse like good money management to cover up their racial prejudices.

Unfortunately, some people face off with the ECK to play the power games of the Kal when they ought to know better. As long as I don't catch them in cross burnings or crimes (overt) against society, I let them run out the full cycle of prejudice until the ECK calls for the day of reckoning.

You are a chosen one of ECK, and I want to encourage you to walk in the Sound and Light. Keep away from such people and arrange a circle of acquaintances (and ECK duties) that brings you love and goodwill. Ask the woman who manages the ECK Center to find a replacement to sit the ECK Center for you. Just say that conditions in your personal life have changed so that you will not be able to open the ECK Center.

The High Initiates are given the responsibility to keep an honest accounting of all funds, but this check can be made through a comparison of funds with items left in inventory.

I tend to avoid a policy of confrontation and prefer giving people plenty of room to turn around in, if at all possible. It lets them save face, but it's not always possible.

## Facing Family Crisis

*My wife and I are being torn apart by a decision. She wants to move to the Midwest to avoid an economic crisis here on the East Coast. I don't want to go, but I don't want to split our marriage. I even feel this problem could be caused by outside forces. Is there any way we can remain in our marriage and still have spiritual growth for each of us?*

Fear is a destructive thing. Those who envy ECK initiates that live a life of fulfillment will do all within their power to drive the wedge of fear between them.

There are always crises. To know this only requires a study of history. The chelas of the Mahanta are given warning in advance of any problems to come which they can avoid.

There is no crisis of such scope that requires a move for your family to another state. If you want to move somewhere else, fine—but there is no local disaster in the making.

Others use warnings of fear in order to get control over a following of people, whom they wish to manipulate for their own uses. Notice—when fear enters, love departs. Those who love the Mahanta will not let prophets of doom destroy their lives. The travesty would be in the destruction of a love bond.

Love the Mahanta and all will be well with you.

## How to Love

*Fear has paralyzed me and left me cold and unfeeling. Mahanta, I want to learn how to love. Can you show me?*

There is a lot of pain that goes with love, as you surely know firsthand. But the fire of love brings a change in spiritual outlook that cannot come by a shorter path. So, without love, we die; but with love, we are face-to-face with the agonies that burn the heart deeply.

On the one hand I see a chela without love, who wants it. On the other hand, there are many who've had it, have lost it, and must decide whether to gamble on it again.

The secret is that one cannot live without love. You've got to find the kind that agrees with your spiritual makeup. Once you have it, you find it a delicate thing that can slip away like water through the fingers.

## How Does an ECKist Grieve?

*It's been five months since my son was killed in an airplane accident. Although I have accepted his going and see him on the inner planes often, I miss his physical presence. Tell me, how does an ECKist grieve?*

The pain of losing a loved one is a sorrow common to all people, regardless of belief. It's natural to miss someone who has been so much a part of ourselves.

How does an ECKist grieve? There's no one way because our feelings about each loved one who leaves are different in each case.

To deal with the pain of separation, make an effort to help others. Offer to babysit someone else's children or pets. Or call the local hospital and say you have a few weeks free in which you could be a volunteer.

Right now you have to go beyond your sorrow. Time heals all wounds, so be a volunteer for a while to give yourself time to heal. And write again, if you need to.

## Fear of Losing Love

*When a relationship starts to spiral downward, I panic. I can't bear to see all the time and love I put into it be for nothing. Why do I experience this turmoil? Why can't I let go more easily?*

The turmoil of lost affection that you are experiencing is actually Soul's desire for God. It makes you almost panic when a relationship goes other than what one could rightly expect from it. There is a lesson in all this, which is simply for us to trust the ECK to bring to us the conditions that are for our best advantage. I wonder if it's ever possible to get complete security in the lower worlds due to their impermanent nature. Every time we seem to have the world going our way, something comes up to upset our plans and leaves us in an emotional upheaval.

Yet, we know that life is ECK and ECK, in turn, is love. When a relationship with a dear one ends for whatever reason, the ECK already has something to replace it. The interval in which we wait is the difficult one, where our hearts cry out for understanding. When it doesn't come at the very instant of our need, we rush about in a blind fury, as if that will make things better.

Please remember that the Mahanta is always with you, even in the darkest of times. We tend to forget that, remembering his presence only when things are on a steady keel. The ECK is already working things out for you at this very moment, but it's not possible to say that everything will remain smooth for you from now on.

The nature of life is to face us with ourselves, until we are able to handle the problems that knocked us into the dirt yesterday. The higher you go into the states of consciousness, the greater will become the problems you encounter. This life on earth is a golden opportunity for Soul to make important strides toward Its goal of self-mastery in ECK. Although the way may be hard at times, know that the Mahanta is as near to you as your heartbeat.

Your goals in ECK are in the right place, for you strive to do the best in all things. A reminder is the power of the spiritual exercises to give you a strong aura that cannot be easily broken by outer events, which will always try to pull you from the love of ECK.

I am always with you in all your concerns.

## Missing a Loved One

*My precious husband passed away recently. We were married for twenty years and loved each other very much. It is unbearable to live without him. I need your help.*

Your love for your husband and his for you shone on his face for all who know what love is. Words of condolence do not begin to put salve on the bite of separation.

We love our dear ones deeply and miss them when they leave us. But in ECK we know that the bond of love is greater than death.

He lives in your heart. When you are lonely and cry, look for him there, for he is happy to walk by the side of the Mahanta. He is now able to taste of the freedom he knew was there.

The sorrow of parting heals slowly. Let your tears fall, because they are tears of love too. And in your darkest hours, I am with you—giving all the love of SUGMAD to you.

## Your Personal Life

*I would like to know the implications of homosexuality from the spiritual viewpoint. I have not found an answer to this in the ECK books or my contemplation, and I cannot speak to anyone about it. I have been in ECKANKAR for a few months and wonder if homosexuality affects spiritual unfoldment.*

Thank you for your letter regarding homosexuality and living the life of ECK. Your personal life is for you to choose.

The ECK begins uplifting Soul from Its present state into higher ones. As this happens, those practices which are obstacles on your next step to Self- and God-Realization will dissolve through the purification given by the ECK.

Whatever one does in his personal affairs is a matter solely between Divine Spirit and himself. I do ask the ECK leadership, however, not to bring personal convictions and lifestyles to the attention of others in the ECK Satsang classes and ECK Centers. The reason is that the Living ECK Master wants to direct Soul to Its true home in the Ocean of Love and Mercy. He has no interest in social issues or reform, only in the preservation of the individual throughout eternity.

## Soul Is Eternal

*Eleven years ago, our son committed suicide. This year our neighbor's boy did the same. What happens to those who do this? Can loved ones help by forgiving and releasing them to the ECK? I just don't understand why he wanted to leave so badly.*

We can only do so much when our dear ones shut out love and destroy themselves. Yet, take comfort: Soul is eternal.

You did all that was humanly possible to encourage him to anchor himself in this life. Please do not feel that you have failed him in any way. He knows you haven't and does not want you to carry an unnecessary burden of grief over time.

For a while, these unfortunate Souls wander on the Astral Plane, lost. Some must relive their act of self-harm again and again. Thereby they learn how precious life is.

Eventually, the wheel of karma turns, and they are reborn. Their new life may be harsh, but it is to teach them love.

Your son's act of self-harm is of a temporary nature, for finally he, as Soul, will recognize his responsibility to life and serve it gladly without regrets. The Mahanta is working with him even now to help him adjust his spiritual viewpoint, so that he may become worthy of service to God.

*I have been deeply depressed since an ECKist friend decided to kill himself. I think it was stupid. Ever since then, I haven't been able to contemplate or even hold a job!*

Your friend's suicide was tragic, because he knew better. However, it did not end his spiritual existence but an all-important chapter in his life.

Why do people do acts that seem irrational to the rest of us? They are exercising their free will in light of their survival instincts. Many incarnations develop a fierce drive toward survival. But many, even in ECK, are only on the bottom rungs of this ladder of the survival factor.

There are chelas in ECK who have physical disabilities many times worse than those your friend had. Yet these people, some of whom are Vietnam vets, are cheerful, upbeat people. Why? It's a difference in how much more love they can show themselves. Your friend will learn to love himself more next time.

Remember—love is all!

# Where Is Love?

*I have many physical problems this lifetime and have had to overcome many obstacles. I've come to the conclusion that love is not for me this time around. How can I begin to have love in my life? Is it too late for me?*

Your life certainly is an extraordinary one, and its uniqueness might let you think that love is only for others and not for you. You may find this hard to believe, but people can live together for years in a relationship and still not know love.

It would be wrong for me or anyone else to try to change your mind about anything that is between the SUGMAD and you, so I won't. This world has its torture camps (as in World-War-II Germany and elsewhere) and places for breaking the human spirit. Yet for some reason, a few among many who faced the same prospect of fear and death on a daily basis had a fierce desire to live. Why? Who can say? Perhaps the survivors were those with the strongest spiritual heartbeats.

Where is love? Again, who can say? We know it's all around us like an ocean, but where's the little stream to nourish the garden of our heart?

We don't mind if all the world has love, but we'd like a little too. Sure, we know about Helen Keller, who became blind, deaf, and mute at the age of nineteen months. With the help of Anne Sullivan, who was her friend and teacher, Helen became a renowned writer and lecturer. She raised funds for training the blind and other projects.

What I'm saying to you here is that people with exceptional problems like yourself must work many times harder than the average person for love or for anything else. But your success can also be much more than that of others.

Love begins in a small place in your heart. Love your music, which can reach out to bring love to others, and so the love in you can grow larger.

There are other people with handicaps who are looking for love as much as you. Some have found it. How? Can you connect with an organization of handicapped individuals to see how its members cope with their search for love?

Love is something we all need as much as air and light.

## Can I Have Love and ECK Too?

*I've recently begun a relationship with someone whom I love deeply. But it's making me question my belief in ECK. I don't understand the role of human love in terms of ECKANKAR, and I've often convinced myself that I'm not allowed to have it. As a result I often fear that devotion to ECKANKAR would carry me away from this person I love. It's gotten so I am reluctant to do my spiritual exercises.*

The path of ECK is actually for those who want to reach the God Consciousness in a certain, direct line. There are many paths to God, and I feel everyone should have the choice of his own religious way without fear from any outside source.

Motivation for doing the spiritual exercises is all part of your self-discipline. There is really very little that another can do to help us with that. It is a measure of how badly we want something and what we are willing to do to earn it. No one else can make that decision for another.

Others also have questions about ECKANKAR and the role of human love. The ECKist is not an ascetic, nor does he allow another person to tell him how to conduct his personal life. ECKANKAR is to enhance our lives, open up the sleeping resources within us so we can go forth in life and enjoy it—but with a love and responsibility for all life.

In other words, we don't willfully hurt anyone. If we want a loving relationship with another person, we must look it all over carefully, because that becomes our life. It is part of life to make our experience on earth as rich and interesting as possible.

## What Keeps Me from God's Love?

*How can I get closer to the love of God? I seem to stumble often.*

*Stranger by the River* has a number of good selections to spiritualize the consciousness. Reading the holy works is a preliminary phase, and then the Holy ECK begins to unveil the individual's vision to the opportunities all around him that offer a chance to both give and get love.

First, one must learn to love, to give love to someone or something else. This means a sacrifice of one's self in the little things for the better interests of another.

The next part is one which few reach, because they cannot jump the hurdle of giving. This second step involves the art of receiving love from another. It takes humility to accept it with an open heart.

The third, unspoken part is when the love that is given or received is transformed and passed along to somebody else. No one can hold on to SUGMAD's love and expect to get any more of it.

In summary, first one learns to give love; second, to receive it; third, whether it's given or received, the sender or recipient must pass it along.

It takes enormous courage to follow where love leads. Its fruits are bittersweet, most certainly. I doubt whether the love of God can really be known by someone who avoids human love.

## Getting Along with Others

*Is it important to be friends with fellow ECKists? I am a Higher Initiate and have wondered about this for some time.*

Many Higher Initiates are beginning to build bonds of friendship and respect among themselves. I've observed so often that when the love of ECK comes into the heart, all sorts of transformations take place in both people and groups.

Love is the balm that overlooks impatience and slights. Work in harmony with all life, even those who do not agree with your understanding of God and Divine Spirit. The ECKist, with his greater understanding of the spiritual pattern, is tolerant of others.

## Family Harmony

*I am very interested in ECKANKAR and would like to participate on the outer as well as the inner. The only problem is my parents are against it. Is there any way I can become an ECKist without their knowing?*

Usually when someone wants to join a different religion than the one of the others in the family, it is best not to do it hastily. Later, there may be more direction for a decision such as this.

It is interesting to see that Divine Spirit actually tries to keep families together. One can advance himself spiritually by reading widely in books of other ways of thought. Better yet, if there are contemplative exercises available he can begin with these.

There is always the assurance that once anyone makes a deep commitment to Divine Spirit, no matter what pathway he chooses, his best interests are handled.

Divine love is without limit, not bounded by the limits of fear about the unknown. Such a person as this, the devotee of Divine Spirit, may rest assured that the Inner Guide will always be with him, both in this life and the next. His spiritual welfare is always in the hands of God.

## Helping Children Grow Up

*I raised my son alone, being both father and mother to him. Now he is married and has a family of his own. But he has always been a source of fear and concern to me, being very unstable mentally. I have found a man I like and would like to be with, but I am afraid of my son's reaction. Can you do a reading on him and find out why he is this way? Can you help me get over this fear?*

Spiritual law prevents me from getting into the background of your son without his permission. However, I can address your problem.

As you said several times, your fears are holding you back spiritually. They are keeping you from having a clear mind about what you would like to do for yourself. You've been both mother and father to your son, which was a noble but difficult task. The problem is that you've given so much of yourself to make him happy that you've neglected your own happiness.

See if your son can understand that you did everything possible to give him a good start in life. He is now healthy, has a good wife, and is the father of two children. He has the basics for happiness. Now that he's taken care of, you would also like to have a companion and happiness. Would he let you have that?

You can only do so much for someone else. You also have a right to be happy. There is no reason to feel guilty about that. Everyone has to grow up sometime, and your son can now do for his children what you tried to do for him. And you will always love him, but he cannot expect you to give up your whole life to him anymore. He's no longer a small, helpless child. Now he's an adult who must give his love and help to his growing family, as you once did.

We like to be with our own even after they've grown up and left home. But then the relationship between parent and offspring is that of two adults, no longer of adult and helpless child.

## Passing through Grief

*I am presently going through a period of enormous grief over the death of my husband who passed away a few weeks ago. The extremely loving relationship we shared was rare and exquisite beyond description. I am hoping you can help me overcome some of the despair that I feel.*

I've been carrying your letter with me for a week on a trip, trying to find words to fill the void left by the passing of your husband, whom you loved dearly. I find no words for a loss as deep as yours. The love you shared is a genuine and rare thing that will not be replaced.

If you are sincere in wanting to find a way through the awful despondency that has settled upon you, I can only suggest something that may turn your love for him so that others may share it through you. Love must have someone to go to, and the love you have for him must be given to another, one who needs it as much as you did.

This is your choice, of course, and you may find an alternate plan that suits your feelings better, but go to a retirement home and ask one of the people there to tell you what they learned about grief in their long life. Pick the person carefully. It should be an alert, sensitive individual whose face shines with goodness, kindness, and humor. Imagine that you are a child asking a teacher a difficult question, but that you are humble and want to know the answer.

I'm happy for you in the joy that lit your life, and I cry with you at your loss. I do send my love to you, with spiritual blessings.

*Why do loved ones die and leave us here? My husband died suddenly, and I am bereft with grief.*

Words alone cannot heal a broken heart. Only time can. Your husband went into the cave of purification by choice, because Soul makes Its own decision about the worth of God's love for It.

He knew that pain is a cleanser, but also that he could leave it behind by rising into a state of consciousness where it simply can't exist.

He's happy now. I'm sure you already know that. Let time and his love heal your wounds, for they surely will.

## Loving Service

*In the last two or three months I have been immersed in the Sound Current. I have been able to perceive It at any moment I wanted. But only in this instant have I suddenly realized I have been standing in the middle of the gift of God, the Audible Life Stream.*

I'm happy to hear you are conscious of being in the Audible Life Stream. There is simply no way to do justice to the reality of SUGMAD in writing, so I won't try here.

ECK opens our hearts to love. We can now love life and all living things. Its gift makes us joyful, satisfied to serve It with humility. Others may not see Its Light in us—even as we hear Its Sound—but we are now clear channels of divine love.

Such a role does not require either the approval or understanding of others. We are content to be the chosen. Our lives are ever afterward those of loving service.

## God's Mercy

*You refer to the Ocean of Love and Mercy when speaking about SUGMAD. You have made great efforts to give us a feel for divine love. I don't recall, however, anything said or written about divine mercy or compassion of any kind. Would you please discuss mercy and how it fits in with your mission?*

Mercy and compassion are two very important qualities, but love is the greatest of all.

From top to bottom, SUGMAD is the Ocean of Love and Mercy. "Life has no existence," says *The Shariyat,* Book One, "but for the love and mercy of God." Yet one can only find the Mahanta, the Living ECK Master if he has love and humility, and shows compassion (mercy) toward others.

"Love is the passkey to the Kingdom of Heaven," says *The Shariyat,* Book Two.

To date, the focus in ECK has been on divine love. There is a reason for that. So many people, inside and outside of ECK, have the upside-down notion that mercy is a divine quality that God and others owe them. Such thinking is part of the push for "entitlements" that has gained favor in society since the founding of ECKANKAR in the mid-1960s. The imprint of this attitude upon the minds of Western society is spelled out in an old prayer: "Lord, have mercy upon me, a poor sinful being."

Such a view of mercy put out the creative spark in Soul. It makes for passive people.

In ECK, we go in steps. Love and mercy are equally important in the ECK doctrines. Yet our attention so far has been upon divine love because of what mercy implies: a position of strength from which to show compassion for the less fortunate. An ECK Master, for example, speaks from a position of spiritual strength. Thus, mercy from him can do miracles, like opening the gates of heaven for an individual with a mere glance. Yet mercy from a slave counts for little, because he has so little control over his own destiny.

The second of the four Zoas lists compassion among the qualities of a Mahdis, the ECK High Initiate. It does so with the understanding that all who reach the Atma Lok know their mission: to become a Co-worker with God. That role means giving love and mercy to all.

Further, the Spiritual Exercises of ECK impart wisdom. They give an insight on how compassion shrinks the walls between Souls, for how could anyone not have compassion for another Light of God in need of a smile, a kind word, or even a meal?

## Human Love, Divine Love

*What is human love and what is divine love? How can I learn to live divine love?*

You want to know the difference between love and divine love. Begin with love, and that grows into divine love. I know that's not the answer you look for, but the mind has nothing to do with love.

You must have read the chapter "Love" in *Stranger by the River* tens of times, but use it now in contemplation for the next ten days. Then your heart will begin to open to love.

Begin with the love you have. Love gratefully. This love expands your heart into a greater vessel which can hold yet more love. On the outside, divine and emotional love may look the same, but divine love is joyful, thankful. It gives itself fully.

Let love be what it will. Don't let the mind tell you one is human and the other divine. Just love without expecting its return. I am always with you—and that is love.

There are thousands of forms a Soul can take.

# 4

# What Animals Teach Us

*I have many questions about the nature of Soul. For example, do minerals, plants, and animals have Souls?*

Since Soul is invisible, for the most part, and not subject to analysis in a scientific laboratory, Its nature remains a matter of speculative belief or personal experience.

The purpose of the ECK teachings is to give the individual proof of the nature of Soul in a way that is meaningful to him. When and how this is done depends upon the Mahanta, who determines the best time and place.

When the time is right, each question you have will be answered to your satisfaction.

## Soul's Choices

*What life-form comes after the human?*

Cat or dog, I think (joke).

Actually, there are many choices for Soul. We think of the human body as the highest form on earth. Yet sometimes I wonder whether some animals, birds, or fish are not spiritually ahead of some people.

At times, I also wonder what people would do if they found that our first space visitors were dolphins (joke again), who came to earth by thought instead of rocket power. They are surely smarter than a lot of people.

There are thousands of forms a Soul can take. But finally, Soul drops all the outer forms and becomes the pure Light and Sound of God. That's the Soul body. It's a far higher form than that of any human, ghost, or angel.

## Animals and Heaven

*I want to know if there are animals on the Astral Plane, Causal Plane, and so on.*

Yes, there are. As above, so below. That means cats, dogs, and turtles have a heaven, just like people. It makes you wonder why some people get so angry to hear that animals go to heaven. That's where we all come from.

## When a Pet Dies

*Will I know what to do as the condition of my dog worsens with age? Specifically, will I know if I should help in her translation, as is commonly practiced today by veterinarian injections? I don't want to incur any karma by interfering with her life, but still want to honor our relationship in love.*

When the time comes, use the ways available to help a pet have a painless translation. How do you know when the time is right? When your pet is no longer able to partake of life; whenever pain or disability no longer allows it to love you as it would.

Talk this matter over with your pet first, and ask for dream guidance to make the right decision. No karma will be involved if you put your pet into the hands of the Mahanta.

## Pets Reincarnate Too

*Our beloved family pet died recently. Since then we have found a new Lhasa apso puppy. Could Soul have reincarnated in such a short time?*

Yes. Soul moves freely between the body forms that suit It. Soul reincarnates into animals both on the physical and higher planes. Families may choose to reincarnate together and so may their pets.

## Spiritual Nature of Animals

*What's the spiritual nature of animals? Do they help us with our spiritual growth?*

Not everybody owns a pet, or can. Some apartment managers won't allow them, nor can all parents afford them. But if you do have one, you'll find your pet a wonderful companion for teaching certain ways of the divine ECK.

There is an interesting book about how animals think and feel. *What the Animals Tell Me* by Beatrice Lydecker (Harper & Row) tells how she learned to "talk" with her pets by using visualization methods.

Over the years, animals in Beatrice Lydecker's family included dogs, cats, cows, ducks, and other farm animals. The mental pictures she used to talk with them are like the visualization techniques explained by Paul

Twitchell in *The Flute of God.* Lydecker's methods of teaching animals are formed from the spiritual wisdom of ECK, but her pets taught her a lot of lessons about life too.

The author once tried to teach her dog, Princessa, to speak. The author wanted the dog to bark for something it wanted. Hours passed as she prompted it by saying, "Woof, woof," but the dog sat in silence, a puzzled frown on its face.

Finally, she asked why it would not speak. By the inner language, it said, "You already know what I want. Why do I have to bark?"

In other experiments, she found that animals do not understand negative words, such as: *don't, can't, shouldn't, couldn't,* and *wouldn't.* A dog that jumps on the bed and is ordered off with the command, "Don't go on the bed!" will probably stay on it. The pet drops the word *don't* and hears, "Go on the bed!" So it obeys, happy to please its master. Then it becomes confused when it is scolded for disobedience.

To teach your pet obedience, try using sentences with only positive words in them. First, visualize a picture in your mind of the dog on the floor beside the bed. Next, say, "Sit on the floor!" That command is a positive image and will work for most dogs in time.

*What the Animals Tell Me* gives sound tips for training pets. Anyone who is twelve or older should find the book easy to read. It is full of stories, examples, and tips on pet care centered on the ECK precepts. But the real message is between the lines: how you can open your eyes to the ECK.

The book may be in your local library. Call the librarian, and ask for it by title and the author's name. If it's not there, ask how you can find it.

If you don't have a pet of your own, make friends

with cats and dogs near home. Then look at the world through their eyes, which is a Soul Travel exercise. You will see old things in a new light. Each time one sees with new eyes, he is nearer to being a Co-worker with God.

## For the Good of All

*My daughter saw an animal shelter in our city in which the dogs suffer from very bad care. They live in extremely small boxes made out of concrete blocks. Some of these dogs have gone crazy. Since we both love animals, my daughter wants to know why these dogs have to suffer so badly and live under such cruel conditions.*

*When people suffer and live in bad circumstances, I can explain it with the Law of Karma and rebirth. But how can those animals have broken the spiritual laws? I didn't know how to answer her question. Could you please explain if animals do create karma too, and if so, how?*

Suffering is not always a direct result of breaking a spiritual law. Even though everyone gets *adi karma,* the primal karma that starts us off in our first lifetime, there is far more to the spiritual journey. A Soul may intentionally choose a hard life to learn more about love, wisdom, and charity. Pain, like joy, is simply a tool in the toolbox of karma and rebirth.

To grow spiritually, we move beyond a strict acceptance of karma and thus take the high road to God.

You can, as spiritual beings, try to make your city shelter a more livable place. Talk to the owner or manager. If that goes nowhere, visit or call your city hall. Each time, ask the Mahanta what steps to take, then go one step at a time until the conditions in the city's animal shelter are more humane.

An ECKist need not be a helpless cog in the machinery of life. You answer to a higher law: divine love. Use your spiritual powers of creation for the good of all.

## Bird Stories

*I love your talks at seminars about the animals and birds. We have many birds at our lake home. I feel so peaceful when I listen to their songs.*

The sound of birds is one of the Sounds of ECK. That's why I like birds too.

## Protecting Oneself

*I am concerned about the karma involved in this situation: while on duty as a police officer, I had to shoot a vicious dog that had attacked someone. I love animals. Why does this happen?*

While one protects life whenever possible, we must trust Divine Spirit to guide us to act for the good of the whole.

Some of the animals that law officials confront in the line of duty have been trained to maim and injure. It's unlikely that they can ever be useful as family pets. Police officials are entrusted with preserving the peace and safety of citizens. This is a warring universe and sometimes it is needed to fight for our freedom and well-being.

The difference comes in our attitude. If we must discharge our duty and destroy a vicious animal, we do not let guilt set in our consciousness. We can act in the name of the SUGMAD. Although we strive to act in peace and harmony with all life, there are ECKists bearing arms in the service of their country. There is no guilt with this.

We must exercise great care with human life unless ours or another's is in jeopardy.

## A Hunter's Guilt

*I have been an avid hunter and fisherman all my life. But the ECK discourses speak of having love for all of God's creation. Does this love mean we will not take life as in hunting for deer, elk, or shooting predators? How about fishing? I have come to the point where shooting a predator brings a feeling of guilt, but then I think of the fish and cattle beef we eat every day that have been killed. I am confused.*

I greatly appreciate your question about the taking of animal life. Some religious followers walk with their eyes to the ground not as a sign of humility but supposedly as an indication of their great love for life. They don't want to crush an insect.

But one must decide for himself whether to hunt and fish. If there is a need for food, I would hunt too. But for sport, that again is a personal decision.

I make no restrictions on meat eating. Some people would get very ill if they suddenly dropped a lifelong diet and chose to become vegetarian. But plants also afford a habitation for Soul.

What is important, however, whether or not one decides to hunt and fish, is the attitude. The attitude of guilt might prove more harmful than the act itself. Do what you will. The Inner Master will give you the necessary insights, step by step. You may choose the way that is right for you.

## An Attitude of Gratitude

*I am fifteen and I like to hunt. What is the karma in doing this? In* The Wind of Change *you said you broke your arm because you shot a deer. Does this mean I'll die because I shot a pheasant?*

Life feeds upon life. In the eighth century B.C., the Greek poet Hesiod said, "Big fish eat little fish."

Some Native Americans offered a prayer before the hunt, thanking Divine Spirit for the gift of food they hoped to find that day. The prayer showed a respect for life, while still recognizing the need for physical life-forms to feed upon yet other life-forms.

During my deer hunt, I did not have this sense of detachment and thanks.

There was a lot of social pressure in my home community for men to go hunting and prove their manhood. Deer hunting was an annual rite of passage, but I was starting to have a problem with it. My deepest regret later was about going hunting to please others. The karma that followed was due to ignoring my own strong feelings.

You can hunt and fish. Just hold an attitude of gratitude to ECK for Its gifts of food.

## Special Friend

*I am eight years old, and I had a dream about a cat with a crystal in its forehead. Are animals really this special?*

The cat with the crystal in the middle of its forehead sounds like a special cat to love.

A neighbor's black cat comes over to say hi when my wife walks our little dog, Molly. The cat is Nubby.

She likes Molly and my wife, so one day she brought them a gift. It is a smooth white pebble. Nubby laid it on the lawn by the front door, and she comes every day to see if her gift is still there. It is.

Nubby is a special cat. She can hear you talk when you speak to her on the inside, like a whisper.

The little dog, Molly, seemed ready for her walk once this afternoon, so I opened the door to tell Nubby we'd be right out. Of course, Molly changed her mind and lay down again.

I forgot about Nubby, who was waiting outside the front door for us. Nubby is a polite lady. She has good manners. But finally she meowed through the door. Were Molly and I coming out? I was busy and ignored her. Then she scratched the door. So Molly and I went outside before Nubby tore the door down.

## The Orange Cat

*An orange cat came to my house and I took care of her for a while. She was pregnant and had kittens, but soon after she got hit by a car. I took her to the vet, then nursed her at home, but since her spinal nerves were crushed, she had to be put to sleep.*

*I dearly love animals and thought I had done the right thing. But maybe I should learn a lesson from this. Was I negligent in some way? Why does this hurt so?*

You did everything in accord with Divine Spirit. Much as you might want to, it's just not possible to take in every stray animal that comes to your home. But the cat saw what love could be when it met you. It knew now what it hadn't before, that a completely new lifetime was needed to enjoy such love, because it chose its present life without the knowledge of love.

So it will indeed return so that it may enter into those conditions that will allow it to give and receive love.

You both know that you did all you could humanly do for it. Now rest in the comfort of the Mahanta's grace and let the ECK's law of manifestation provide the orange cat with the life it needs next time.

Experience will earn us a place of honor among the Vairagi Adepts, but only if we master the lessons in all sides of life.

# 5

# Youth and Families in ECK

*How do the ECK youth take a leadership role in the face of views that we're inexperienced, underdeveloped, or naive—without coming across as self-righteous?*

Do the ECK youth leaders really accept the idea that they are inexperienced, underdeveloped, or naive? That would lead to hopeless stagnation. Yes, it is true that we are all cubs, greenhorns, or rookies while first learning something new. That's life.

Does a high-school basketball coach put a raw freshman on the A-team simply because the new kid thinks he belongs there? Why shouldn't he earn his place on the team, like everyone else?

How does a flutist get to play first flute? She earns it, doesn't she?

All this agrees with the ECK teachings. Experience will earn us a place of honor among the Vairagi Adepts, but only if we master the lessons in all sides of life. Some people never seem to learn, and for them it takes longer.

Leadership means a strong sense of responsibility. It is a commitment to seeing a project through to the bitter end, no matter what the odds. Some people are natural leaders and thrive on those challenges, but the rest of us can learn.

To sum up, we must prove our worth, both here on earth and in heaven. That's what makes life so interesting.

The youth program is coming along, and some future date will find us ready to respond to the young people in even fuller ways than is possible today. When one has the vision of how the stage will be set a few years from now, there is a sense of urgency to be there today. Of course, such sudden movements are not possible because they get ahead of the consciousness of today's youth.

## Questions about God

*My seven-year-old son has asked me when God started. I have told him God is without beginning or end, but he wants to go to the time God started, in a time-travel machine. Mahanta, how do I answer his questions?*

The questions from your son have been on my mind for some time. Children do want to know the ultimate mysteries of God, sometimes astounding adults who pass them off as foolish.

Tell your son that the Inner Master will have to show him why God did not start like everything else. To do this, help him draw a time machine on a piece of paper—one that satisfies him as being a worthy space vessel to undertake such a noble venture. Put a seat in for the Mahanta, the Living ECK Master.

Tell him to think of his time-travel machine at bedtime and ask the Mahanta to show him what he needs to know about God. If this is the will of the ECK, he will find the need for that question to be fulfilled.

## Light Bodies

*I am twelve years old. I was walking in the hallway of my house when I thought I saw a body of light in front of me. My mind said it was just because I was in a dark hallway, entering a brightly lit room.*

*But the next time I had to go down the hallway, I got scared. Was there really a Light body in my hallway?*

There are always light bodies around us. The Astral Plane is at a level of vibration just above the Physical Plane, but sometimes there are dips or drops in vibration. Then people catch a glimpse of the neighboring plane.

Right now, on the Astral Plane, there is a twelve-year-old girl who also thinks she saw someone in the hallway.

When you walk in your hallway, chant HU. Then whisper to her, "I didn't mean to frighten you either." Don't worry, I'll be there with you.

## The Goodness of ECK

*My two-year-old son has suddenly become afraid and distressed about ECK, the ECK Masters, and HU. In the past he liked the HU Songs that are held at our house once a week and even sang HU to his stuffed animals. Now he asks us not to HU with him and he says, "No Z!" before going to sleep. When I put on an ECK audiocassette, he ran screaming to me to tell me to turn it off. I don't know what to do.*

115

While often such a turnabout in a two-year-old can be a reaction to something on the inner planes, it may simply be linked to physical pain. For instance, a toothache. Since he can't express himself well, he rejects something he knows you regard as both good and important. Later, as the pain lessens, his reaction to ECK will also reduce.

But it depends upon how the parents respond when the child rejects an important value of the family, like ECK. He'll remember your reaction and may use it in the future as a way to control you. Children do that.

Be compassionate to his pain, but be *firm* about the goodness of ECK.

## Learning Discrimination

*I am twelve years old. I had a bad dream where I was attacked by the Kal in the form of bad vibrations from a cartoon on TV. How can I avoid frightening dreams like that in the future?*

You asked how to avoid frightening dreams caused by a certain cartoon on TV. Watch other cartoons instead.

Don't let anything into your life that hurts or frightens you, if there is something you can do about it. That means not just a cartoon show, but also people, food, habits, etc. You'll be much more at peace with yourself.

If you want something positive in your life, then look for something more positive. If all of a sudden a lot of things are going wrong at school, it could be because of the negative thoughts coming from a TV show or movie.

## When Children See Their Past

*My four-year-old daughter wakes up every night screaming and crying. It goes on for hours. She can't*

116

*tell us what's wrong, and we have tried everything we can think of to help her. I am afraid. Can you help?*

Sometimes a child may not be able to handle the influences of her past as they appear in her dreams. In this case, I would suggest you find a counselor to help her deal with her inner problems. It's important to find a caring and sensitive person. Ask your family doctor to refer you to such a counselor, if possible.

The ECK uses all kinds of doctors and healing to let us have a better life. Accept the guidance of the ECK to help you find a counselor for your daughter.

## Wheel of Life

*Does the Wheel of Awagawan ever end?*

Yes, it does. The Wheel of Awagawan means an endless round of births and deaths. People go around the wheel many hundreds of times, and each time is one lifetime. They must meet the Mahanta, the Living ECK Master if they ever hope to get off it, though.

The Mahanta shows you how to do the Spiritual Exercises of ECK. They help you work off the karma that has kept you on the Wheel of Awagawan.

The spiritual exercises make you (Soul) pure.

When you become pure enough in this lifetime, you will never again have to return to earth unless you want to help others find spiritual freedom too. That's what the ECK Masters do.

## Sharing a Dream

*Are the friends and family members I meet in my dreams actually sharing the experience? Is it as real*

*for them as it is for me (though they may not remem-*
*ber)? Or are they only present as mock-ups in my mind?*

You may all have the same dream experience. Yet
there are times when your mind will create a fantasy
world, like a dramatist who moves characters around
in a play. How do you tell the difference? What is
illusion, what is truth?

The key is the Spiritual Exercises of ECK. They
help you sort out the real experiences from the false
ones.

Some people tell other people about their dreams
in order to control others. For example, a man tells a
woman about his dream where she agreed to marry
him. It's a choke hold. His intentions should stand on
their own merits. That means he should simply say he
loves her. Then it's up to her to decide whether the
relationship holds anything for her without the pressure of trying to live up to his dream.

As I've said before—the inner is for the inner, the
outer is for the outer.

It's unfair to others to say they've agreed to something that happened in your dreams. You may have
been under a spell of illusion.

Each person has many dream experiences every
night, and no one can remember them all later. So just
as others don't remember their place in your dreams,
you are likely to draw a blank on your role in theirs.

Each recalls the events that strike his or her
imagination.


## Learning about Life

*Who do you listen to if your inner guidance tells you*
*that something is all right for you to do, but your*

*parent or someone else deserving of respect tells you that you may not?*

That depends upon what our so-called inner guidance tells us to do. The guidance may be from the Kal, instead of from the Mahanta. The whole purpose of the teachings of ECK is to teach us the difference.

Growing up, spiritually and physically, means that more and more people are affected by what we do. When a four-year-old boy hits his younger brother on the head with his hand, his parents see no great harm is done, because the child has so little strength. Therefore, the child gets a mild rebuke.

But let's say the child grows up. Now he's fifteen. He strikes a classmate in a fit of anger and hurts him. Will his punishment be as light as when he was a child? Again, it depends upon what provoked his anger—belligerence or self-defense.

Most people make impulsive decisions while under the control of the passions of the mind. This has nothing to do with the inner guidance of the Mahanta. They are selfish human beings who think only of their own gratification. In this case, they must suffer the consequences of their runaway emotions.

There's a hard way and an easy way to learn about life. If you've ever tried a new game in the video arcade, you can lose a handful of quarters in no time while trying to learn the game by yourself. A better way is to watch someone who has played the game before and imitate him.

Parents and teachers are role models for us. They do not have all the answers, but they are responsible for their children's entry into society as mature individuals. If they cannot do the job, then the Kal sees to it that the courts limit the destructive behavior of their children.

The older you become, the more you find there is no right or wrong in an absolute sense. The guiding rule that will stand you well throughout life is this ECK saying: Is it true, is it necessary, is it kind? Unless the answer is yes for all three, then you would do well to reconsider your intended action.

That saying will resolve many of the problems that are facing you now in trying to understand the conflict you feel between your inner guidance and the guidance of your parents and others.

## Age of Sensitivity

*I have a lot of trouble in my room. I am fourteen years old and still have nightmares or see things, such as a ghost. I do a visualization technique in which I put the ECK Masters around the windows and doors, but it doesn't always work. I still get afraid. What can I do?*

You're at an age of high sensitivity. It can take the form of nightmares or seeing ghosts, a problem that my sister and I also ran into from about the age of twelve to fifteen.

A small night-light or two for your bedroom is a way to keep the powers of night at bay. Another is to have a pet in your room overnight. And keep up the spiritual exercises. Don't watch horror shows on TV at all, but try to watch upbeat programs of comedy, nature, or sports. Many soft drinks are high in caffeine, which makes for tense nerves — so replace harmful soft drinks with teas or fruit drinks. Take multivitamins and multiminerals. Be sure to get enough rest and exercise.

The above suggestions can bring you more calm. Put extra attention on peace and quiet for another year or two, after which your sensitivity will balance out.

## Family Harmony

*I would like to become a member of ECKANKAR, but my parents don't want me to. I am in high school now. What can I do?*

For the present time it is better to study and read the books of ECKANKAR rather than considering membership. I like to keep families together. It's best for a person to reach legal age before considering membership unless the rest of the family are already members.

If you find a spiritual exercise in one of the ECK books that you would like to do on your own, until you are earning your own way, you are certainly welcome to do so. If you want to practice the Easy Way technique or another exercise in the book *The Spiritual Exercises of ECK,* you will find the love and protection of the Mahanta are always with you.

I can understand your hunger for truth. But remember that the ECK actually keeps families together and does not separate them. As long as you are in your parents' home, it is more honest to respect their wishes that you not join the outer membership of ECK.

I do not want to see a family quarrel about ECK. We try to live as quietly, discretely, and harmoniously with our kin as possible. There is no advantage in making our beliefs the center of controversy at home. Parents have a duty to society to raise their children in the way that's right for them, and I cannot interfere.

## Responsibility

*Like other ECK youth, decisions await me about
how to handle responsibilities—either in career, in
college, or in personal relationships. I see responsibility
as another face of love. But is there a way to tell if I'm
using responsibility as an excuse to avoid experiences?*

Responsibility is a big word, and it can frighten us.
It tries to take a snapshot of us running through life
and put a caption to this single picture, which is so
small compared to all life that it's nearly invisible.

But what does a word like that tagged on to what
we do after it's done mean? As you say, responsibility
is another face of love. Every time a decision faces you,
the question is: "Will you be responsible or not?" But
responsible to whom?

The usual definition of responsibility is what society expects of you, but that may not always be the
right thing to do. At the crossroads of decision, ask the
Inner Master what to do. He will tell you by intuition,
by knowing, or by direct speech what decision is spiritually correct.

For now, get experiences in work, in education, in
your spiritual exercises, and in your personal relationships. When you turn decisions over to the Mahanta,
you will do the responsible thing. The point is to live
life with a loving, grateful heart.

## Working for Mastership

*Was becoming an ECK Master hard?*

Yes, it took a lot of work to become an ECK Master,
but I like to work with the SUGMAD.

## Love Bond

*I have been in ECK almost two years. I come from a very traditional Catholic family, and my parents are very upset about ECK. They say I will go to hell, and they want to disown me. I feel like I am being torn in half. I love them, and I don't want to lose them. What can I do?*

The ECK will sometimes cause a ferocious reaction in people. I found the same was true when my parents learned I was leaving the Lutheran church for ECKANKAR. It was a painful time. The rift with my family continued for over ten years and is not healed yet.

I am being more lenient today than in the past about initiates, like you, who are caught in the unfortunate no-man's-land between their family's religion and ECK. So if it would help things to remain a Catholic and continue your ECK studies, by all means do that.

If the family pressure is too strong, you also have my blessings if you feel it better to rest from the ECK teachings. Mainly, you have to be able to live with yourself, so let your inner feelings lead you to what you can live with. My love and thoughts are with you during these difficult times.

## Having Personal Freedoms

*I'm having trouble with my life. I am tired of everything I'm doing. It always feels like I am following someone else's rules rather than a natural extension of my own spiritual nature. Where is the freedom I want from life?*

I can appreciate your frustration. You have so much energy but haven't found a place to put it to use or how.

Something that bothered me in college was the fact of having to tell somebody so early what classes I wanted to take that would fit my career plans. I had no plans. There was so much freedom and so much energy, but I didn't know what to do with my life.

Then the U.S. got into Vietnam. The draft board helped me make a decision: better to join the Air Force than be drafted into the Army and land in Vietnam. I lost some freedom in service, but the Air Force taught me skills and gave me direction in life.

You have youth, health, and energy. If you can marshal your self-discipline, the world is at your feet. You have many things to be grateful for, despite all the uncertainty.

*My parents make me study some things in ECKANKAR that I do not believe. What can I do about it? How can I let them know that I don't want to study certain things?*

They probably also make you do some things you don't like apart from ECKANKAR.

No two people will ever see anything exactly alike. The problem can be worse in a home because it is like a pressure cooker. You and your parents have to live under the same roof and see each other every day.

As parents, they have the job of preparing you to be a responsible adult in today's society. For a while, my daughter and I had the same problem. She thought she could live any which way she pleased. I agreed but also told her there was a price to pay. Did she know what it was, and was she willing to pay it?

Most young people don't know the price. They need advice, but they don't want to get it from their parents. After all, their parents are the very ones from whom they are trying to win more freedom. This tension exists in nearly every family.

I have no single answer for you. If your parents are paying for the housing where you stay, then they have quite a bit to say about the rules of the house. Learn what you can from them. In the meantime, begin to plan for when you are of legal age and can have your own place. Read the classified ads and see what the cost of rentals is.

Then look in the classified ads again, this time in the Help Wanted section. See how much you'd need to earn to afford the kind of place you'd like to live in. Your parents can help you learn about the many costs involved in having your own place. Ask them about the cost of insurance, heating, and food. It may give you a common ground of understanding.

You may then find that you also have a lot in common about the teachings of ECK too. See if you can work something out.

## Drugs—A Spiritual Dead End

*Where is one when one is on drugs?*

Drugs are a rose-lined lane to misery and unhappiness. I can't say this strongly enough.

Few who dabble in drugs want to admit that there is any danger in using them. They use them to escape boredom, and boredom itself is a crime against the creative power of Soul.

Every act has a consequence, so are we ready to pay the piper?

Drugs bring unreal experiences in the elementary Astral world—some good, some bad, but all petty. What good ever comes from putting our sanity on the line for little pills and powders?

How do you say no to "friends" who push drugs at you? That happened to me in a house where I once lived with thirteen other people. I just said no. God Consciousness was my goal, and I did not want to turn into a druggie like them.

Have you ever noticed the cute names the Kal Niranjan has put on drugs? You know most of them—angel dust, coke, buttons, smack or horse, orange sunshine, and the like. The cute labels are to hide the horror that catches Soul once It falls for them. Drugs are a shortcut to more unbearable incarnations, and they hardly bring more than simple light and color, at best.

Chant HU or SUGMAD if you want to see Kal's face behind the face of a "friend" who pushes drugs at you. Soul Travel is better—it puts you in control of your life and is completely safe.

## Cleaning Up Your Act

*What happens to those who use foul language? I hear it all the time at school, and I want to understand the consequences of it.*

Foul language, no matter how you spell it, is for the barnyard. The simple ECK principle is this: where your attention is, so are you. What you hold in your thoughts is what you become.

Since you're an expression of the Sound Current, do you want to bring beauty, joy, love, and harmony to the world? Then choose words that do that. The words you speak are an expression of what you are and what you'd like to be.

*Almost every day people come up to me and speak negatively of someone, or I hear people around me gossiping. I have noticed that even when I do not support what they are saying, they lower my opinion about that individual.*

*What can I do to avoid getting involved in this gossip?*

Once when I was a freshman in high school, four of my roommates were gossiping about our other roommate. Their comments were sharp, biting, and largely untrue.

I was only half listening to them but noticed, as you have, that their opinions were having a bad effect on me. Suddenly, these words dropped from my lips: "Won't anybody here speak up for Bill?"

All four turned to glare at me. It was very uncomfortable, because I had not meant to embarrass anyone, especially since two of them were sophomores. But my question broke up the group. After that, they chose their words more carefully around me.

Was it courage that had made me speak up for Bill? In a way, yes. The Mahanta had given me the words to speak, but I had to speak them. He was already guiding me then, years before I had first heard of ECKANKAR.

This may not work in your case. But listen to the Inner Master the next time such an occasion arises, and you will know what to do or say.

## Discrimination and Inner Guidance

*How can someone tell whether he is being guided by the ECK or by the mind?*

You can't ever be sure.
Why?
The mind has a power to make you believe you are

127

always right. That's why a headstrong person acts so smart. He thinks he's always right, though he's often wrong.

So, then, what is the good of ECK?

If guided by ECK, we are more likely to change our minds when new information comes along. We're quicker to admit that an earlier decision based on sketchy information needs to change. Those under the guidance of ECK are always alert. The purpose of ECK is to have chelas at the peak of awareness.

## Mistakes of the Past

*When I was a child of eight, I stole food from my father. This was during the war when food was as precious as life. Now I am an adult and have great fear of being called a thief. How can I reconcile these mistakes of my youth and free myself of this shame? I am now twenty-nine and working as a lawyer in our small town.*

Let the mistakes of your youth remain in the past. Everyone has things in the past he would like to forget. What is important, however, is that you've done something to improve yourself. Through the practice of law and your experiences as a youth, you can be a better and more useful Co-worker with the Mahanta.

Be fair in your dealings with people, and you can do much good.

## Anger

*I'm a thirteen-year-old boy. How can I learn to control my temper and stop fighting with my brother?*

A big reason for anger at your age is that you want to have more freedom in every way, to get more independence to do what you want and not what others tell you to do.

The anger comes because we think we know more than we do. But important lessons that lie ahead during the next few years include: What knowledge do you need to prepare you to leave home after high school? How much do you have to meet halfway the opinions of co-workers in order to have a life filled with rich spiritual adventures and growth?

The parents' duty is to give their children a firm foundation in the principles of ECK, so we can learn ways to live in harmony with people around us, including brothers. Get into some sport you like a lot to work off some energy, and go into contemplation for the rest of the answer to your question.

## Telling Right from Wrong

*If you do something wrong, but do it in the name of the SUGMAD, is it still wrong? Like if you're with friends and doing drugs, but doing it in the name of the SUGMAD?*

Drugs, in any case, don't help you out. They are stopping you on the most direct way to God.

Any act that holds someone else or yourself back is wrong, whether you say you are doing it in the name of SUGMAD or not. The words don't make it right.

## Contemplation Time

*Do you have any suggestions on how to start good patterns for doing spiritual exercises? I set a time, then something else to do always comes up instead. When I change the time to do them, it feels like the pattern gets goofed up.*

It's better to do the spiritual exercises at different times than not do them at all.

You can also try choosing a time when other things might not interfere, like right before bedtime.

As you practice the spiritual exercises, pretty soon you will be able to tune in to the ECK anywhere, no matter what time it is. You will be able to do it easily, no matter where you are.

*In contemplation, when I place my attention on my Third Eye, it always begins to sway and move around. This makes me yawn and disturbs my spiritual exercise. Do you have any suggestions?*

The mind gets bored fast. So if it makes you yawn when you place your attention on the Third Eye, then put your attention on your crown chakra instead. That's at the top of your head. That spiritual center is actually the easiest place to succeed at Soul Travel.

## Remembering Dreams

*When you have a dream, why do you forget it the next morning?*

There can be any number of reasons. Sometimes the mind wants to protect you because the dream would shock you. It's a different world with different rules. You wake up and right away this world crowds in on you and you say, "I've got to get up, go to school."

You can set a dream in your mind before you wake up by repeating the main points of it, then talking about it out loud or writing it down as soon as you wake up. Dreams are real but like fluffy clouds in that they'll float away unless you try to make them more real.

## Competition

*Is it "un-ECKish" to like games such as chess, since the very nature of such games is based on war, power, and egotistical competition?*

Not in my opinion. The ECK teachings say this is a warring universe. To survive here, one must know its ways.

Chess is simply another way an individual can test his survival instinct. Competition is not necessarily a bad activity. It forms the very basis of many societies today. Their members must know how to move in such an environment and how to provide a protective shield (a home, for example) for themselves and their families.

Competition is all right as long as a person develops and follows a code of fair play.

## Staying a Virgin until Marriage

*Why is virginity until marriage suggested by the ECK Masters?*

First of all, it is a suggestion, not an order. A young person is in intensive training the first eighteen or more years of his life, learning the responsibility of self-discipline that is needed for him to be self-supporting in the world.

There is a time and a place for everything. It is natural for us to chafe against the rules that hinder our freedom. But society puts restraints on us until we learn what consequences we will shoulder for certain actions. Ignorance is no excuse under the Law of Karma.

When one is an infant, he is often a self-centered,

131

selfish person. Because he is helpless, he is used to the world catering to his whims. All the baby has to do is cry or whine to get attention. Of course, sometime between infancy and adulthood, the individual learns that he's got the workings of the world backward: He is to serve life; life does not serve him. Until this lesson hits home, he is not understanding the purpose of Soul's reincarnation, which is to become a Co-worker with God.

Virginity is suggested for the youth because without a fair grounding in life, an individual is hollow inside and mistakes sex for love. Sex takes, love gives. Unless there is love, life can be a miserable and sad experience: an unnecessary detour on the road to God.

## Meaning of ECK Initiations

*I recently learned that youth in ECK under eighteen aren't eligible for initiations beyond the Second. For those of us raised in the days when whole families were given initiations together, does our initiation accurately describe our spiritual status? Where are we?*

A chela receives the next ECK initiation when he is spiritually ready for a richer, more rewarding life.

The ECK initiation is not just a family experience. If a youth has earned an initiation beyond the Second before the age of eighteen, the Master will see that he gets it.

Yet, all initiations must be won again daily. The Second Initiation means that for now a chela's home in the other worlds is on the Second Plane, the Astral. But even at that, he may often reach a higher spiritual plane on any given day, like the Causal, Mental, or Soul Plane.

## Learning about ECK

*What are some ways to get my two daughters (five and seven years old) more involved with learning about ECK from the discourses?*

The parent can make it interesting for the little ones by letting them help read. For instance, a five-year-old can supply a simple word like *ECK* while the parent reads the ECK discourse. The seven-year-old might want to try a paragraph with help from Mom or Dad, or even a full page if the child is especially advanced in reading or wants to.

Children usually have a more direct link with the Mahanta than many adults do. They do appreciate, once or twice a month, the chance to participate with reading the ECK discourses. For example, ask them, "Would you like to read ECK tonight?" They can also be shown how to send a monthly initiate report. Usually little ones draw pictures.

## Can the Inner Master See Me?

*Can you see me when I'm watching TV?*

A lot of times, when you're just going about your regular activities, I don't come into your space and bother you as such. I never intrude in any way. I'm not always looking over your shoulder.

But if it's something of a spiritual nature that you need help with, I'm always there spiritually. If there is ever an insight you need or you want to understand something, I can help in this way.

*If I have a dream about you, do you see me at the same time?*

I always do, but sometimes I remember.

## Remembering Inner Experiences

*Is there anything I can do to help me remember experiences that I have inwardly?*

You could write things down, but that's a hard way to do it. Sometimes you don't feel like writing. Another way to remember is to study the details of the experience while it's happening.

For instance, if you're at a baseball game on the inner, you could study the uniform of one of the players on the other team, see what kind of shoes he's got—cleats or whatever—and what color shirt he has on. Even notice the stitching on parts of the shirt.

Become aware of the little details. Notice a tree, a cat—and the cat's ears, how he twitches them. This exercise will help you remember dreams.


## Can You Work in Harmony?

*I have noticed that, in their quest to be channels for the ECK, the youth in ECK have sometimes proceeded without first obtaining approval from the ECKANKAR Spiritual Center, or they have taken a broad interpretation of the ECKANKAR guidelines.*

*Is it possible that following one's inner guidance might sometimes be in conflict with the leadership structure and guidelines in ECKANKAR?*

Yours is an honest question, so I will do my best to answer you.

Spiritually, everything in ECK starts from above. As the spiritual leader of ECK, it is my responsibility to make sure that the ECK teachings and practices go in a certain direction. This would be easy to do if all the people in ECK were ECK Masters.

My point is that every person has a unique state of awareness. Another fact is that hardly anyone is God-Realized. Vain people, who run roughshod over others, may defend themselves by saying, "I got it on the inner." Usually that's an excuse for a lack of responsibility.

Every day, to keep the teachings on track, I give directions to the ECK staff outwardly. Things that come down from above (from the SUGMAD and the ECK) are naturally always changing. As the chief agent for these changes, I inform the ECK staff, the ECK leaders, and each individual ECKist what needs to be done now. Some can hear me, others cannot. It all depends upon each individual's ability to hear the Master spiritually.

Therefore, the process of change reaches the consciousness of people at various times. As a result, people must balance their inner communications with what comes to them outwardly.

They must also be willing to listen to the understandings of other people within the ECK community. It is through such interaction that people unfold and work out karma in the easiest way possible.

## Getting Guidance

*Have you ever listened to the guidance of Divine Spirit, followed it, then watched everything go wrong afterward? I wonder if sometimes I misunderstood what I got.*

Divine Spirit wants you to learn and have experiences. The result may not be what you want but it's helping you learn and grow.

It's not what happens to you but your attitude about what happens that's really important. When something happens to you, ask, Since this is what Spirit got for me, what does it mean? How is it helping me grow?

## Giving Others Freedom

*Can I use the ECK to get someone to be my friend?*

You mean if you wanted someone to be your friend, could you make that happen?

A better way is to let the person have complete freedom to make up his or her mind. You don't really want a friend who doesn't want you. It never works. But you can be a good friend by allowing others space.

Anyone who is worth his weight likes freedom, and as soon as we take away the freedom the person doesn't like us anymore. It causes a lot of heartache for us. Friendship has to be two-way.

## In the Mahanta's Name

*What is the most valuable thing which the ECK youth as a group can offer as Co-workers with the SUGMAD?*

Individuals make up a group. Therefore, all in ECK—regardless of age—must check whether they are directed by Divine Spirit or ego.

Do everything in the name of the Mahanta. How? Here come the old standbys: Is it true? Is it necessary? Is it kind? Ask yourself those three simple questions every time you are in doubt about any action.

Before a group can be of true service to the Mahanta, each person in that group must know how to listen to the inner voice of divine love. These three questions will help you do that in the best way I know.

## Ancient Teachings

*I'm nine years old. I'd like to know where, or in what country, did ECKANKAR begin?*

In ancient times, the Living ECK Master gave the ECK teachings to his disciples by word of mouth. Rama was among the first of these Masters. *The Shariyat-Ki-Sugmad* says he came from the forests of northern Germany.

From there, he traveled to Iran (ancient Persia), where he gave the secret teachings to a small band of mystics. Their descendants were later to become the followers of Zoroaster, around 600 B.C. But the first ECK writings did not appear until much later, around the thirteenth century. Rumi, the Persian poet, was about the first writer to hint at them, which he did in his famous poem "The Reed of God."

After leaving Persia, Rama moved to India, where he settled down. *The Shariyat* says he taught people there about the chance to have the experience of God in that very lifetime.

So where did ECKANKAR begin?

Even before Rama, the ECK teachings were in Atlantis and Lemuria. Modern scholars scoff at the existence of those two lost continents, so we don't talk much about them in ECKANKAR today. Yet proof does exist. Under the waters off the southeastern part of the United States are huge stone blocks in the shape of a wall or an ancient road. Somebody put them there a long time ago, when that part of the ocean was above water.

## Soul Just Is

*Did SUGMAD create all Souls at the same time? If yes, why? And if not, why not?*

In our world, we must think about time. Even your question says "at the same time." But SUGMAD created Souls before time began, so it is not a question of Souls made sooner or later. As humans, we find this hard to understand.

Yet even when studying the origin of this universe, scientists run into a problem of how to determine the age of the "big bang." It's a theory about the moment of creation. But creation happened before there was time. So scientists work from there and accept the fact of creation, because the evidence is all around. However, they cannot fix a date to the beginning of time. It's simply not possible.

SUGMAD created all Souls before time began, so there is no answer to your question of when. If God creates more Souls, that also happens beyond the laws of time and space.

Soul just is.

We know that Soul exists by the evidence of life around us. When Soul inhabits a body, that body lives, moves, and has being. When Soul leaves, the body no longer lives, moves, or has being. What has left? By direct and indirect evidence, we know that some unseen force gives life to a physical body.

What is that something? Soul, of course.

There is no simple reply to your question. But spiritually, there is an answer. In contemplation, ask the Mahanta to let you see and know about the creation and nature of Soul. If you are sincere, he will show you.

The most important point of all is that you are Soul. Know that you are a spark of God and can exist fully only wthin the realization of that profound truth. As such, you are a light and inspiration to others.

Take each step in your physical life as it comes, with the assurance that the way has already been prepared by the Mahanta. It will be resolved in the best way for all concerned.

# 6

# Spiritual Healing

*A*t a recent seminar, I was approached by an ECKist I had never met. She shook my hand and thanked me for healing her of a very serious illness that she had been suffering for some time. This came as a big surprise to me. I was quick to point out that it was not me who did the healing, but the ECK, through the vehicle of the Mahanta.

*Still, my question to you is: Did this really happen? Or could this woman have been mistaken?*

Yes, it really happened. What you report is a fairly common happening. Other initiates have said the same thing.

As you correctly told her, it was the ECK, through the Mahanta, that did the healing. The Master often comes in the likeness of an initiate to give the healing. He then arranges for an outer meeting later between the initiate and the person who was healed. This is so the initiate can tell the other in plain language something important about the ways of the ECK.

## Karmaless Healing

*How do healers stay free of karma? What is karma-less healing?*

The safe way to handle requests for healing is to turn the person with the request over to the Living ECK Master. You will perform the karmaless action if you instruct them to write to me so that the healing may be accomplished through Divine Spirit if It so wills.

Spirit acts in a way that is for the good of the whole, sometimes bringing a healing of the emotions or the mind instead of the body, because that is in the best interests of that particular Soul's unfoldment.

For one to put himself in the healer's shoes is to unknowingly accept the karma of the person who requests the healing. At some time in the future, the karma must come due if it is not passed off into the ECK Stream.

## More than Band-Aids

*I'd like a greater understanding of the difference between psychic healers and other kinds of healers.*

Regular healers help fix problems people cause themselves by putting a Band-Aid on them. If you go to a doctor for a cut, he cleans it and applies a bandage until it can heal naturally. He does not try to tamper with a spiritual condition he is not qualified to heal, which psychic healers often try to do and thereby set up more causes to be worked out as more problems.

A difference between psychic healing and spiritual healing is that psychic healing leaves you in the same state of consciousness, perhaps temporarily alleviating symptoms caused by an attitude you hold. However, spiritual healing helps change the attitude which caused the problem, so it can go away and not recur.

See the difference?

## Healing Broken Laws

*What stand does ECKANKAR take on healing? I was a spiritualist before I came to ECK. I often healed others but now wonder if I should continue.*

The problem surrounding healing is karmic. The ill person once broke a divine principle through ignorance. Psychic healers can ease the symptoms for a while, but eventually the sickness surfaces again with a new face.

In the meantime, the healer is accruing the karma from all the people he heals with the psychic force. Someday the debt comes due. There is more to healing than erasing the outer symptoms for a few months or years, or until the passion of the mind that lies behind the illness produces the next symptom of arthritis or cancer.

The Living ECK Master puts the entire matter into the hands of the ECK. It, in Its divine wisdom, sees whether or not the individual has learned to control the mental aberration that made him ill. If not, there is no healing. After all, Divine Spirit wants only the education of Soul so It can be a Co-worker with God.

ECKists learn to perform the karmaless action. That means telling the afflicted one to write directly to the Living ECK Master. Healing with the psychic power is a thorny path; karmic burn-off is speeded up for one on the path of ECK.

## Searching for Health

*I am plagued by rheumatoid arthritis and don't know where to turn next. Can you give me any direction toward healing this problem?*

By now you've probably seen a lot of doctors about it. There is always somebody on earth who knows more about a certain condition than anybody else.

If you haven't already, try to find a homeopathic chiropractor who has some knowledge of nutrition: the effects of foods on the body. For instance, nuts and seeds (raw and roasted) are not good at all for some people, while others thrive on them.

This isn't much of a lead, but your search for health will be guided by the inner principle that I am, the Mahanta. Divine Spirit acts in Its own way and in Its own time to bring about what is for the good of all.

At times Divine Spirit heals directly, at other times It leads one to the right medical doctor. Sometimes It will assist in the healing and treatment we are presently undergoing. On the one hand we must inwardly turn everything over to the guidance of this Supreme Force while making every effort to find the most suitable medical help.

## Spiritual Fasting

*Can you give me some idea how enlightenment comes into Soul and heals the inner bodies, and what techniques help this?*

Enlightenment is a gentle thing if it's right, if you're ready for it. It gives you a different viewpoint, a different state of consciousness.

This also occurs when we do a spiritual fast. This

144

is why Fridays have been set aside for you to do a mental fast where you keep your attention on the Inner Master for as much of the day as you can.

You'll notice that when you are on a spiritual fast, you treat people differently at work and at home. You're in a different state of awareness that day. You're pulled out of the routine or rut that the mind likes.

This actually works off karma. The hold of the material world, the attachments, are not as strong on you. This gives you a little more freedom of choice. It puts you in charge of your own life in subtle ways. Other people can feel this.

Sometimes there is something going on at work, something that's not too smooth for you. You can do a spiritual fast for a couple of days. You'll find that your attitude and your very words are different. You're not creating karma the way you were before.

Most of our problems are self-made. When things go wrong, if we take responsibility and do something that gives us greater understanding, life becomes easier.

This is how it should be, rather than having someone always giving us spiritual, emotional, or physical healings.

## Action by Divine Spirit

*How do you solve a matter of healing for a chela when someone writes you with a request?*

The problem is turned over to Divine Spirit which goes to work immediately, even before your letter reaches its destination. I do nothing of myself, but it is my responsibility and spiritual duty to act as an instrument for the spiritual power to flow out to all and help anyone who makes a request.

I cannot tell if a person's request will be fulfilled as he desires. Spirit will use Its own divine wisdom to help each one for his individual welfare. It may guide him to the proper medical doctor or in some other way address Itself to the condition behind the problem.

If the chela will surrender all of the problem to the Mahanta, the Inner Master, the problem will be taken care of in due time.

## Breaking Free

*I am at a crossroads spiritually. And I feel stuck. Is it possible to be a member of a spiritual organization without surrendering to a master? I have blocked myself inside for fear of spiritual traps which abound in different paths—I've encountered quite a few myself. A few years ago I abandoned all gurus and took to Mother Earth and gardening.*

You've gone through some hard times, trying to understand what part those past experiences played in your spiritual growth. Some people have a very delicate inner mainspring, like that of a watch. They are hurt more easily by things which another might take more in stride.

Inwardly, you saw the need to heal yourself. That's why you took up T'ai Chi and gardening. We all need to feel in touch with something stable, and you did too. But now that you've healed to a certain degree, the inner nudge from the spiritual side is again offering you a chance to grow. The idea is not to hide from life: It is to live life, but without making the same mistakes we did before.

The question you're now asking is whether you need to join an organization (like ECKANKAR or

146

something else) to grow spiritually. No, you do not. But don't be a hermit either. People need people. That's how things are. Join recreation groups or study groups, even take classes—if that's what you want. But be with people when you need to.

Some people do not fit within an organization like ECKANKAR, and I respect that. You've come a long way in healing yourself, but try to understand that earth is not a rose garden. We all get hurt and cry, but then we must get up tomorrow morning for those who depend on us.

## The Pace of Healing

*I have asked repeatedly for healings from my terrible cancer. Please help me understand why I am still afflicted with it.*

It is not I that do the healing, but the ECK—if It sees any to be done. You stare at the negative side of your life as if nobody else in the world has any troubles.

Do you recall the story of the distraught mother who lost her child and came to the Master beside herself with grief? He said, yes, he would help her if she would but go door to door and find one household that had never been touched by sorrow or death. After spending a great length of time in doing this, she returned to the Master a much wiser woman. It became clear to her that the things in our life are not our own, merely things that are lent to us by the Spirit of Life for our growth.

You have a wonderful husband who loves you dearly. There is not anything more precious in this world than love—not health, youth, or beauty. If your ill health were ripped away from you in one day, there would no longer be the tie between you that you have today. And it is a good one in that both of you are able to give your love to each other if you so choose.

The Mahanta wants to show us how to make our life a bearable one by the application of the rules of common sense, which are those of the ECK.

When calls for help come to me from victims of cancer, but the Law of Karma says that this is the best way for them to get purification of the mind so that they can get liberation of Soul, then that is the will of the ECK. I cannot interfere. There is help for you, but you must really stop and listen to the help that is coming to you.

## Inner Attention

*I noticed an uncomfortable pressure in my head and wrote to you for help. Over the next few weeks, I began to notice times the pressure was stronger or weaker. I also noticed it was stronger after drinking certain herbal teas. I held to the thought that the situation would improve, and it has. I was able to give my first solo talk at an ECK presentation recently.*

I am happy you opened yourself to Divine Spirit for an understanding of what caused the pressure. The ECK will bring healing in subtle ways, often by suddenly giving an insight into certain food or drink that is the source of the discomfort.

That is why I often recommend a person go to a doctor for a routine checkup, for that frequently reveals a minor dietary adjustment that makes all the difference in the world.

If your condition requires more attention to dissolve the symptoms completely, please consider a checkup, if only for your peace of mind.

It is noteworthy that you went beyond yourself to speak at the ECK presentation. Obstacles arise to prevent our growth in new areas. Yet when we put our fears and ills in the background, implicit trust in the ECK carries us through to success.

It's always a test. If it's not met today, there's no worry, for another opportunity will come.

## The Healer's Protection

*Recently I signed up for a Japanese Reiki workshop. But when I arrived at the first meeting, I discovered that in order to get what I'd paid for, I was required to attend all of the meetings and take their four initiations.*

*I am very upset over this and wonder if it will reverse my unfoldment in ECK.*

To put your mind at ease, the workshop will not jeopardize your ECK initiations because you put your attention upon the Mahanta.

You wanted to know what to do when you find yourself in this type of situation—of having to sign a paper promising to complete the seminar and get all four initiations. We all get put into those spots, because the Kal agents are full of tricks.

But no matter what kind of corner we find ourselves in, whether here or in the invisible planes, the way out of the trap is to instantly put attention on the Mahanta or the ECK. Full thought or immersion in the spiritual principle, which is love, pushes out fear. When fear is pushed from our consciousness, then the hunter's control is broken and has no power over us.

I would caution you to not lay hands upon another during the healing process. This is to forestall one's taking on of another's karma through ignorance of the impartial laws of ECK. These simply work like mathematical principles. Of course, medical people use their hands in treating patients, but their protection comes from being in the healers' guild. They are taught well in school how to keep detached from their patients' sicknesses.

Despite the training given to doctors, many of them are not as detached in their healing as they have been trained to be.

Self-made healers do not have the advantage of such training—impartiality coupled still with compassion, which any good healer must have. Therefore they are like babes among the wolves when it comes to knowing the spiritual laws the sick person broke and which are responsible for his illness.

As far as I am concerned, people can do as they please. But it is my job to point out the dangers. Some things actually hold people back in their journey home to God. But they are so caught up in human sentimentality that they never understand how they interfere in the workings of karma and thus take on the karma themselves.

Since you put your attention upon the Mahanta, there is no harm that will come to you from the Reiki workshop.

### Spiritual Tangle

*I'm having scary visions. I have talked to an ECKist friend, who explained to me about the psychic I've been going to. He also said you may be able to tell me why I'm having these frightening visions.*

The cause of the disturbing visions is mixing the psychic field with the spiritual way of ECK. A terrible storm develops within the human consciousness.

The safest thing to do is, first, get the psychic centers in your body closed. Call the United Way (see the telephone white pages in larger cities) or your local counseling referral service and ask for advice for your problem of scary visions.

See what counseling is available to you and the cost. If you take the step to seek qualified counseling, then Divine Spirit will begin straightening out your spiritual tangle.

## How to Ask for Help

*I would like to have license to be a spiritual healer in my country. Please open me so that I can let the wonders of God flow into myself.*

I am happy that your chief goal remains God-Realization. Once the initiate reaches these heights, he finds the truth contained in the biblical words: "But rather seek ye the kingdom of God; and all these things shall be added unto you."

The Living ECK Master never appoints anyone as a spiritual healer. The chela can learn the art of spiritual healing, but it must be for self-healing alone. Thus I am not able to appoint you as a spiritual healer in ECKANKAR.

However, whatever you choose as your profession is a personal matter strictly between you and the Mahanta. You must meet the licensing needs of your country of residence, whether the profession is as a medical doctor, mental counselor, or dentist.

I do not let the initiate use the works of ECK to make a personal profit. The chela can tell uninitiated people to write a personal letter to the Living ECK

Master to request healing. His training for the Mastership has revealed the secret of turning healing requests over to the ECK.

Thus the ECKist gives a service to his neighbors without accepting another's karma. The Living ECK Master accepts healing requests only if the person making the request has exhausted every traditional source of healing, without success.

## Gifts from God

*I am not an ECKist but am writing you because my interest in ECKANKAR is growing and I need your help on a problem that is devastating to me. Both my sons have been diagnosed with cystic fibrosis, a life-threatening disease. The doctor says they will live only to their twenties or thirties. My heart breaks daily over this, since they are truly beings of light. Can you give me some insight into why they chose this or what I did to cause it?*

Science is making new discoveries all the time about the cure of diseases. The Holy Spirit, or ECK, works in many ways to bring healing, even through the wonders of science. The doctors give your children a number of years in which science may find a way to help them. As a parent, I know that your children are as dear to you as your own life.

While the doctors and scientists are racing to find a cure for cystic fibrosis, ask Divine Spirit to show you the reason for their illness. What can you learn spiritually from it that cannot be learned another way?

Our children are a gift from God. Though we do not own them, we do love them with all our heart. Until the doctors find a cure, be thankful for every moment you have with them, but remember to let your sons breathe and grow into their own dreams.

My thoughts and love are with you in these troubling times. I'm turning your problem over to the ECK to handle as It will.

## Love of God

*I was in an automobile accident that paralyzed me from the neck down. Can you reach out and help me get through this period?*

You were asleep when I called today, but I want to reassure you that the love of Divine Spirit is with you still. Especially now, put your attention on the Spiritual Eye and sing HU or your own word. Look for either the Light or Sound, also the Inner Master.

You know what to look for. You will come to know that the love of God surrounds you even in these dark hours.

## Weathering Spiritual Storms

*What happens when chelas in ECK become involved in psychic healing? What kind of karma do they have to work off when they leave the psychic groups? How can ECKists protect themselves from psychic attacks or heal themselves afterward?*

When chelas leave former spiritual groups, attacks may be made on the inner planes by promoters of these groups. They see nothing wrong in doing this. For them, it is like a holy war. Their belief is that anything done to those of another system of consciousness in the spreading of their own belief is all right.

The first and most important step when leaving

these groups is to have absolutely nothing to do with these people in the future. Destroy mailings from them, ignore calls by telephone, and certainly do not attend meetings for the sake of old friendships. This is complicated when family members are part of these groups, but one's reliance on them can be diminished gradually over a period of time.

In place of using these groups as a crutch, as in the past, the attention is now placed 100 percent on the Mahanta. The Mahanta can bring relief only when a chela has cut all emotional and inner ties with the people in the organization he used to belong to.

## White Light

*An ECKist in our area has been using the white light to heal other ECKists. Isn't this an invasion of their privacy and a misuse of the white light?*

I am concerned when an ECKist misuses the ECK teachings through ignorance of the laws of Divine Spirit. As the present Living ECK Master, it's my duty to point out the pitfalls to the individuals involved. Whether or not they decide to follow the path of ECK based on the information I give them is purely their choice.

*The Shariyat-Ki-Sugmad* says, "To practice ECK out of curiosity, in search of new sensations, or in order to gain psychic power is a mistake which is punished with futility, neurosis, or worse. . . . Also to try praying for someone else or to use any type of healing, such as putting him in the white light, is to bring a lower power into being. . . . Prayer and healing in any other way than through the ECK of Itself is to deal in the psychic worlds."

154

## Healing from Inner Attacks

*How can I heal myself from psychic attack?*

Psychic attacks can be severe against leaders in ECK and can actually produce real illness. If this happens, get a diagnosis (if it is a safe procedure) from the medical profession or from an alternate branch of healing, to track the progress or deterioration of health.

The ECK will lead one through a labyrinth of specialists (it seems endless at times) until the right combination comes face up and help is given to relieve the ailment. The long process of discovery is one of a continual broadening of understanding about the causes of illness.

## Healers in ECK

*Will there ever be healers in ECK?*

There will be healers in ECK some day. This is one of the service fields laid out by Paul Twitchell. A select group of people will work themselves into it over a period of time and perform a valuable contribution to their fellowman.

The Living ECK Master will seldom ever tell somebody how to make a living. Healing is something only a few people can do right, because there must be a deep understanding inside them as to how karma, cause and effect, works.

One can always be a channel for the Holy Spirit. This means putting aside the need for fame and glory, and being willing to be a humble servant of the Divine Power, saying, "Let thy will be done."

Medicine is one way that Spirit brings healing to people. So is dentistry and psychology. Each profession

155

plays an important role in the coming together of Souls to reach an idea of the meaning of the hidden laws that have brought on an illness in the first place.

## Finding the Reason

*My eyesight has failed because of glaucoma. Can you heal me?*

Your failing eyesight and glaucoma has been put into the hands of Divine Spirit to do with as It will. The healing is not done by myself. It is all done through the ECK if this is best for Soul.

Soul is eternal, without beginning or ending. It comes again and again to get every experience so It can become a citizen of the high worlds of God while still alive here on earth.

Divine Spirit works in many ways to bring about healing, if that is what It chooses to do. It may lead you to a doctor who is very good at healing your illness. Or you could be led to the right herb or herbalist.

All I can do at this point is suggest you go to the Mahanta during your contemplation. There you can find the reason for this affliction and what must be done to resolve it. The answer may come quickly, or it could take days, weeks, or months.

Many times there is a karmic condition associated with the problem. The way of healing may include an opened understanding of the cause of the health problem. One may also look at his responsibility to live a life that takes into consideration weaknesses inherent in every family stock.

Please know that the Master is with you always, but it is the Inner Master, the Mahanta, which we must look to in all problems of life.

# Path toward Healing

*My son is recovering from a long illness—can you help ease his pain? Would it help if I did the spiritual exercises twice or more a day?*

Your request for your son's health has been turned over to Divine Spirit. It works in Its own way and in Its own time. How It will handle this, I cannot tell, for I am only Its vehicle.

It may guide you to the proper medical doctor or in some other way address Itself to this condition. All healing comes from the ECK no matter what vehicle It uses. Medical doctors and psychologists are legitimate healing agents on the physical plane. Once we seek professional help, then the ECK will guide us from one doctor to another until the proper help is given. This is how the ECK often works, although there are the rare instances of miraculous healings.

Take your time with the Spiritual Exercises of ECK, for it takes each person time to build spiritual stamina. It's often helpful to keep a dream notebook, if your inclinations run that way. The path of ECK enhances our life, to guide us along our own path to God. With that I can help you as the Inner Master.

In time the curtain is drawn back, and we see the purpose of hardships that we have had to endure. There is a reason for everything that happens in our life, even though the greater picture may be withheld from our spiritual eyesight for the present.

Take each step in your physical life as it comes, with the assurance that the way has already been prepared by the Mahanta. It will be resolved in the best way for all concerned.

Well-being is physical, emotional, mental, and spiritual.

# 7

# How's Your Health?

*I* *have tried everything to relieve myself of a deep depression. I feel I am drowning. Please help.*

I received your request for help. You've asked God to give you vision and the light to see with. It will be done as you asked, but in His time. Again, it will be done, but in your time. This means, God's gifts are already yours, but only as soon as you can open yourself to accept them.

Well-being is physical, emotional, mental, and spiritual. If there is an absence of well-being, there is a deficiency in one or more of these four areas. Always start with the physical, because it's easiest to begin with what's closest.

If you have worries about your health, have a doctor give you a checkup. Also, review your eating and drinking habits. Alcohol, for instance, leaves one doped and depressed. Sweets, especially chocolate, can be just as bad for some people.

It is ironic that when we're depressed we want to eat something sweet, which can cause depression. A vicious cycle.

# Loud Sound

*I am having some health problems after enjoying a strong body for most of my life. The divine Sound Current is very loud. Am I going through a spiritual or physical change?*

You mentioned a change of health and the increase of the Sound Current. We in ECK recognize the natural effect of changing consciousness. It can show up as both physical and emotional. It requires us to adjust our habits of eating and perhaps even the spiritual exercises.

In my case, I've found that aging had an effect upon my feelings of well-being. It forced me to develop new dietary habits. I eventually gave up caffeine stimulants, such as are found in coffee, many soft drinks, and even chocolate. The stimulants, on top of my increasing spiritual awareness, made me be too sensitive to the Sound Current.

We want the Sound in our lives, but too much of It can render us physically unable to carry on with our daily life. That means we must find a new balance. This means changing our habits.

Go about this rationally. Look at the foods you eat, for instance, then eliminate just the one food or drink that seems least useful to you spiritually. Continue to eat and drink your other foods and beverages. Watch for a few days if the removal of a certain food had any beneficial effect upon your feelings of well-being. If it did, don't use that food for several weeks. Later, you may wish to experiment: try to eat it again, but observe the effect it has upon your feelings of well-being.

Follow this plan with a second item of food or drink that seems *least* beneficial for your physical or spiritual good. Go slow. You don't want to make massive changes to your diet. It could be too much of a shock to your body, and that would create unnecessary health conditions.

In effect, you're treating your body as a science lab. What you see there is unique: a reflection of your expanding state of consciousness. While making observations on your food and beverage habits, be sure to get any help you see necessary from experts of nutrition, etc.

We *are* a state of consciousness. Everyone and everything in our personal and universal world has an effect upon us. We want to become aware of what these effects are. Then we can sort through them, nurturing the good ones and discarding the bad.

## Too Far Open

*My mother complains of an inner sound like people wailing or crying. She is not an ECKist and finds the sound distressing. Could you please give me a suitable explanation which I can pass on to her?*

It's hard to explain some things to people who do not know the geography of the inner worlds, as many ECKists do. She is hearing the cry of distressed Souls caught in a purgatory midway between heaven and earth. This means, between the Physical and Astral planes.

People who are open to such inner sounds are often quite sympathetic to the suffering of others. They are likely to take in homeless animals and offer soft shoulders for the troubled to cry upon.

But their sympathetic nature actually works against them. They do not understand that people have caused their own troubles. This does not mean we should be cold about the sufferings of others, but it does point out that some people secretly like to injure themselves spiritually so they can complain to others about their problems.

Your mother is hearing the cry of lost Souls. These are generally people who died under stress or unresolved personal circumstances. Let her know God provides for their deliverance from purgatory (she is likely not to believe in purgatory) when they are ready to stop clinging to the sadness that keeps them there. They are in a temporary state, and angels will take them to heaven soon enough.

Then have her sing the name *Jesus*, if she is unwilling to use HU.

A final note: Faulty nutrition can also open up some people to psychic phenomena. Have your mother check with your family doctor to see that everything is in order in the health department of her life.

## Your Responsibility

*I am not an ECKist at this time, but I hope it is OK to ask you, as the Mahanta, for help with a problem. I have a severe allergy in my eyes which is very painful and affecting my eyesight. I have been to one doctor and am going to another, but the problem is still there. Can you help me?*

The ECK began to work upon the conditions of your eyesight the moment you mailed your request for help. The ways of healing by Divine Spirit are truly endless. Often, the individual who has received relief does not connect it back to Spirit, but feels he has stumbled upon help by chance.

The ECK today often heals through the field of

162

medicine. It guides one to the doctor who is right for the condition.

The purpose of healing, however, transcends the cure of a bodily condition. There is a spiritual reason that the illness occurred. The process of spiritual healing teaches us something about ourselves that we didn't know before. When the eyes are in trouble, we have to ask, "Mahanta, what am I *not* seeing about my spiritual life that is causing me difficulty with my eyesight?"

You see, the approach assumes responsibility for whatever is wrong. Once we're willing to shoulder the blame for our thoughts and actions, then the inner forces can begin to heal us, even as our understanding of the causes becomes known to us, perhaps through our dreams or other means of understanding.

Leave your problem in the care of the Mahanta, continue to look for a doctor to help you (don't overlook a good nutritionist), and write to me again in three months about your progress.

## A Cure for Insomnia

*I have been in ECK since the days of Paul Twitchell. Over the years, I've had a problem with insomnia that has gotten more severe. I have called on many specialists but the insomnia is so all-prevailing that it is literally ruining my life. Can you point me in any direction?*

I don't often like to bring up past lives, because people usually have enough resources at hand in their life to get a start on their health problem. With science so much in the forefront today, people tend to overlook influences from past lives because the idea seems hokey.

Nevertheless, perhaps a look into your past will give you an understanding of your inability to rest.

Today, some geologists poke fun at the notion of Atlantis, because none of their drilling into the ocean floor shows it to ever have been above water. Anyway, the civilization was very advanced in many ways that would make science today envious. But, as a whole, the people at that time were spiritually in what we'd call a state of infantile emotional development.

In short, they were efficient to a T, but the consciousness then had only the beginnings of what today we'd call compassion and humanity. Thus it became a common practice during the decline of Atlantis for doctors to perform euthanasia upon patients who were old, sickly, or malformed according to the standards of beauty in vogue then.

Somehow, you escaped notice of the authorities, even though you had a misshapen back, which left you in a constantly bent-over position. No one was too concerned about your appearance because you were a rural laborer, the equivalent of a migrant farmworker. Such labor was necessary because the maturing Atlantean society was much like ours today in that everybody was becoming too refined to dirty their hands at manual labor.

Of course, carried to its extreme, no society could exist for long under those conditions. Therefore, you and other members of the lowest class of laborers were not measured by the standards of beauty that applied to a growing segment of the population.

But you grew old and fell sick in the fields. This brought you to the attention of the medical people. It was determined that your useful life as a laborer was at an end. As with so many other unfortunates, a day and hour was set when you would be administered a drug that would put you into an eternal sleep.

The medical people treated you like an object without feelings, speaking clinically—without grace—about the removal of your body and belongings the morning after. You were terrified of what amounted to a death sentence, and this fear is the reason for your fear of sleep. And while you've suffered from insomnia for a long time, it's gotten worse as you approach a condition of aging similar to the one in Atlantis. The aging is the trigger.

From the ECK teachings you know that Soul cannot die. You did not know that in Atlantis. To bend this condition of fear back to a more reasonable place, I suggest you find a way to be an aide or a volunteer who works with small *children*. (Best of all would be to work with emotionally—not physically—handicapped children, so you can come to terms with the emotionally bankrupt Atlanteans who caused you so much trouble in the past.)

You need to feel and see the continuity of life. Mainly, you must find a way to give your love to little ones. It must become unlocked and flow out into the world.

You now see yourself as the center of your world; you must make others the object of your love, which has to pour out from you. It may be hard to do this at first, so start small.

## Reliable Knowledge

*How reliable is the information we get from telepathy? Can it be affecting my health?*

While it is true that telepathy is one method of communication between the mind and senses, it is also

165

under the unstable psychic law. That means the knowledge will be reliable until you trust it. By that time the individual is certain that he's the reincarnation of Christ or some other departed Master. Then society will put him under psychiatric care in order to be rid of his nuisance. That's life.

If you know anything at all about the workers of the negative field, you will see immediately that the Dark Force has tricked you and is playing with you. I sincerely suggest that you visit or call the United Way for referral to a licensed professional counselor (see the white pages of the phone book). See if they can direct you to someone who can give you insight into this problem.

### Curing Winter Blues

*I have been very sad lately, but try to put on a happy face for others. Nothing seems to help, not even an ECK Spiritual Aide session. Recently I lost both my dog and cat, plus my husband's been down with the flu.*

It's easy to see why you'd feel down because of losing your dog and cat, and having your husband sick with the flu. Since your letter in January, you'll have seen changes in your situation.

Winter causes some people to be depressed because of less sunlight. So they try to balance that with eating more carbohydrates. Often they substitute soft drinks and other foods with a lot of sucrose, table sugar. Better would be complex carbohydrates like pasta, cereal, and potatoes, and other vegetables. There are also full-spectrum lightbulbs to give you more of the correct light.

Back to sugar a moment: If you feel depressed and

take it in some food or drink (to feel sweetness), it'll actually make you more depressed shortly. Diet can play a major role in how we feel. Chocolate can cause severe depression in some people and should be avoided if that's the case with you.

Since you wish to make an effort to find the reasons, consider getting a checkup from a competent physician to insure your health is as it should be. Private counseling may be more difficult to come by, but if it's available and affordable, consider the option.

## Longevity

*How can we live longer? I have been studying the use of herbs as stabilizers of well-being, as mentioned in Paul Twitchell's books.*

By watching nature, we learn the reality of aging. Everything gets older and eventually returns to the soil—everything except Soul.

There are many ways to improve our nutrition and have a long, happy life. Don't overlook the offerings of science. It has increased the average life span in many countries from forty and fifty years to better than sixty and seventy years.

## Grip of the Mind

*If I don't do the Friday fasts because I don't feel good when I do them (I get mild headaches, colds, and feel a little faint) am I lacking the spiritual discipline or right attitude to unfold? Does this change for me as I get older?*

It's a real surprise how the human body does not want ECK to make us into greater spiritual beings.

The Holy Spirit wants to tear loose all the old stick-in-the-mud attitudes that have done nothing but make bad karma for us in the past.

The Friday fasts are the Mahanta's way of breaking the mind's grip on us, to let him lead us to all things that are good.

The headaches, colds, and faintness are the mind screaming against the refinement of character that is going on in Soul. Don't let the discomfort discourage you, but switch to the mental fast. This means keeping the mind completely off negative thoughts all day. Also look for the Mahanta in people's faces.

If you do the disciplines—such as the spiritual exercises and the Friday fasts—I promise that life will open doors for everything you do.

## Attitudes about Friday Fasts

*I need to approach the Friday fast with the proper attitude. Please tell me: Why Friday? Is there a mass readjustment of sorts for all ECKists on that day? Is it more for spiritual growth than physical cleansing?*

Friday is the date established by the Vairagi Order. It has been imitated by other groups in a corrupted form, such as by the Catholic church in its former days of fish on Friday.

Yes, there is a mass readjustment of sorts for all ECKists on that day.

It is solely for spiritual growth. It lifts Soul above the social consciousness; it is the easiest way to dissolve past and present life karma.

*If my doctor says it's better not to fast, how can I do the Friday fast?*

The Wisdom Notes tell about the three different kinds of fasts. Follow your doctor's advice. If a full fast is not good for your body, it is possible to do a mental fast, keeping one's attention on the Mahanta. A partial fast suits some people who are not able to drink only water for twenty-four hours.

So do what your doctor suggests is best for you. We do not want to hurt ourselves. That is not the way of ECK, for It brings fullness in all things.

## Roots of a Cough

*I have an awful cough that began after my wife translated. It is embarrassing to be at ECK meetings; I have to leave until I stop coughing. I have seen four different doctors without getting help. I am asking for spiritual assistance and would appreciate your help very soon.*

You have done the correct thing by seeking help from four different M.D.'s, even though none was able to help you with your problem. I am not a licensed physician and so cannot pretend to offer a cure where they have failed.

It is interesting that this problem began *after* the translation of your wife. While it is possible that you contracted something in the hospital during your four-month stay, it is also possible that since your wife left, your diet has changed for the worse. This may or may not be the case: you are the best judge of that.

In my own experience, I have found certain classes of food cause phlegm in my body. This does not mean that another person will have the same sensitivities. Any kind of a dairy product causes mucus: cheese, yogurt, cottage cheese, or milk. Bread and crackers do the same thing. It even got so that fruit caused phlegm.

A body needs protein. I avoid beef and pork (except for bacon on occasion), but I do eat chicken, turkey, and fish—broiled or baked, never fried. Baked red potatoes seem to sit better than brown potatoes, although I do eat mashed potatoes with a homemade sauce of fresh garlic, sunflower oil, and water shaken in a jar or a blender.

Flours (the bread, crackers, and gravies) also cause congestion. But I'm able to eat salad—except no iceberg (head) lettuce—and hot and cold vegetables. In addition, a nutritionist might recommend a balanced vitamin-supplement program.

This is only my control diet, when regular eating has given me too much congestion. (It may not be good to someone else.) Otherwise, I eat many of the things I used to.

## Dangers of the Kundalini

*Years ago, I was initiated by another master, and after much meditation, the kundalini power was awakened. My health has deteriorated ever since. Why? Can you help?*

The kundalini is a powerful force that is better left asleep. Once it starts to move up the spinal column, there must be some place for it to go—or like a flooding river blocked from its usual course to the sea by a landslide, the water overruns the banks and causes great damage to the farmland on either side.

Meditation is a passive discipline that shows a disciple how to see the Light, but then what? It's like the pilot who knows how to take off but never bothered to learn how to land the plane! There must be a way to return this love or it will burn and damage the inner and outer bodies. This is why I suggest the ECK contemplations be kept to no more than twenty or thirty minutes a day. The rest of the day is for one's job, family, and recreation time.

Now, what to do? The Law of Karma is exact in its measure. To cure a health problem several years in the making often takes a like amount of time for healing. There is no magic way to get an instant, long-term cure without our taking a part in the rebuilding.

Find a good doctor who knows nutrition; an expert in this field can help you back on the road to recovery. Be assured that the Mahanta is always with you to steer you to people who can help you to better health and the happiness that comes with it.

## Inner Circle Defense

*Recently at a seminar I got food poisoning. This was unusual for me. Any insights?*

Out here it may be food poisoning, but the real reason is often that you were a guard of the inner circle and got into combat for love of the ECK.

For this I thank you.

## Wrong Advice

*I have been having blood-pressure problems. The doctor has given me a prescription for the condition. An ECKist friend advised me not to take the medicine, and I'd prefer not to. What should I do? I've also been forgetting my dreams lately. Why?*

Please listen to your doctor and take the pills he wants you to take for your blood-pressure problems. If you are not sure about his diagnosis, get the opinion of another doctor. Don't take the advice of an ECKist who says to ignore the doctor's prescription.

You want to get good medical advice from a doctor for health problems, not an uninformed opinion from a layperson, even if it is an ECK initiate. The ECK also heals through physicians, dentists, and other kinds of doctors.

Regarding your concern about not doing Soul Travel or remembering dreams as you used to: Often I allow you to forget your inner experiences for a while, even during the higher ECK initiations. Some experiences take getting used to. You are doing well spiritually, and your dreams will return in time.

## AIDS Question

*What is the truth about the phenomenon of AIDS, and how can we protect ourselves from it?*

AIDS is just another of the serious illnesses that periodically sweeps the earth.

In the fourteenth century, for example, the Black Death, or bubonic plague, killed from a quarter to a third of Europe's population in three years. Standards of hygiene were much lower then than today. Bubonic plague was transmitted by the fleas on black rats. The waste of its victims gave others pneumonic plague. Europe had no defense against either, because of its low consciousness about hygiene.

The problem with AIDS again is a matter of awareness. Health agencies have made available much information of how to be careful with sexual intimacy. It means taking the trouble to first find out the state of your partner's health and other considerations.

## Wave from the Past

*Some extraordinary fear and pain has been activated by my recent motherhood. I am at the bottom, feeling trapped. Can you please take me to a healing place in my Soul body and wash me of this agony? Perhaps give me an understanding of its source.*

The fear and pain which have resulted after your recent motherhood is due to both outer and inner conditions. In a recent life in New England you gave birth to an illegitimate son. The late 1600s were not very understanding times for a girl in your condition.

The childbirth in this life triggered a recall of that life, and the old feelings of shame and abandonment that made you want to end it all. To your credit, you raised the child and learned the spiritual lessons that accrued from that experience.

I would encourage you to follow up with counseling by a professional. Also have a nutritionist make sure that the demands of motherhood are not outpacing your normal level of nourishment.

## Spiritual Boosts

*Why do some of us have to live with chronic disease in this life? I am an epileptic.*

It has been difficult for you to cope with epilepsy for most of your life, but it is exactly that which gave you the spiritual boost to find ECK. In this case, your burden proved to be your ladder into the higher states of consciousness.

## Mixing Paths

*I am having trouble sleeping. I try using the mantra I got from my former TM teacher and also ECK words, but it doesn't help.*

First of all, I suggest you go to a good doctor and make sure your health is as good as it should be.

By using the former TM mantra and also the Spiritual Exercises of ECK, you're actually mixing two paths. This shorts out the effectiveness of both and can also be the cause of tiredness. You are thus pulling yourself in two different directions at the same time.

Read in *Letters to Gail,* Volume I, perhaps one letter a night. At the end of the first several letters, Paul Twitchell gives some very simple techniques for reaching the spiritual consciousness. Use these when you are unable to sleep.

## For Kal or ECK?

*Here is a preamble to give a clear understanding of the issues involved in my question. Western medicine is gaining a foothold in Third World countries such as mine, but traditional doctors still dominate. The latter give the patient herbs, roots, and other extracts, but they often go beyond this—and this is the part that bothers me. They perform invocations, incantations, and rites of killing animals and birds to appease their gods.*

*A good number of ECKists in my country go through rituals of this sort. I am worried about the effect such practices may have on ECKANKAR, which has a good foothold here. I believe we need only the Light and Sound of ECK to protect us from psychic attacks, which are commonplace in this country.*

*My question: Is it right to visit such traditional doctors, and if so, how far does one go with them? Sometimes they give their patients certain things to wear for protection.*

You describe people in ECK who won't surrender to the Mahanta, the Living ECK Master. Their faith in the power of an evil mind is greater than their assurance in the Sound and Light of ECK. All of us go to doctors at one time or another, but who is in charge of our treatment? We let the doctor treat only what is needed. Therefore, look for a doctor who treats with herbs, roots, and extracts; one who respects your wishes not to play with invocations to his own god.

There are no two ways about it: We are either for the ECK or for the Kal. Initiates who accept the traditional rituals for banishing evil spirits are weakening the future of ECK in their hometowns. One does not have to be an evangelist about his ECK beliefs, but is it not possible to quietly ask the doctor for a healing with only the herbs?

ECKists who support the black arts by accepting the traditional rites to counter them are corrupting the ECK teachings. They would be shocked if this were brought to their attention. The Mahanta tests his chelas in many ways, and this is one of them. How far will we go with the Master? Where is our faith?

Thank you for bringing up this issue. One who is strong in ECK is beyond the power of evil spirits to harm him.


## Year of Spiritual Healing

*During the Year of Spiritual Healing, we received some important health information we needed. What is the key to good health?*

There is an endless stream of healing that the ECK provides to those who love It. It seems there is no limit to Its capacity to nurture and restore anyone who is to continue on in his mission on the particular plane where he finds himself.

Having passed one wall, we meet another. We exercise our full powers of creativity to get around that one too. The experience leaves us always a little more capable spiritually than before.

# 8

## Doubts and Tests

*I feel I'm not very spiritual. I am doing the spiritual exercises faithfully and can hear the Sound Current, but I'm sure I'm not Soul traveling. Am I doing as well as I can?*

Please know that your spiritual life is in order: you do hear the Sound of ECK, which is more important than remembering dreams or doing Soul Travel.

Our real quest is to reach a greater state of consciousness. The Sound, for those who hear It, is always at work, expanding their understanding of life. More than anything, the Sound increases one's ability to love God, the SUGMAD.

That's the most important thing of all.

### Fear of Death

*I am eighty-seven years old and not a member of ECKANKAR. I am asking if you could help break the terrible fear of death I have carried with me since childhood. I want to have this burden gone forever and the assurance that someone will meet me when my time*

177

*comes. I want it to be the beautiful experience it was meant to be.*

Please be assured that your loved ones will meet you on the other side, so there's no reason to hold on to your fear.

If you'll keep in mind that love and love alone is the reason for living, it will calm your heart and free you from your worries. And, of course, I am always with you in my spiritual self.

## Nothing Is Wasted

*When my book was rejected for publication by ECKANKAR, I was initially at a loss. But the pain of failure or rejection was very minimal because truth is far more important to me than having a book published just to have it published. I did my best with the awareness I had and committed myself totally to the project. In writing about an ECK Master, I realize that there is much I have still to learn.*

It was heartening to receive your response to the rejection of your book. Heartening because you've seen by means of the inner channels what could not be put into words about the manuscript.

You recognize that the experience of writing the book has hidden rewards which are not apparent to superficial scrutiny. Believe me, I was rooting for you as I read the story, but it unraveled near the end as you were put into a position of speaking about something that this ECK Master may have to do himself someday.

Writing a spiritual novel is one of the hardest things I can think of to do. Whenever the manuscript of an ECK initiate comes to my attention, I'm in his corner, cheering him on. It is perhaps as great a disappointment for me as for the writer when the story cannot be published.

If the ECK wants you to write, you will again.

Your travels in pursuit of knowledge are not wasted. It's not the end of the journey that counts, but the journey itself.

## Surviving a Great Loss

*Our five-year-old daughter translated unexpectedly. She lit up my life to a degree I cannot describe. I would like to believe that my love for her is the love of the SUGMAD and the Mahanta. Please help us during these difficult times.*

The hand of sorrow has touched your family deeply. The wisdom of your son is right: Your daughter came to teach you all to love each other more.

We understand that life is a series of comings and goings, but somehow the passing of a child is harder to accept than is the passing of one well along in years. It is hard to see now, but life will replace the joy you have lost with even greater joy. But first you must heal your sorrow, and that will take time.

Any words I write to you about the loss of your daughter cannot heal the ache of your heart. I would suggest that in contemplation you ask to meet the Mahanta as a family, including your daughter, of course. You will receive the understanding you need about human love being the link to love for the SUGMAD and the Mahanta.

I am with you in your days of sorrow, but will remain with you in the happier days to come. This I promise you. Look for the Light, listen for the Sound— in your heart.

## Helping Others with Grief

*How can I help a friend whose child recently died? She is not an ECKist.*

It would help first to understand the consciousness of people in this Christian society as they face death with their families and loved ones. They are trying to come to grips with their beliefs about God.

They have been taught that God gives only good, but now all of a sudden here comes something bad. And how do you pray to God to take away the pain, they wonder, when maybe God gave them the pain? These are questions in the hearts of people like your friend.

As you are carrying the ECK message, you may not always speak ECK words but they can feel the light you carry. At times, we try to give comfort to others but say just the wrong thing: "Your child is now in heaven, and he is much happier there" or "God gave you this cross to bear because you were strong enough to bear it." "Oh, that I had been weaker," the friend cries.

Nothing can heal your friend's grief but time. Man grapples with the meaning of life, and eventually he comes to certain terms with it.

## New Freedom

*I am a Seventh Initiate. I have recently felt that I was missing some key part of the ECK teachings. While involved in a local ECK project, I felt wonderful and alive, but once it ended a numbness grew. Can you help me understand what is going on?*

I just want to thank you for having the diligence to be the instrument for ECK that you are. This letter could end right now, and you could go on in your enjoyment of living without any fear that you are somehow missing a key part of the ECK teachings.

Are you active enough for a Seventh Initiate? Somebody who listens to the ECK follows the natural ebb and flow of the comings and goings, the ups and downs, the silences and activities that are a part of living. Cycles fall upon cycles, and each is a degree of oppositeness from the part of the wave cycle that has gone before it. I'm not being vague or heady, but want to instill in you the natural rhythms of life. "To every thing there is a season," said the Preacher in Ecclesiastes. "There are rest points in eternity," said Rebazar Tarzs to Paul Twitchell.

A funny thing happens with people who can help in the projects of ECK. All is fine while they are caught up in the sweep of activity; they never know that at this moment they are living life as they have never lived it before. But they are doing it as a satellite of somebody else's universe.

Then when the Master has lit the fire and steps back to see if Soul can keep the spark of creativity going by Itself, there is a test for It: How much is the linkup with the Sound Current instead of with the personality of the Master?

Most people struggle with that one, and it brings anguish of the deepest kind that leaves them striking out blindly in all directions. They suddenly awaken to the emptiness within their heart when they imagine they are cut off from the Master. But he is standing quietly aside to see what the initiate will do with his new freedom.

## Giving Love

*At a recent seminar a panel seemed to say that to achieve wealth one should give money to the ECK Temple. It upset some chelas to hear that. They felt the original focus of the ECK teachings on spiritual unfoldment and service to all life had now turned to the creation of wealth and power. Would you comment on this, please?*

The panel did not mean to impose its spiritual values and goals upon others. Certainly, the ECK missionary work does need gifts, but there are many gifts other than those of a financial kind.

Love is the most important element behind any gift to ECK. Sometimes love causes a person of means to give what is most suitable for him or her: funds or property. Yet, as often, love for ECK shows up as a gift of service: the hospice volunteer, the Arahata, or the person who opens the ECK Center.

Sometimes the most precious gift of all is the spirit of understanding. Tell the panel members how you feel. But do it with love, because they are unfolding on the path to God the same as you.

If you were in their shoes, would you rather have someone speak to you with kindness or anger?


## Straight and Narrow Path

*I have been given the idea for an invention on the inner, and I want to offer this opportunity to other ECKists as an investment.*

I greatly appreciate your report about the proposed invention and the plans to get investment money from ECKists. Please don't do that. It mixes the spiritual with the material and will only lead to reverses. I cannot allow ECKists under my care to be approached for investment funding, no matter how the idea developed.

Remember, every experience is given only for our spiritual growth. Sometimes the occasion is a test. We are only too willing to believe that the ECK Masters would come to lay out the plans of an invention that will bring us untold wealth. It is a trick of the negative power.

As far as the invention itself goes, putting aside any other lesson that might be put forth by an entity from the other side while masquerading as a spiritual traveler, that is something that is approached quietly. You study it each step of the way. If there is capital needed, do not get money from any ECKist and you will never go wrong. If the invention has any true merit, investors will see the possibilities too. If it is too advanced for the present consciousness of technology, nobody with "outside" money would invest in it. Then you would have invested a lot of money in an idea that is not believed in by the big money needed to make it pay off the investment.

If you have an idea from the inner planes, work quietly with it. I hope that you understand that I have no objection if you personally go ahead with this plan. But I do not want any other ECKists giving money toward this project.

## Inner Discrimination

*Soon after I got my Fifth Initiation, I was supposed to give a Soul Travel workshop, but the night before I became very ill. You came to me on the inner and told me not to do the workshop. That night in a dream my cofacilitator accused me of trying to get out of a com-mitment.*

*I ended up not doing the workshop and felt fine. Why did you not want me to go? Was this a test?*

Welcome to the Fifth Circle of ECK initiates. The tests are ongoing.

The Inner Master wanted you to stay home from the Soul Travel workshop because your health was of primary importance.

Sometimes it's easier to ignore the ECK than to listen. To test Soul's growing power of discrimination, an impostor from the Kal will come at other times to give advice that's spiritually harmful. But love for SUGMAD will help you to decide if it's the Mahanta or an impostor.

You will learn much as a Fifth.

## Sacredness of Initiate Reports

*There are a few initiates in the area who worry that the Living ECK Master might not read all their initiate reports, and that maybe someone else reads them. Would you care to comment on this?*

The answer to your question is in a book of my seminar talks to ECK initiates, *Be the HU.* Have the initiates read chapter 13, under the subhead "Sacred-ness of Initiate Reports." Tell those with concerns about this book and where they can read my answer for themselves.

## The Real Truth

*I've been in ECK for almost a year and a half. If ECKANKAR really works, how come I can't Soul Travel, even after so many months of trying? Please give me some proof that ECKANKAR is the right path to follow. I want to know truth.*

It is possible that ECKANKAR is not for you. That is for you to decide. Whatever path you choose, consider carefully: Do you want truth on your terms?

Truth never is what people would expect. It challenges, catches off guard, or gets the seeker leaning the other way. I hope you see what I'm driving at here. There is *belief* in ECK. That leads to *experiences,* which brings *awareness.*

To return to the point made earlier: One who expects truth to come on his terms will never find it at all. That's the cause of dissatisfaction. To paraphrase Rebazar in *Stranger by the River:* Open your heart so that you may find love. It's worth more than all the experiences put together. But first you must find humility, for truth won't enter an impure heart.

## When Others Leave ECK

*Are people getting burned out in ECK? Why do some leave it?*

Growth takes time. The earth can move an inch a year a mile under the ground, and nobody cares. But when it jolts twenty feet in a minute, that's a destructive earthquake.

Growth takes time, and we are going along at a fast clip. Behind all the outer trappings, the tests go on.

I don't worry about dropouts from ECK, no matter what rationalization they give for leaving ECK. Those who have a strong bond with the Mahanta will stay with the Outer Master also. Any who leave for reasons such as "There was no organization in ECK" are using that as an excuse to go where their hearts are anyway, outside of ECK.

The Master-initiate relationship is above good or evil, adequacy or inadequacy, right or wrong. It is either there or it's not. I prefer that an individual find out early in ECK if his heart is elsewhere, so that he can go to another teaching. No excuse for leaving the Mahanta ever hides the fact that one did leave him. This separation of Soul from the Light and Sound shows one thing, above and beyond the excuses It makes to Itself: This Soul is not in agreement with the ECK.

A person gets taken over by the social consciousness: he is too sensitive about how he looks to others in his relationship with the Mahanta. He cares more about what people think than he does about piercing the veil of illusion that makes him uncomfortable around other ECKists. What will be, will be. What is, is.

## The Inner War

*I have a problem in dealing with the ECK. I was a member for a while but always had the most horrible anxiety, worry, and fear about this path. Finally it got too much, and I canceled my membership. Do you think all these feelings are caused by Kal? They're so real, so terribly strong!*

Your reaction to dealing with the ECK comes from the conflict between the spiritual and negative forces waging war in your consciousness.

This nagging fear in the back of the mind is: What if there is only one heaven, and my path's not going there?

Numerous heavens are scattered throughout creation, and Soul *earns* Its place in one of them. No chela of the Mahanta, the Living ECK Master need worry about eternal damnation. A more powerful law than even the Law of Karma is this: The Law of Love supersedes karma.

When love enters the heart, no room is left for fear or doubt. But this change in heart takes time and resists force in any way.

Continue with the studies of ECK when you have the inner strength. Then read *The Spiritual Notebook* from cover to cover, but only a little every day. Take half a year to finish the project. Meanwhile I shall be with you as the Inner Master if you wish this to be so.

## An Orderly Life

*I have come to the realization that I am responsible for my own spiritual unfoldment, and I feel uncomfortable depending on the Mahanta to take care of me. I do feel I have guidance, but I don't understand truly what the Mahanta is. Should I stay in ECK?*

I greatly appreciate your sincere questions and will not try to make up your mind for you.

It's true that one can arrive at an awareness of the presence of God every moment. A mistake is to withdraw from life to sit in contemplation all day, convincing ourselves it's done because of a great love for God, when really we're hiding from the lessons of living. A God-Realized person, if you're looking for a rule of thumb, has his physical life, as well as spiritual, in order. He earns his keep.

The only purpose of the outer teachings of ECKANKAR is to lead you, in the most direct way, to the inner worlds. That's the source of personal

Mastership that develops through the actual experience of the Sound and Light of God.

A common reason for failure with the spiritual works is a lack of discipline in the practice of the Spiritual Exercises of ECK. They must be done as stated, and regularly. Experiment occasionally with them; after all, they are *creative* techniques.

## Self-Discipline

*Can you help me with my self-discipline?*

Each one of us in the lower worlds is struggling with self-discipline. We find it in everything we do, in our job or at home. It means, Can I get up in the morning on time? We have all these little things in our lives which are teaching us greater discipline.

I can't give you self-discipline, motivation, or even spirituality. In fact I can't give you anything. All I can do is help you in your own efforts. First of all, you have to figure out what your goal is.

Your goal can be anything, but it should be God-Realization. Not in the limited sense we've understood in orthodox religions, but in the sense of becoming one with Divine Spirit. Once we set that as our goal, then it depends on how fervently we want it.

Every so often you'll see a high-school student going down the street with a basketball in hand. Everywhere he goes he's got his basketball. He dribbles here, he dribbles there. It looks like the guy's lost his mind, but it's that kind of devotion that's needed to get to a goal. He wants to be the best player.

What are you really looking for on the path of ECK? What are you expecting it to do for you, and how do you expect to be different?

Often we want enlightenment because the life we have today is hard. We have pains, aging starts catching up with us, the body won't run like it used to. But the true reason for spiritual enlightenment is not to escape this life but to learn how to live it richly, to enjoy it.

It's up to us to put the effort into it, to develop the self-discipline to practice the spiritual exercises.

## Facing Doubts

*One of my closest friends has chosen to quit ECKANKAR as her path, and I was left dealing with a lot of ideas which are very challenging to my beliefs. I believe a situation is often created to test our strength, and what kept coming to mind is that the spiritual works cannot be judged by outer standards. The path continues to be a slow one for me, and I know that is my own choice. I feel somewhat apart from the path at the moment, but inside it is always there when I turn to it.*

I greatly appreciate your note about the doubts you recently encountered about ECKANKAR. You're right, we all face the test about the Mahanta and his embodiment. Yet there is little reason for one to try to influence another in his beliefs, and you didn't.

We must all gain our own understanding of what part we will allow Divine Spirit in our life. It is different for everyone.

Spiritual law does not allow one to perform miracles to gain followers. This is as it should be, for miracles only place the individual's attention on the fleeting and passing things.

How many are really ready to let go and enter the realms of the ECK that lie above the Fifth Plane?

Considering the percentage among all the world's inhabitants, it is only a handful. These are the ones we reach.

## How Badly Do You Want God?

*When I have doubts about the path, I lose the motivation to do my spiritual exercises. I am not sure about the role of ECKANKAR in my life.*

The path of ECK is actually for those who want to reach the God Consciousness in a certain, direct line. There are many paths to God, and I feel everyone should have the choice of his own religious way without fear from any outside source.

Motivation for doing the spiritual exercises is all part of our self-discipline. There is really very little that another can do to help us with that. It is a measure of how badly we want something and what we are willing to do to earn it. No one else can make that decision for another.

## Short Fall

*I feel badly because of not turning in the money I've collected from three Satsang classes. Who am I trying to kid? Facing how short we fall from being good ECKists is not easy.*

You spoke of "not turning in the money I've collected from three Satsang classes." If such is the case, I recommend most strongly that you make matters right.

Something like that goes into the hands of the Lords of Karma, and there is nothing that can be done to stop the manner in which they exact payment.

*I believe I have reached the Eighth Initiation inwardly, although I have not received any outer initiations. I had an experience where I saw God. Can you confirm this, please?*

Though the experience you had was of a certain kind, it was not the ultimate experience of God. There are many tests initiated by the Kal, as the servant of the SUGMAD. They are designed to mislead any individual on the path to God.

When one has earned true Self- and God-Realization, he must first have received a number of initiations on the physical. The ECK Masters bring a person along slowly to insure that he gets every opportunity to absorb the increasingly greater Sound Current and not go out of balance.

Thus the first eight initiations are given by the Living ECK Master on the physical plane, after a good many years between each initiation. The reason is to see what the chela does at that level before he is allowed entrance into the next plane.

Anyone who has earned God-Realization is self-sufficient and has his life in order in every degree. A yardstick for the God-Realized individual is that he is able to pay his own way in society and take care of himself.

## Out of Control

*Lately I've hardly been able to cope with my out-of-control emotions. I've always been tormented by emotional storms—depression, tears, fierce anger, strong anxieties. I've been contacted inwardly by something called the Irona Group, who seem to be guiding me along a specific path of development. But my latest outbreak of emotional distress coincided with the Irona*

*Group's trying to give me direct mental contact with an entity. I'm asking for your help to understand this.*

You asked for help to contain the emotional storms that have affected you from an early age. Some of the things I will suggest you may have tried and may sound elementary, but look over them again.

The Irona Group says they made contact with you after you suffered an injury or blow at the age of eight. It might be useful to find a good chiropractor with holistic training. A routine X-ray could pinpoint health problems caused by impaired nerves. Not every chiropractor will do, only one who is comfortable with the latest scientific instruments and has a knowledge of related fields, such as acupuncture. That combination, or something on that order, is hard to find. He or she should also know nutrition.

You, in the highest state of consciousness, are Soul; and It rebels at the control that the Irona Group is hoping to impose on you. The Higher Self is like a teen who rebels when his parents want to make him live their values, when all he wants is freedom to live and think for himself: hence, the emotional distress.

So my suggestion is for you to first make sure your physical health is in order. Automatic handwriting is the means for Irona to control you, which is all right if you want that.

See if you can get help from your dreams.

## Doubt's Role

*What is the role of doubt?*

Doubt provides a stabilizing factor that prevents one from going too fast in the spiritual works and losing control. The Mahanta pulls the curtain on the memory, oftentimes, of experiences in the Light and Sound of God. The shock would be too great and throw us into emotional disorders, as happened to certain saints who briefly tasted the love of God.

If a hockey player or baseball team didn't practice their sport, they could not compete in the league. They must play or practice their sport daily during the season in order to meet the competition and be successful. The same with the Spiritual Exercises of ECK.

## Is Rebazar Real?

*I feel that I'm drifting spiritually, that there's no linkup with Divine Spirit in my life anymore. Although my deepest desire is to be God-Realized, I feel angry and resentful. Is there something fundamental that I'm doing wrong?*

There are about as many spiritual needs to fill as there are Souls. The whole point of ECK is to reach first Self-Realization, then to go on to God Consciousness. Once we get to the top of the mountain, we find that freedom, charity, and wisdom are our due.

But only love can bring us to the heights of realization, and only love can bring the qualities of freedom, charity, and wisdom. So where do we start?

The idea is to set an image before us that fulfills the ideal we want to reach. All the abbots of the Wisdom Temples were once the Mahanta, the Living ECK Master before they began their duties as guardians of the Shariyat.

Before contemplation, get a sketch pad or notebook and, from memory, make the best drawing of Rebazar Tarzs possible. At first, you may just end up with a bushy black beard, black hair, and coal black eyes.

Work on improving the details of his face the first month. In the second month, start putting Rebazar in the middle of some setting (by a river, on a road, in the mountains, etc.).

Then go to sleep at night with your mind lightly toying with the question "Is Rebazar real? If he is, what can I know about him?" Try this for three months, and write to me again. Ask him about spiritual freedom.

## Finding Heaven Anywhere

*Recently while walking the hills and talking with you, the Mahanta, I realized I was being limited by life within the society of ECKANKAR. I could no longer accept the idea of initiation levels. I love the ECK, and I love you. I ask your blessing in stepping away from the outer path.*

I appreciate your courtesy and thoughtfulness in sending your recent note. You, of course, have the freedom to follow the call of Soul to your destination.

A thought occurs to me that Soul in the lower worlds is always bounded on all sides. No matter where we go or what we do, things are so created that we always bump into a wall somewhere. Sometimes it's our own wall, other times it is someone else's. No matter what, what matters is not the wall, but what we do about it.

Having passed one wall, we meet another. We exercise our full powers of creativity and get around that one too. The experience leaves us always a little more capable spiritually than before.

Limits, inner and outer, bound Soul in the lower worlds, so It finally learns to rise above them. In doing so, It can find heaven in hell; or anywhere else, for that matter.

# Just a Guide

*Recently I found my inner balance gone. I had been given a book on cults by a friend, and I read the chapter on ECKANKAR. It was very biased against Paul Twitchell, and although I follow the inner path not the personality, I found myself irritated and questioning ECKANKAR because of some of the comments made about Paul's life.*

As you so rightly see, the core of the ECK teachings is from the inner instead of the outer.

In the late 1960s, when Paul was introducing the ECK works to the public, its consciousness was quite low. He found that people were bored with pure truth. The Living ECK Master's mission is to find a doorway to Soul. Partly as protection for his family, Paul created the town of China Point, which does not exist. Paul dressed up some outer writings, like a myth form, to acquaint seekers with underlying truth. He had to reach them at their state of consciousness, which was very low when compared to people's understanding today.

In my talks at the 1984 World Wide of ECK, I addressed Paul's gift for recognizing the great truths and putting them into one place for people to find. It's easy to criticize his gift once we have it. His mission was to lead seekers from the outer, changeable things to those spiritual realities of God that are found only on the inner planes: Sound and Light, Soul and dream travel, etc.

Only through the inner channels can a person even hope to approach the ancient wisdoms. The outer works are thus simply a doorway to the hidden, spiritual things of life.

Therefore, we recognize the fallibility of outer writings, which do serve as the best guide available until we can make the inner connection with the Audible Life Stream.

All great teachings seem to have a cloudy history. In the case of older ones, the passing centuries have given the church fathers plenty of time to cut away anything that did not support their later doctrines. More will be learned about Paul's life in the future when scholars find new records.

## More than Pat Answers

*Having been active in ECKANKAR for the past six years of my life, it hurts me to have to express some real doubts and concerns about the path. I recently read conflicting information about Paul Twitchell and his writings. Can you understand that I want truth and not pat answers?*

Your questions about truth are sincere, so I will try to give you an idea of what to look for—and without pat answers, for there are none.

To review your position, it seems you want truth to fall in line with your previous ideas of what it should be. For instance, when outer evidence conflicts with what you expected to find, you are ready to discount the whole experience of illusion as a blind trail.

Maybe I'm being too general for you to catch the image I'm trying to get across to you: real truth will always be other than what you think it is; otherwise wouldn't you have it and know it? Since you know you do not have truth, it must be other than what you think it is. What does this mean?

Unless you give up old ideas of what you expect truth to be, it will always elude you. It is a principle in ECK that one must give up the dear values again and again if the veil hiding God is to be pierced. When one reaches Self-Realization, he finds the world that he's been so comfortable in (in an unsettled way) is really at a right angle to truth. And the same conventional truth seen from the vantage point of God-Realization is 180 degrees off the mark.

Now all this philosophy won't help you, nor will the reading of any book, nor the practice of any spiritual exercise, unless the desire for truth and God is absolutely pure. Have you been misled in the past in your search? Hasn't everybody? That is the nature of this life experience, which is educational for Soul.

The outer writings serve only one purpose in their lack of perfection, since perfection is not in an imperfect world: to show Soul the inner path of ECK. No one can find the Sound and Light by memorizing *The Shariyat*. It can only inspire the individual to exert himself to meet the Mahanta on the inner planes. This is not really so difficult, because others are doing it.

I've found it a waste of time to convince anyone to stay on a job, or in ECK, in the face of serious doubts. If the individual is inclined to leave, he should. Unless he does, he is not following his inner guidance. Some people learn better in places other than ECK. Go into contemplation to see if you are one. I won't hold you if it is your sincere desire to study another path.

### Feeling Trapped

*I'm contemplating from a sense of duty rather than love and not doing it regularly. I think of the Mahanta only when I have a problem. Only when I meet with my ECKist friends are my feelings reaffirmed. I love the ECK and couldn't do without the Mahanta, but I feel trapped. Am I losing my faith in ECK, and how*

197

*do I overcome this inner barrier?*

It would be easy to beg off the question with "Don't worry; life will teach you better."

You are at one of life's many crossroads which cause these feelings of doubt about your faith in ECK. But you can safely pass through this cycle by keeping your heart open to the Mahanta's love.

Each life cycle has a growth and fulfillment stage. We switch back and forth between them. The growth phase begins with a restless feeling that urges us into a new and greater opportunity, but fear holds us back. Finally, the need for growth outweighs the fear, so perhaps we risk taking a new job, enter a relationship, or return to school to improve our skills.

The growth phase then moves on to the fulfillment stage. Here, we master the new routines that come with change and plunge into the options of our unexplored life. All our attention is upon the challenges and rewards before us.

However, the old restlessness will return. It's nothing to worry about, though. It simply means that Soul is ready to embark upon a fresh adventure of growth and fulfillment.

The company of other ECKists will help you move gracefully from the state of growth to fulfillment. The community of ECK initiates passes along the love and support of the Master whenever your fears try to shut him out.

How do you overcome the inner barrier of doubt and fear?

Put your heart into every new venture, for the Mahanta has led you through a gateway of opportunity to help you reach a higher level of ability, love, and compassion.

You also need to address the habit of thinking so much about yourself. Remember the goal: becoming a Co-worker with God. It includes seeing the good qualities in others as well as yourself.

## Is the Imagination Always Helpful?

*When I try to do a spiritual exercise and travel out of my body, my imagination always brings in unexpected things. For example if I am in a forest on the inner planes and the tree leaves remind me of eucalyptus, immediately my imagination puts me in a eucalyptus grove. Is this helpful or should I try to control the experience more?*

The only way you can tell if it's helpful is to ask, What effect is it having on me? Is it something beneficial that gives me insight?

Sometimes it's not important that you end up at a place you wanted to go but merely the fact that you end up someplace. The next part of learning comes in trying to figure out where it is. An easy answer, whether it's in healing or Soul Travel, isn't always the best because it overlooks the whole purpose of the experience, which is for learning.

As long as it's a positive experience, go with it. You may not always know where you are. If you feel bad when you come back, you know right away that it wasn't good. I wouldn't worry about it; all you're doing is getting experience, and that's fine.

## Censor

*How does the censor work in our dreams and in our daily lives?*

A dream usually applies very directly to what's happening in your outer life, often something right at the moment. But the dream comes through disguised because it would shock us.

Divine Spirit is trying to get a message through to the lower bodies to give us a hint of how we should change our lives a little bit. But the mind says, "No. If we let that message come straight through from the chief, it would be too much for them down here. We'll reword it a little." So by the time it gets down to the physical consciousness, you can't figure out exactly what it's supposed to say.

Change usually comes gradually. It's not usually an earthshaking thing like, Go out and start your own business now. And you wonder, How will I pay my rent on the thirtieth? Whatever you're doing right now is just right for you. When there's a change to come, it can come gradually.

Soul tries to make this gradual change but by the time the censor finishes with the information, it's diluted so you can't make heads or tails of which direction to take.

Just remember, the inner is directly related to the outer. If you get help in the dream state, it generally applies to your immediate outer life, what you're doing right here and now. It will also put you in positions to grow in understanding.

## Love Is the Only Way

*How can I tell new chelas that ECK is truth when my life is so filled with money problems and other troubles too numerous to write about here?*

All problems come from the inner to the outer; therefore, we want to find out what is being done on the inner planes that is bringing about the problems out here, which seem to be too much to endure at times.

There is no need to run through the clichés such as "There is no such thing as an accident," "All that befalls us is for a reason," or similar sayings. But what is causing all the trouble in terms that can be understood and accepted, and what is the solution?

The individual must be honest with himself and ask, "What did I expect from ECK when I took up the teachings?" The path to God is the path to God. It is not an easy one, otherwise many would be on it. Life is truly meeting ourselves. The complaints we have of others are a mirror of our own deficiencies. The more complaints there are, the greater the amount of deficiencies.

It makes no sense patching up our spiritual life with Band-Aids. The teachings of ECK are to give one a deep spiritual healing that touches all aspects of our lives. The magic wand, however, is not the instrument by which this is done. Has one kept up the spiritual exercises, not with the robotic diligence of a person on the prayer beads, but with a real desire to open himself to the secrets of God?

There are two basic paths for one to take in the lower worlds in an effort to find God—the path of love or the path of power. Most opt for power. This direction is the breeding ground of all the ills that come out of the five passions of the mind. Life is for him a disaster, and he wonders what keeps him from taking an easy way out.

Love is the only way to the SUGMAD. The only way. If you want to go this route, ask the Mahanta in contemplation to be shown the way. Most people in ECK have not found it. Otherwise there would be less gossip coming from their lips, fewer complaints, less of the power plays in the ECK Center.

But the individual's heart must be pure in this request. There must also be a complete surrender to the Inner Master, no holding back and having opinions of what is right or wrong about what is given him in order to light the Golden Heart.

The ECK is real but Its altar must be approached with humility and love, if one is ever to see Its ways.

## Just Listen to Serve God

*I've been in ECK for more than twenty years and was very active when I was younger. I am now ninety years old, in poor health, and living in a senior citizens' building. I am depressed because most of the other residents here have closed minds and are not open to hearing about ECK. Also I cannot get out to a Satsang class.*

You *are* a Co-worker with the Mahanta simply by your presence when you let the love of ECK fill your heart. Others will feel it.

I know it is difficult for you to talk about ECK in your senior citizens' building. But you don't have to. It's enough to *listen* to others when they need to talk, because in doing so, the divine love of ECK will flow through you to them, giving comfort and love where it's so much needed.

It will also strengthen your faith in ECK.

## Three Tests

*A couple of years ago you spoke of three tests we would all have to deal with as ECK chelas. I believe the first one was seeing ECKANKAR as a religion and acceptance of the ECK Worship Service. The second one was acceptance of the Temple of ECK. Can you tell us what the third one was?*

The third test is more stringent than the first two in the sense that it involves believing in yourself as a follower of ECK. The first two involved a belief in something outside of you: ECKANKAR as a religion and the ECK Worship Service, and the need for the Temple of ECK.

This third test coincides with the third part of my mission, which is to tell people everywhere about the Light and Sound of God. It will take ECKists of heart and courage to help do that.

Test three is the hardest of the lot because it puts the beliefs of the individual on the line. Is an ECKist confident about the love and power of ECK or is the main concern what society feels or thinks about the ECK teachings?

The third test asks, Will you stand up for ECK?

When the Sound and Light of ECK comes through an individual, he or she stands out as a leader and is an example to others. While it is imprudent to throw our spiritual beliefs in the face of people from other paths, there is still a need to stand up for ECK principles.

This third test puts your ECK beliefs on the line.

## Calling for Help

*If you're going through an unpleasant experience in the dream state which you determine is a test, and you call on the Inner Master for help, at that moment have you passed the test or failed it?*

You've remembered to ask, and that is an important step because you've remembered the Inner Master. Every answer is within your grasp, some are very close to you.

When you're wandering around the lower worlds, it's possible for those beings Paul Twitchell called the Time Makers to cloud your memory. They can wash your memory so that you forget there is help available simply by calling for it.

But if you have one little thought stuck away that reminds you that help is there if you ask, then you'll find another thought will come: how to extricate yourself from the situation. You'll remember the laws of the inner worlds that you may have forgotten. You'll remember, As Soul, I am free!

All is therefore of Divine Spirit. The degree to which we realize that is the degree to which we aspire for even higher things.

# 9

# Climbing the Spiritual Ladder

*If one does not recall many of his dreams, how can he find out about the First Initiation in the dream state?*

The First Initiation is the first real guidepost on one's journey home to God, the initial linkup between Soul and Divine Spirit.

Many people recall some part of the First Initiation, though others do not. Whatever the case, the Mahanta gives it to all during their first year of ECK study. This dream initiation occurs in a place you may visit again by singing *Alayi* (ah-LAH-yee) during a spiritual exercise. This word is for the physical plane.

If you sincerely want to learn about your dream initiation, sing this word daily for a month. Keep a dream journal. In the morning, allow the extra ten minutes in your schedule to jot down any impressions or dream memories, no matter how faint or silly.

Above all, be patient. Stick with this plan for a month. Soon you will catch a whole new outlook on the First Initiation and your relation to ECK.

## Our Unfoldment as Soul

*If the Soul Plane is above the realm of time, how does Soul progress after It reaches the Soul Plane?*

It doesn't, in the way we think of movement. The most we can say is that Soul unfolds spiritually.

As you suggest, if we create a world where space or time does not exist, then there can be no travel or progress. Travel or progress means going from one point in space to a second point, and that also requires duration.

Space, time, and matter collapse when Soul reaches the Soul Plane. Spiritual development continues, however.

The problem is human language. It originated on the Mental Plane, the last refuge of space and time. Since our spoken communication is based on the concepts of space and time, which are limited, we must use limited terms to address even those things that are beyond limitations.

For this reason the spoken word, even in ECK, is useful only to a certain point in learning truth. Finally, we must learn by direct perception.

## Evolution

*Can you explain evolution?*

Evolution is a guess by science about how a life-form changed since its beginning. A key word is *change*.

Evolution is the idea that everything changes over time. One example is the family of elephants, which includes the mammoth of thousands of years ago. The mammoth and the elephant came from the same ancestor. Today the mammoth is gone, and the elephant remains. Change is natural. So evolution fits right in with the ECK teachings.

## Toward God

*How can I reach God-Realization if I don't know what it is or what to aim at?*

A definition of God-Realization in all its details would fill volumes. But, in short, it is the state of seeing, knowing, and being from the highest spiritual plane.

That is one definition. Getting to that state is a whole other matter, of course. Here are a few guidelines on how to reach God-Realization: (1) do everything in the name of the Mahanta, (2) do even the smallest act with love and attention to detail, and (3) above all, give others the right to find their own way to God.

How do you accomplish that? The road to God begins with the Spiritual Exercises of ECK. Do them with love. Also pay close attention to the daily instructions, insights, and details that the Master will give you about reaching God Consciousness. He gives most of the training via the inner channels. Yet the details must prove themselves in everyday life.

## Inner and Outer

*How is it possible to have such a radiant, joyous communication with you at an inner level and yet be in such disharmony with the outer organization? In trying to help a friend and fellow chela, others mistook my actions and I received serious chastisement. Now I doubt whether I am truly a channel for the Mahanta.*

You asked about love instead of chastisement, and it is understandable because love sustains us. It is the ECK.

By the time one becomes a Higher Initiate, most of the communication between the Living ECK Master and the individual is done through the inner channels. One of the stages that we come to is learning to work in harmony with all life. This sounds too pat, too flat. But when we can see the Mahanta in all we meet—can see the Light of ECK in the eyes of people passing us on the street—then we can only give love in return to all life.

To qualify for the Order of the Vairagi, Soul must know discrimination in Its love. Warm love for our dear ones, charity (detached love) for the rest of creation. No one has the capacity to love all life without injury to himself. That is the purpose of discrimination.

The ECK Masters practice detachment, but this does not mean lack of compassion. Nor does this mean interfering in somebody else's affairs. Perhaps the hardest part of my duties is picking up a letter on my desk where someone asks relief from a crushing weight of karma, and I know it must be worked through and there is no shortcut available to him.

Of all who work in the spiritual field, some are able to move quietly and cooperatively among people while others generate a storm of controversy and disruption wherever they go. Why is that, all Souls being equal as the spark of God? There is always more to learn about acting as a vehicle for Divine Spirit and what it means, and how it's done.

The ECK Masters works strictly through the spiritual hierarchy. That is step number one. They are not in competition with each other. They know their common mission is to serve the great SUGMAD. Secondly, they do so in harmony, nurturing the plus factor, the building element in all they do.

We are all learning and growing. You also share the love and protection of the Mahanta at all times and need only be aware of it. I am always with you.

## Remembering the ECK Is All Life

*I have heard that some ECKists are upset about ECKANKAR keeping track of initiations on a computer. I don't know what to tell them.*

We get caught up in the mechanics of how Divine Spirit, the ECK, works. Some people don't understand the ways of Spirit. They go chasing off to the Philippines looking for a psychic healer; they get upset when they hear we work with computers. "My spiritual life is in the hands of computers," they say. As if the computer can overrule the ECK.

They forget that Spirit runs the whole show, from the Kal Niranjan down, even to the computer system we're using. ECK encompasses and surpasses all life; It runs life. I don't make rules regarding initiations; I carry out the laws of ECK. Sometimes I want to carry something out, but It'll do something else because It is the ECK.

To become an ECK Master means to learn the laws of Divine Spirit and live within those laws.

Some people come through the initiations very fast in this lifetime, but it could be because they had almost made this level in another lifetime then left the path. The people who may be standing back right now are those who in another lifetime are going to move very fast. There's no hurry. You can't get lost in the ECK.

You don't have to try to convince anyone. Things change as we go down the road. This is the nature of life; it throws us from one pole to the other like wheat in the wind. The chaff blows away, and what's left is the mature Soul. This is when we are no longer swept back and forth by the psychic waves, when we look directly to the Mahanta for our guidance and take measured steps out here. We don't let anything shake us; as Rebazar Tarzs said, "Nothing should move the dweller in ECK."

## Personal Goals

*How do you tell when a goal you're striving for is the right one, and the methods you are using are also right?*

One must have trust in ECK, and then follow through to manifest the good things in life. When you simply act "as if" you'd get your goal and trying for it hurts no one else in any way, that is one test of whether something you do is ECK or not.

I think you used good sense and used the principles to allow Divine Spirit to manifest for you what It would. Nothing wrong in that. Keep on with your personal spiritual experiments in ECK.

## Fine-Tuning

*After years of experience with the Light and Sound, I guess I have gotten used to being in Its presence, and It's not as vividly obvious as It used to be. What is happening?*

You're getting into an area where there's fine-tuning to be done on the inner. This is why people

212

have experiences when they first get on the path of ECK and later they go away. They've become used to their own state of being at that level.

I illustrated a similar principle in *The Wind of Change* with the story on invisibility. You can, for your experience sometime, come into such harmony with the outer vibrations of the people around you that you walk among them in such a way that you don't disturb their field force. Their senses aren't alerted, so for all purposes you are invisible to them. What you've really done is raise your vibration.

Before you come to this understanding in your spiritual unfoldment you get used to your dream state and your spiritual experiences so they no longer register upon the mind. The mind is the vehicle usually used to translate the vision of the higher worlds down to the lower worlds, but if the mind gets too numb or tired or accustomed to the experiences, it simply doesn't register them anymore.

So we have to be creative in our spiritual exercises. We approach everything in a fresh, new way, like a child would. I do this sometimes too because I want to do certain research or put myself in a discipline so I can easily slip back into a state of remembering the other planes. Usually I don't bother, but sometimes when I'm writing I have to verify things or get ideas.

But most important is to live here, in the present.

## Open Your Eyes

*I am an eighty-seven-year-old who has not yet succeeded in opening my Third Eye. What do you recommend?*

You asked to have the Tisra Til, the Spiritual Eye, opened. When it begins to open, you start to have experience with the Light of ECK in some manner or other, or else with the Sound. When both come together in a single matrix within the Spiritual Eye, the fortunate one is seeing the Inner Master, who has stationed himself there to purify the negative stream that wants always to flow into the student.

The question then is: Are you aware of any Light or Sound during contemplation or the dream state? The Light may be a blue star, disc, or globe; It may even be white, yellow, or green. The Sound may resemble a rushing wind, a symphony, a humming of bees, or the sound of a flute. Some hear the distant chirping of crickets. Others may have none of these manifestations but simply recall a meeting with one of the ECK Masters.

Other people find something quite different when the Spiritual Eye is opened. An awareness grows, not of the other worlds, but of the love and protection of the Mahanta. It settles about their shoulders like a warm cloak of love. Other ECKists carry a knowingness that their spiritual lives are directed by the great hand of the ECK.

So, you see, when the Third Eye opens there can be a wide variety of ways that Soul becomes aware of it.

*Thank you for your gentle touch on the inner plane which assured me of my initiation. Try as I will, I cannot figure out what you meant when, as you touched me under the left eye, you said, "You don't need this anymore."*

The left eye symbolizes your old reliance upon material things. At initiation, the Mahanta opened your Spiritual Eye. Material interests have bowed to a new, higher vision of life.

## Initiate Reports

*Is it possible to write a "wrong" initiate report? In Satsang class, a Higher Initiate recalled a letter that Paul Twitchell once sent him in response to an initiate report. Paul took him to task for too many "personal desires."*

*This is in opposition to what I have been told by other sources. They say, "Put any problems you are experiencing into the report." Now I'm puzzled. How much help can I ask for with my problems in a monthly report? Especially if I understand the help is to come not through the physical, but the inner channels?*

Paul's letter was for that Higher Initiate at that time. It does not apply across the board. The Master will sometimes make a sharp point to a chela when gentler means have failed.

You may include anything in your monthly report that comes to mind. Indeed, new chelas often do ask the Mahanta to fulfill personal desires. When they put such feelings on paper, it lets them see their unvarnished thoughts, often for the first time. That process burns away old karma. And if the Mahanta sees that it will benefit the individual, he may grant the personal desire. It never hurts to ask.

*I have been in ECK about seven years and am a Second Initiate. A friend told me it was not necessary to send in my initiate reports. I hope this is not what kept me from getting my Third Initiation. Can you straighten me out on this matter?*

215

I greatly appreciate your letter and the service you give to bring the ECK message to the uninitiated. All that's important is that the initiate undertake the self-discipline to write a monthly report concerning his spiritual affairs. It is not necessary to mail it to the Living ECK Master if the individual is comfortable with his linkup with the Mahanta, the Living ECK Master.

One gains inner initiations through the spiritual unfoldment that comes with regular practice of the spiritual exercises. To receive outer initiations, however, the completion and balance for those of the inner, one must keep up the outer membership and study of the ECK discourses. The inner initiations are not complete without the outer ones.

The sincere initiate, who wants the experience of Self- and God-Realization, must also begin to work with one of the Friday fasts listed in the Wisdom Notes. Not everyone will have vivid inner experiences, but will instead see Divine Spirit working in their daily affairs.

## Help with Takeoff

*It has been eight years since my Second Initiation. I have not to my knowledge seen the Inner Master or the Blue Light, or felt the presence of the Master. I love the Master and the ECK teachings, but I'm frustrated that I'm not able to have these experiences.*

*Paul Twitchell mentioned in his writings the feeling of anticipation one has when going to meet a loved one at the airport. I have had that feeling for a long time but cannot take many more canceled flights.*

*I know I have to be patient and persistent, but I'm very tired. I have an awful lot to learn, so please, will you help me get started?*

It was good to hear from you. In response to the lack of success in ECK with the spiritual exercises, I can only say that each person is unique, and Divine Spirit brings him along at the proper speed for him. You will find a greater understanding of this in *The Shariyat-Ki-Sugmad,* Book Two, pages 211–12.

Success comes from one's exercise of self-discipline. Contemplation must be done with joyful expectation. Before dropping off to sleep at night, it's possible to make a request of the Inner Master like this: "I give you permission to take me to that Temple of Golden Wisdom that fits my spiritual state, or any place else you choose." Then go to sleep and forget the permission you gave to the Mahanta.

It is a spiritual discipline to do the spiritual exercises daily.

## Soul's Separate Path

*What happens to our newborn baby if he translates before getting the Second Initiation? As new parents, we are very concerned about this.*

Understand that each Soul comes to earth along the lines of Its own destiny. A parent cannot get a child into heaven by proxy. Nor is a Soul ever lost in the arms of the ECK. Divine Spirit makes ample provisions for everyone to find Its path, Its Voice, when all the preparations are done.

Know that the Mahanta watches over Soul in a newborn baby as carefully as he does an adult. Nothing is impossible for the Holy ECK, for all things are within Its hand.

It is no blind accident that your son came into this lifetime after you received the Second Initiation. There are no loopholes in the school of ECK where a child can fall through and be forgotten by the Master.

How far can a parent carry a child in life? When must each Soul meet Its own experiences from the past? Do we delay Its progress when we let our emotions cloud the spiritual principle that each of us must stand before God in our own right?

Indeed, it is a privilege, for Soul is an independent unit in substance like the SUGMAD ITSELF. The potential for spiritual greatness is therefore in all of us, but it must have the chance to mature in its own time.

I hope this gives you a broad view of God's plan for Soul.

## Choosing to Return

*If a Higher Initiate translates, then chooses to reincarnate on this planet, what happens to his initiations? Is he automatically born into a family of ECKists? Does he have to do his initiations all over, or does he get them faster than others?*

Let's take Paul Twitchell as an example. Why did he choose to return? The spiritual hierarchy felt that his training until then made him uniquely qualified to become the Mahanta, the Living ECK Master in 1965.

He had reached the Fifth Initiation in his previous incarnation, but he chose to return anyway. Why? Because his love for the SUGMAD outweighed any desire for titles, such as Fifth or Sixth Initiate. His birth in 1908 was an opportunity for him to reach a greater state of spiritual awareness.

And, yes, he had to go through all the ECK initiations again. A veil shut off memories of his earlier lives, so he was largely unaware of past accomplishments. Often a person like Paul is born into a family where at least one of the members has a good understanding of ECK.

This system may look harsh, but it works. Soul cares only for experience. Titles and position mean little to It, and Its desire to serve God results in the purest love of all.

## Go at Your Own Pace

*I am not a student of ECK but my husband is. I have come to realize that he is in a changed state of consciousness. I've read in some of the ECK books that one person can drag the other down, and I don't want to be that sort of person, since it would put a strain on our marriage. How do I go about letting him grow at his own rate and me at mine?*

Thank you for your letter of concern. When one's love for God is so strong and leads us into unfamiliar areas, it is best to go slowly and give love and goodwill to all life.

ECK moves to bring harmony to families. By *ECK* I mean the Holy Spirit as you are more familiar with it. Stay with the Catholic teachings of your youth. The love and protection of Divine Spirit surmount any distinctions of religious paths if the seeker is sincere in wanting the experience of God.

Don't be alarmed, for you are unfolding along with your husband, even though you are more comfortable in your childhood religion. After all, any religious teaching must fit you; not you, it. If you'll accept the fact that you can see the spiritual unfoldment of your spouse because his is only a reflection of your own, you will enjoy your family in your daily duty as well as recreation.

The first two years of membership in ECKANKAR are purposely set aside for one to study its suitability to oneself. After two years of study one can better make the decision of whether or not to follow ECKANKAR or Catholicism. The choice must be based on what you learn is right for you.

## Stone Statue

*I feel frustrated because I am having such difficulty with Soul Travel. I am new to ECK. Can you help?*

The problem, as you state it, is the inability to get out of your body. The methods of ECK work sooner or later for most people. But, of course, owing to the individuality of us all, Soul Travel experiences may be dramatic, routine, or nonexistent.

I do my best to help everyone who is serious about being a channel for the ECK to reach a higher state of consciousness in the way that is best for him. It is a foregone conclusion in ECK that whatever can be imagined can also be accomplished.

Therefore, I am happy to hear that you are keeping up with the spiritual exercises. In doing them, you are building up the inner stamina needed to go beyond the physical body, and to remember the result.

Try this exercise, which has worked for some people who regard themselves as too practical in nature for having Soul Travel outings.

Before you go to sleep, imagine seeing yourself as a statue. Visualize the ECK Masters Peddar Zaskq, Rebazar Tarzs, Fubbi Quantz, and Wah Z gathered around the statue with moving equipment. Wah Z and Peddar Zaskq each have a crowbar, while Fubbi Quantz and Rebazar Tarzs are operating a tow truck.

Visualize Peddar and Wah Z prying up the edge of the statue and the hoist from the tow truck being slipped under it. The tow truck groans under the dead weight of the statue, but it lifts it. How high it lifts it doesn't matter.

The Masters now move the statue from one place to another—from the Physical to the Astral to the Causal Plane. Fubbi Quantz then drives the tow truck up a ramp into a Temple of Golden Wisdom where they have a restoration room. In this big, empty room the ECK Masters turn statues back into living spiritual beings.

The ECK Masters are all very happy that they have gotten the statue this far. It's a lateral move but better than no move at all. Fubbi Quantz carefully lowers the statue and sets it down in the center of the room. He brings in a few plants, including large ferns, and places them around the statue to make it pretty.

Now watch carefully to see what the ECK Masters are doing.

Each Master has a little can, which he pries open with a screwdriver. Inside is a very special oil designed to dissolve crust, the crust of ages, the kind of crust that gets on Soul after being hardened by the problems of daily living.

The ECK Masters very carefully put this dissolving oil all over the statue. Remember the statue is you. Shift your viewpoint from watching what is happening, to being the statue itself. Feel the dissolving oil being smeared all over you. After a moment, the crust of ages begins to crumble, and underneath it is healthy skin.

The ECK Masters stand back and look. "There's somebody in there," they cry jokingly. They watch as Soul breaks free of the human consciousness. When this happens, the ceiling opens up and the sun, or

Light of God, touches the real being that was trapped inside the statue of human consciousness.

Repeat this exercise for one month. As you progress in the Light and Sound, the ECK will begin to enliven your spiritual pulse. You will begin to listen, and you will hear the Sound of the spheres, which may sound like the wind in the trees.

## Using Right Discrimination

*I have recently begun a new business and would like to sell my product to ECKists I know in my area. Can you advise me on whether this is all right spiritually?*

Concerning your question about mixing your profession with the spiritual path: It is never good to go to a party and talk politics or religion if you want to keep friends. It holds more true in business. You'll get yourself and others in a lot of grief if you cater to ECKists.

One ECKist I know has her own small business, but she makes it a point not to sell to ECKists. Instead, she refers them to another supplier where she gets no commission.

I do appreciate your thoughtfulness in asking about this. Whatever anyone does as an individual is not my concern. But when someone begins to profit from the ECK membership, then it is, and I must discourage the practice.

## Perfect Freedom

*Is it true that one outgrows ECKANKAR when he becomes a Fifth Initiate in ECK?*

When one goes through the lower planes toward the Soul Plane, the Mahanta walks in front to point out the pitfalls that might snare Soul on Its way back home to God. A change happens on the Soul Plane when the individual becomes Self-Realized. Now he can choose to walk the rest of the way home by himself or extend an invitation to the Inner Master to accompany him.

From this point onward, the Master walks with him right into the very heart of God. This point is often overlooked by the chela as he raises his eyes to the final goal. At every step, however, the Master gives perfect freedom for one to step aside from the ECK works if he really wants that in his heart.

*It is my interpretation as I walked the ECK path that as one came closer to mastership that one would drop the path of ECKANKAR and take up the path of ECK, or as I call it now, the path of Spirit. Does this mean I should leave ECKANKAR?*

Your decision must be your own of course, and will be respected.

*The Shariyat-Ki-Sugmad,* Book Two, page 240, says that "The initiate of the Seventh Circle . . . now has the right to choose whether he will pursue the rest of the way on the path of ECKANKAR." The initiate of the Eighth Circle is stretched even more: "he has the right to choose whether he will sacrifice himself to remain upon the earth to help with the progress of humanity; or whether he will pass onward to the realm of spiritual development outside this planet . . . into the spiritual regions" (page 241).

The first eight ECK initiations are given in the physical, and those beyond on the inner. If one steps aside from the path of ECK, the individual loses all his ECK initiations. If this is your wish, I will respect it.

## Who Is the Mahanta?

*Can you tell me more about the Mahanta? Is it a universal force or a person? I am new to the teachings of ECK and thinking of becoming a member.*

I greatly appreciate your letter that showed interest in ECKANKAR. About the Mahanta, it is best if you make up your mind yourself in this matter. I suggest light research in *The Shariyat-Ki-Sugmad,* as well as *The Spiritual Notebook* by Paul Twitchell.

The topic to put attention on is the Rod of ECK Power. Take what you find into contemplation in a gentle way. You may develop an understanding of who the Mahanta is for you; a more direct answer will come in the dream state.

You must remember that your relationship with the Mahanta is for you alone. It really doesn't matter if another person sees your reality the way you do or not. It is easier to follow the dictates of your own truth by adhering to the Law of Silence, which is known as Kamit.

Most of your questions will be answered in time if you continue with the spiritual exercises. Take your time, go slowly, and let your feelings or intuition steer your course rather than any outside influence. If the course is right, you will feel good inside about it. That is one of the best tests for truth that I can give you.

## Secret Word and Karma

*What if you don't use your secret word given in your initiations? Does that mean you'll have a lot of karma to work off when you become a High Initiate?*

People who don't use their secret words might never become Fifth Initiates.

The secret word is indeed for working off karma. It is a spiritual gift. The Mahanta has given it to you to make your way easier in this life, because it lets you tap the power of ECK to help you unfold spiritually.

Karma blocks a person from the higher worlds. The secret word helps you sort through your baggage and toss out the junk. It makes your life easier.

So remember to use this gift of the Mahanta.

## A New Word

*I seem to have gotten my spiritual name on the inner planes. Can you verify this?*

One's spiritual name is given at the Ninth Initiation. The name you received is your secret word for the present level of spiritual growth. It is the key that unlocks the powers of the ECK, to lift you into the sublime states of spiritual consciousness. It must be kept to yourself or the power of the word will be lost.

*If it is appropriate, would you speak about having a series of spiritual words, not just one? I had the secret word from my Second Initiation for only a few weeks. Ever since, I have been receiving a new word about every six months to a year. I worry that I am not doing something right.*

Your question illustrates how each person in ECK walks a unique path to God Consciousness. The Master gives a new secret word every time the chela unfolds in awareness. The Astral Plane, for example, has many subinitiation levels, and each of them requires a new password for entry. Each new word permits access to a special area of instruction.

The fact that your word changes so often indicates an inquisitive and spiritually adventurous nature.

## Importance of Outer Initiations

*Since my husband translated in 1979, I have met with him often on the inner planes. He says he is now a member of the Vairagi Masters and has many good writings to pass on from Rebazar Tarzs and Fubbi Quantz. Should I send them to you?*

Spiritual unfoldment is a highly personal matter. All members in the Order of the Vairagi were required to pass through the outer initiations under the direction of the Living ECK Master of the times. Your husband had made good progress in his spiritual unfoldment, but never got the first eight initiations on the outer and thus is not a member of the Vairagi ECK Masters.

You are free to send in some of his writings to ECKANKAR if you feel it is helpful, but that is your decision. Your husband is well and happy on the inner planes, and himself makes no pretensions of being a member of the ECK Masters. He has a better picture of his spiritual growth since the translation in 1979.

We do not have the right to hold him back from more unfoldment by our lack of understanding.

## Are You Ready?

*How can I tell when I'm going to get another initiation? How do you know that I'm ready?*

Each ECK initiate must study the ECK discourses for so many years. Then it depends upon how well he or she has been able to open himself to the ECK Current that comes down from the next plane.

A person's unfoldment can be seen in his face and actions. The initiate report is but one of several ways which the Master uses to watch the individual's spiritual progress toward the next initiation.

*For several months now I have had permission for my Second Initiation, but I haven't gotten it. I don't want to get it if I'm not ready. How will I know?*

The Master has sent you the pink slip for initiation. The gift has already been given, but the chela must accept it. You may take the initiation whenever you are willing.

## Attitude of the Loving Heart

*When I got my Second Initiation, I immediately had a bad car accident. Is this aftermath part of initiations? I am concerned about getting any more of them.*

Please do not feel that great troubles are a natural aftermath of receiving the Second Initiation.

When one gets the initiation on any level, the Audible Life Stream flows through him in a greater amount. The ECK uplifts and purifies the consciousness of the individual so that it fits the new level of spiritual understanding that he has reached.

One can have a smooth route through most initiations by listening to the subtle promptings of Divine Spirit trying to steer him past unnecessary karma. The attitude that one can develop is of loving awareness of how the ECK principles are now working in a greater degree in his life.

It is our attitudes that have caused karma. Thus you can see that as quickly as we can identify and let go of those attitudes that harm us, we will move smoothly into the spiritual worlds.

At each level of unfoldment, we realize that we've outgrown some of our previous attitudes. They have no part in the new spiritual consciousness that we have earned. They must go or we must meet the situation until the lesson is absorbed.

I certainly would not walk around with a black shadow over my head. Instead one can look to the Light and Sound of ECK with a loving heart and simpleness in spirit, like a young child trusting its parent to bring it all it needs to survive in life.

An attitude of the loving heart can dissolve much of the unnecessary karma. It becomes powerless to touch us because of the protection of the Mahanta.

## ECK Initiators

*I just had the opportunity to give a woman and her daughter their Second Initiation. I just want to thank you with all my heart for this blessing. The experience of giving an initiation is as profound as receiving one. I am humbled, honored, and filled with the divine joy to serve you and the ECK in this way. Can you tell me anything more about the service of the Initiator?*

The Initiator has a special opportunity to see the power of the ECK. It's a funny thing, but if one occasionally feels doubts about the power of ECK, clear evidence comes to the Initiator during the sacred initiation.

The privilege is his alone because he earned it. Yet he's not able to draw upon these experiences when confronted by an ECKist who still has not earned them.

I always count it a special blessing to serve the SUGMAD as an Initiator, because proof of the divine works is never more strong than during an ECK initiation.

## How Is an ECK Initiation Different?

*How are ECK initiations different from those of other paths?*

A man told me of an acquaintance of his, who was now sixty-seven. He had traveled to Tibet, China, South America, and all ends of the earth to study under the great unknown healers among us. In the process of his education, he took numerous initiations of power and light, some of which would astound the orthodox mind.

Yet all these minor initiations, which are prerequisites to the ECK initiations, had left him an emotional, social, and financial cripple. None of those ceremonies had the power to integrate the different parts of his being and blend them into something that would bridge for him the void between the visible and invisible planes.

Thus he was the receiver of psychic powers, but spiritually he could not put one foot ahead of the other and walk without tripping.

The ECK initiation is a quiet thing. It sets into motion the erratic energy from past-life karma, the impetus that lets one come within a centimeter of the goal only to lose it by an unconscious self-destructive nature.

Outsiders to ECK who know little about the initiations think of them as so much foolish hogwash. They don't know that one earns them dearly. That's why they're so important in one's spiritual unfoldment.

## The Use of Visualization

*What benefits can visualization bring to Higher Initiates in their spiritual growth?*

I had a letter from someone who felt that visualization techniques were not right, that they were from the psychic planes. In *The Flute of God* there's a little bit written about visualization and the importance of it, what it can do to help us along in our spiritual lives.

Everyone's experiences are different, but you may have a hard time getting to the Sixth Initiation. Once you get there, you're so happy to be there that you don't want to leave. You get caught up in a kind of spiritual lethargy. Something which will help you pull yourself along are the spiritual exercises, which are, after all, visualization techniques.

In *Talons of Time,* Paul talks about the Time Makers and their role here in the lower worlds. You may have a spiritual plan for yourself with a starting point, an interval where you try to carry it out, and an ending point where you reach your goal. The Time Makers, or the negative power, try to capture Soul somewhere in the middle and immobilize It. It can show up in a number of different ways: procrastination, lethargy. It serves simply to stop Soul from unfolding.

You can use the visualization techniques to pull yourself free from the mud.

## Making the Climb Easier

*Can you give me some help on how to make it easier to move to the next initiation?*

Each new level of ECK initiation is entering into the vortex of a greater vibration from the ECK. To make it easier upon ourselves, the old rule is to "give up and let go." That means putting aside all our preconceived notions of what is or is not right in line with the initiation.

The ECK always does that which is right for the moment. Each person is treated as an individual. Our opinion of the value of the ECK's workings is of no concern to It, for the thing that must be done will be done regardless.

It is seen that there is only a hairbreadth's difference between the material and spiritual planes. Some cannot tell the difference between them, because it is not the two planes that are so different at all, but our state of consciousness in regard to them. All is therefore of Divine Spirit. The degree to which we realize that is the degree to which we aspire for even higher things.

The Mahanta is thus concerned only that the individual shall unfold in some way. The goal is the ECK Mastership, but on the road one must first master the Physical Plane, then the Astral, and so on.

What does it mean to be a Master? It means to be in full control of the conditions on any plane on which we have earned the recognition as a Master. Being a Master implies having earned the power to control our destiny.

Do everything in the name of SUGMAD, or God.
That means, do it with love and care.

# 10

# Leaders in ECK

*How can we spread the message of ECK without invading the space of others who are not searching for ECK right now?*

Do everything in the name of the SUGMAD, or God. That means, do it with love and care.

Others who also want to live a productive, spiritual life will notice and ask what you believe. That's an opening to tell them about ECK.

Until people seek you out, you can do what so many other ECK chelas are doing. They leave ECK books and brochures where interested people can find them. Some even mention ECK subjects, like dreams, on computer bulletin boards.

If you want to spread the message of ECK, be alert. The Mahanta will provide openings you never dreamed of.

New people really want to talk with someone in ECK who can talk to them about their concerns. Mostly all they want is a listener. While they're talking out their thoughts, insights, doubts, and questions, they are closely watching us to see if we're really listening to them. Or do we use the time to arrange our next speech? If so, it shows in our eyes and manner, and they are quick to pick it up. Then they draw back.

I once worked for a boss who took a printing order from a hospital. He wanted me to strip up the job for the hospital's press because their stripper had quit. It was a press he was obviously not familiar with, so the instructions he gave me were off. The hospital printers were able to salvage the job.

My boss, upset that he'd sent a job out wrong, turned on me and said, "Why didn't you catch the mistake?" I simply told him that he sounded so sure of himself it was possible he knew something I didn't. Therefore, I did it his way just to find out.

After that, he listened to me instead of ordering me from here to there like a warehouseman lugging a carton of soap.

Other leaders in ECK will help distribute the spiritual workload. There are many people who want to hear about ECK, and the members of ECKANKAR are taking more responsibility upon themselves to act as Co-workers with God. I recommend that teachers in ECK go over the *ECK Arahata Book* fairly regularly, to keep in mind the approaches that work when teaching ECK. It tunes one in to the mechanics of divine revelation.

Right now there is a great need to have initiates who are stable and reliable. The public is watching us very carefully, as a child watches a fish swimming in an aquarium and wonders what the thoughts of a fish could be.

But neither the years nor the actions of ECK leaders mean as much to me as does their beingness. That's a ten-dollar word to say that I love you because you're you. Beingness doesn't have to produce or meet quotas.

## A Vehicle for the Mahanta

*Recently I have been experiencing an intense and deep mourning that is not my own. The first time it happened, I learned of two leaders in our Satsang Society with fathers who were near translating. They were both mourning. After I called them, my feelings of mourning left.*

*Two weeks later, the sense of mourning returned to a depth that was almost too much to bear. When I experience this sorrow that doesn't appear to belong to me, is there something else I could be doing as an ECK channel?*

*Or do I just do what I can to survive or endure the experience?*

The feelings you pick up on are from ECK initiates in your region who are facing moments of deep emotion. As a vehicle for the Mahanta, you will feel some of their sorrow, for that is a part of compassion.

However, for your health and peace of mind, you need to release the problems of others to ECK. One way to do that is with an initiate report. It is often hard to sit down when these turbulent feelings come, but if you stop whatever else you are doing and write an initiate report, you will usually get relief within a few minutes. The Mahanta is there right beside you when you do it.

So address your state of unrest immediately, in writing, even if you don't understand all the reasons behind it. Usually, you'll see the problem lessen. And later, you will also likely discover the reason for your experience.

## Dream of Leadership

*Just before my birthday, I had a very powerful dream. I heard a deep voice, first telling me to wake*

235

*up, and then saying, "The lion is loose now, and it* will have its way!" *It startled me so much that I could not sleep, and I have considered this dream many times in the last week. What does it mean?*

Your dream about the deep voice saying, "The lion is loose now, and it will have its way!" means this: The American Indians said the mountain lion was the symbol for leadership. Life is pushing you into that role. There are strong pluses and minuses, because people envy a strong leader. They cannot be a success themselves for a lack of the needed self-discipline, so they need a strong leader to do for them what they can't. But that raises envy. So the leader needs to be strong, with self-direction from an inner source (the ECK). Leadership of the right kind is highly spiritual, for it exercises the power of divine creation.

## Silver Wolf

*I experienced a series of personal losses over a year's time, after stepping back from an ECK leadership position. During a retreat I took in the mountains, I had a very powerful experience on the inner planes with the presence of a silver wolf. The experience lasted several weeks. At one point I heard the words "The transformation is complete."*

*What can you tell me about this?*

The wolf is a good omen among Native Americans, especially so a silver one. You've made an effort to continue your unfoldment since your tenure as an ECK leader. The silver wolf means you've reached a new level of service as a teacher in ECK.

Some people get an outer initiation but then stop growing. You'll feel a sense of the ECK community more than before, but with that comes what seems like a contradictory side: the need for solitude. Go inwardly to meet the Mahanta and learn from him, but then demonstrate that wisdom and truth to others around you.

## Survival Mode

*Sometimes I feel like a soldier in the trenches trying to get the teachings out. What attitude do you hold that allows the ECK teachings to survive in a world not often friendly to them?*

I'm the cautious one, and don't get my hopes up. Once we rest on our laurels, then the end is near. So it's best to run lean and hungry, always looking over your shoulder to see if anyone out there is gaining on you. It's the feeling that a soldier feels when he goes out into combat. He's more alive then than at any other time in his life—although, paradoxically, combat may also end it.

There is much work to do, but it's the good kind. It's a labor of love. Without ECK, what is there?

It's always best to go where the interest is strongest because there is only so much of us to go around.

*For more than a year I have been fighting what has been a very difficult financial situation as well as trying to represent ECKANKAR in this area. I don't understand what is happening and why the problem has worsened in spite of my persistent optimism and sincere efforts to earn a living. I don't have time or places left to turn to.*

There has been a lot of silent opposition to your efforts in your state in regard to the teachings of ECK.

Please look carefully around at all your resources. A way has been opened for you to ease some of the financial burden, but still the responsibility is left up to you to find it.

Look to the Inner Master during the dream state or during contemplation.

## What to Do with Good Ideas

*A lot of people have good ideas, but that's where it stops. How do you plan? Do you have some simple steps you can share to help us manifest the Mahanta's vision?*

Good ideas are indeed a dime a dozen. However, to make an idea work you need a champion and a plan.

Let's say the idea involves a Vahana project. Who brought the idea to your attention? Look closely, for that very person may be your champion. But it's too early to tell for sure yet.

Next call a Vahana meeting. Appoint a *secretary* to keep notes but lead this first meeting yourself. Your goal is twofold: (1) to make a *plan,* complete with steps and due dates, and (2) to select a *team leader* (champion). Give a brief introduction to the idea, then ask the person who first made the suggestion to speak about it. Remember to ask the rest of the team for their ideas, and make sure the secretary gets all the key steps of action down on paper.

A plan has a logical time frame: a right time and place for every step of the plan. Now list those steps in order. Does everyone agree to the plan?

Then ask the most astute, lively person in the room to lead the team on this Vahana project, and name an assistant at the same time. Give them full charge of the project, but ask for an update every week or so.

Are they completing each step of the project by its due date? (You should have your own copy of the final Vahana plan as a checklist.) Also let them know to call you if they run into snags. (They will.)

It takes a champion to make a good idea work. An able champion will get the job done, freeing you for other duties. Wise delegation is the key to good leadership. When you let others help in the mission of ECK, it gives them a chance to grow spiritually. And later, thank them.

One more point: Don't ever hesitate to give the job of team leader to a Second, Third, or Fourth Initiate, even when all the others are Higher Initiates.

Humility is a key word in ECK.

## Golden Age

*I feel the ECK path is changing to make itself more of a home for those who would benefit from these teachings in this lifetime. I hope that the ECK leadership can see this as the great growth opportunity it is. I hope they can offer their services to you during this growth. How can we as ECK leaders help?*

There's a long way to go before ECKANKAR fulfills its destiny. It's like we've moved a shovelful of dirt but the rest of the mountain remains. Most of the groundwork should be done in twenty-five years, which is really a short time when you consider the worldwide base that is in the plans. It all seems overwhelming at times, but this is the age for ECKANKAR to be brought out again. A cultural, social, and spiritual golden age will be the result.

The influence of ECK is moving out into the world. Many people will have the chance to know the Light and Sound of God before it's time for them to leave this earth. More opportunities will be there for the ECK initiates to help in this great mission. One who gives of himself to life without any strings attached is a richer individual, because he is loving something else more than himself.

The ongoing renewal of how we do things is the key ingredient. Take, for example, an ECK seminar. No matter how good the programs are, there's always room for improvement. Keep putting life into it and it stays young, but let it crystallize and it gets old and dies.

The task of coordinating the whole program is something that boggles the mind. Seminar directors from other groups have commented more than once that they don't know how we put on the seminars, especially of such size and run largely by volunteers.

It is a big undertaking. It works because we all work together. The chelas want to give of their time and talents to serve the ECK, and finally there's a chance to do it. All I really care about is giving as many individuals the opportunity for unfoldment as is possible.

As the ECK path becomes broader and more people follow it, more of the everyday decisions will be made by ECK leaders in their hometowns. There will be abuses of power, but there will also be the balance of ECK. Growth means problems because nobody is set to make the decisions at the new level until they have gotten some experience with the conditions there, which takes time.

Every universe is a theater for Souls to do what they must for the purification that opens the heart to God Consciousness.

The challenge the ECK leaders face is to let the

initiates extend themselves in their spiritual unfoldment. There's more to leadership than saying, "That's
the goal over there. Do this and this, and you'll be
rewarded for it. Fail, and the punishment for not
meeting spiritual standards is this."

The challenge is to show the individual how to get
above his personal interests and act in the name of the
SUGMAD. You'll see how closely a good businessman
exemplifies these ideals with his employees.

## Differing Viewpoints

*I recently gave an introductory talk that empha-
sized reliance on one's own experiences with God, that
Soul must seek inner guidance, that we must be original and realize the trap of mimicking other ECKists.
I spoke about going beyond the ECK books—how to
read them, absorb the imagery, and then prepare to
become detached from them so the inner reality will
become part of one's own consciousness. But a Mahdis,
a Fifth Initiate, who attended this talk held a very
different point of view. Was my approach wrong?*

I read your interesting description of the open
discussion. Your insights were deep and to the point.
The Mahdis's concern is that the introductory discussions be kept simple. We do not want to tell people too
much at first, but allow them to make their own discoveries about the ECK works.

You can be certain that the Mahdis has at some
time stood in your shoes. The knowledge from the ECK
poured into the consciousness so fast that it was a trial
deciding what to do with it. Spirituality cannot be
taught, but must be caught. I found myself in the same
situation as yourself. It was easy to speak on the
doctrine of Divine Spirit.

Unfortunately, with so many minds getting in there and misunderstanding the meaning of words, it happened that some people disagreed with my viewpoints. For self-protection I analyzed what it was I said that upset others. What approach could be taken that would present the message of ECK in simple terms for the guest, yet avoid confrontations with the ECK leadership? A solution was to approach the ECK works in story form, either those from the ECK Masters or other ECKists (with permission). That took a lot of work.

Another workable approach in a discussion class is to accept the fact that our ideas are important but to use the class to draw out the insights of others. This is difficult and requires a real interest in other people. Usually a good listener is most successful at this. He allows others to dip into their insights and enjoys their surprise that such gems lay hidden all this time within their being.

I found that there is something more important than being right. The higher path is to work in harmony with every living thing on all planes. It requires real insight to develop this ability.

## Our Focus in ECK

*Can you give us some guidelines on how to work with unofficial special interest groups like gays and lesbians? How can we keep the focus on ECK yet have members of these groups feel welcome?*

Our focus in ECK is the Light and Sound of God. ECKANKAR is not just about relationships, healing, the search for truth, Soul Travel, or any of the many parts of the ECK teachings. It is about all of them. Consider this point: How can the ECK community thrive unless the initiates begin to work together in love, harmony, and wisdom?

We want to give ECKists of like mind a chance to meet. Yet ECKANKAR is for all who want to find their way home to God.

The ECK Centers are not a base for making social statements or for selling products. Those things belong elsewhere. Come together to study ECK and enjoy the company of those who share the high ideal of spiritual freedom here and now.

## An ECK Leader's Spiritual Discipline

*Is fasting something an initiate should do simply because the Mahanta asks him to do it?*

No one is forced to do anything in ECK, but more is expected of leaders. This is only for the spiritual benefit of the initiate—to help him reach Self- and God-Realization in the best way for him.

As you do the Friday fasts over a period of time, you will see an upward move in your thoughts and outlook toward life. You will get a greater control of your life than ever before.

*There are some longtime High Initiates who have status in the ECK community. Often they teach classes and have a following. They are disrupting harmony in the area by not going along with your direction through the Regional ECK Spiritual Aides.*

*Can you give tips on how to work with these people?*

First, gather clear evidence of how they are not following the guidelines in teaching ECK. Then show it to the Regional ECK Spiritual Aide or the appropriate person appointed by the RESA. Some issues will be more serious than others, and the RESA will help you sort through them to come to a decision about the next course of action.

It is very important that Higher Initiates teach ECK correctly, for the spiritual good of many people depends upon it. Thank you for your concern.

*I am a RESA, and I have just discovered that our director of Spiritual Services, an H.I., is a heavy smoker. Sometimes he smokes around other ECKists. It is upsetting some chelas. What do I do?*

You need to sit down with him and have a talk. The Mahanta will not remain where people smoke. Before this meeting, ask the Mahanta for words of firmness, but also of compassion and love. It's better to handle a problem like this now than later, because a leader, especially, who smokes around ECKists does serious harm to them in both a physical and spiritual sense.

You must ask him to step down from this leadership post. His smoking habit is a detriment to the spiritual welfare of others in the ECK community.

## Breaking Inertia

*Even though I'm a leader in ECK, I'm having doubts about the validity of ECKANKAR and my own commitment to Divine Spirit. As a new chela I accepted everything on faith, but now I find myself wanting to reject everything I haven't personally experienced.*

It is not really enough to say that doubts about ECK are a natural step in our spiritual unfoldment. The saints had their different experiences of God, but not all the time. Between the ecstasy, they devoted their time to seeing the Light of God in mundane tasks. Few could understand their happiness in regard to the small and unimportant things of life. The point is that experiences can do only so much for anyone. There comes a time when we have to let go of those which we've had, just so we can exist as a useful human being among our fellows. No path to God is a boardwalk of continuous bliss. Life stretches us beyond what we were yesterday, and we hurt.

Soul works by rest points in eternity. This is covered in *The Far Country.* When we are in a cycle of activity, then all is well. But when everything appears to slow down, our mind is upset and becomes disoriented. Something has changed subtly, and we are at a loss as to what it is. Life runs in cycles. For now, try to find someone to help with your ECK work so you can step back and be the Watcher—Soul—to determine the new direction that Divine Spirit is carrying you. Spirit is going in one direction, and your mind is still off in another. The momentum is left over from the previous cycle which gave you the enthusiasm to work for ECK. There is a new direction, and you have to find it.

To break the inertia that has hold of you, take a pen and a yellow felt-tip marker and read one letter from *Letters to Gail,* starting with Volume I. Do a letter each night or so, underlining and making margin notes as you go. Take your time at this, and do the spiritual exercises found there. They are basic, but useful, if you want to help yourself.

## Using ECK for Personal Gain

*I have a concern about the number of H.I.'s in our area who use the membership of ECKANKAR for their business deals. It's a bit troubling, and I'd like to ask your advice on it.*

There are some ECKists who like to do business with ECKists. I have no problem with that. But sometimes they get into such things as using mailing lists from the ECK Centers. That's not good at all.

If you need a reason why, it's this: We are a nonprofit group, and we have to protect ourselves in a legal way. This is our contract with the state that allows us to exist. This means that a person is not to benefit financially in an improper way from ECKANKAR's nonprofit status as a religion.

If ECKists take mailing lists from the ECK Center for anything like this, it's absolutely wrong. It mixes profit and nonprofit. What they're doing is trying to make a living off a mailing list which would not have come into their hands if they had not been volunteering for a nonprofit religion. This isn't right.

You might have to say something to them. You could say, "You're mixing things here, and I feel you're violating a spiritual trust. Is this the kind of behavior we want going on in the area? Is it ethical?" I know it puts you on the line, but you're on the line anyway.

To me, if a person sets up a business which can only exist because he's dealing with ECKists, then I would have to ask if it's really providing a service. Some people think they're providing a service to the world, but they're really just in it to make a buck.

I sometimes have very little patience with them. I realize that the same thing sometimes happens at seminars because habits are habits. If they do it at home, they're going to bring the same habits to the seminar. If I find out about it, I certainly tell them it's out of place. And if they feel so upset by that that they want to leave ECK in a huff, I'd say let them. They don't belong here.

We always have to remember why we are here. Is

it to gain something for ourselves in some material way? Or is it to love and give service to God? We must have this principle in the back of our minds and use it as the yardstick for all our actions and for those who are working with us. Sometimes we have to call people to task.

## Truth Hurts a Gossip

*How can ECK leaders deal with other initiates who create discontent among the ECK chelas through gossip?*

Truth hurts a gossip.

So I suggest you first get all the background you can on a rumor, then meet with the gossip and ask what basis the gossip has for spreading the rumor. Pin down the facts. And like a detective, check out the whos, whats, whens, wheres, and hows.

Ask the gossip your questions face-to-face, if possible. A gossip is like a rat: He or she likes dark places. Once you shine the light of truth (facts) upon the case, the gossip tends to slink away into the night.

The best weapon against a gossip is truth.

## For the Good of All

*Soon after I became a RESA, a few H.I. leaders got very out of balance. Some are in the public eye. Is this due to a period of cleansing we're all going through, or is it just their own problems?*

*Do I need to speak to them because they are leaders, and how can I help them spiritually as well?*

The longer you are a RESA, the more you'll see how much everything stays the same. There will always be people who go out of balance, even High Initiates. You'll run into this issue again and again.

A person who does not set the dial of his inner TV to the Mahanta will miss out on the latest news from ECK. More than likely, he is out of balance simply because he quit doing the spiritual exercises. Try to steer him back on course in an ESA session.

What do you do, though, if he doesn't ask for help?

Sooner or later, one's inner confusion will always show up in what he says or does. First, sit back and try to get a clear picture in your mind about how bad his behavior actually is. Then, speak to him about it in the spirit of love. Be ready to show, with a specific example or two, how he has hurt others spiritually.

An Arahata is out of balance when he is often late for Satsang class—or sometimes forgets to show up at all. Speak to him about it. If he still won't meet his spiritual duty as an ECK leader, go ahead and find a more responsible person to take his place.

Do everything with love for ECK, and it will usually turn out for the good of all.


## Getting Projects Started

*As an ECK leader I'd like to know, How do you get a project started for ECK? What spiritual qualities should be behind it?*

Most programs are begun quietly so hardly anyone outside those directly involved have any idea that a powerful force for ECK is quietly working behind the scenes. There's no need to push things in such a program because the Mahanta arranges a whole lot of conditions that later all fit together.

Everything depends on the people he chooses, how

quickly the groups can make peace with themselves. Until then, they are of no use to anyone, especially the SUGMAD. But ironically, there's usually no way to speed up this process.

That's why the golden people are chosen for key positions. Most of them go through tests of purification, and some don't pass.

Life has a rhythm that can't be hurried beyond a certain point. It takes patience and understanding and love.

## Term of Service for a RESA

*Is there a right number of years that a RESA should serve?*

There is no given term of service; RESA appointments are annual.

But I suggest you set a personal goal with the Mahanta of what to achieve in your area with ECK missions. When you reach it, either set another with the Mahanta, or ask him for a new direction in your spiritual life.

Few positions offer as much opportunity for love, insight, and spiritual growth as does the role of RESA.

## How the Secret Doctrines Are Given

*How do ECK Masters work with the chelas in leadership positions? How do they give chelas the ECK teachings in an individual way?*

Reading copies of letters that Paul wrote various ECK leaders, I noted that he repeated and repeated things.

For instance, when he appointed someone an area representative, he told a cross section of people about it—up one end and down the other. He wanted to establish the person in the post as an ECK leader.

Paul was confronted with people who were in the program for two years and complained there was no progress. Of course, he could see a difference in them, as could their close ones. He tried to show them how they were different since the ECK had come into their lives. After two years, the person was invited to take the Second Initiation. This initiation is important because here is the point where the Inner Master begins to give the secret doctrines in earnest. How many chelas understand that?

The secret doctrines are given in numerous ways: through the dream state, through Soul Travel, through spiritual insight into all situations, through impressions, through the Mahanta as he speaks through people in city shops and on the streets, through the ECK-Vidya.

People don't trust their own pipeline to ECK and envy the experiences of other people. Spiritual talents vary also. One fellow will pick up the inner message within a day while the slower student struggles with the spiritual alphabet, wondering what is the matter with the ECK writings.

The path to God is a personal one. We can't even walk the same path taken by our Master when he was a student in training. This is shocking and disappointing to some people, but his life can serve only as a general guide. If his example gives us inspiration to find the stillness wherein we find God-Realization, then it is worth the trouble studying his life as well as the lives of all true saints.

For the ECK initiates this means to stand by to

answer the newcomer's questions and give as much support as he allows us to give. He must, however, develop his own spiritual stature through the guidance of the Mahanta. It is the only way to God.

## Soul's Resources

*What does an ECK leader do when he or she runs into obstacles among other chelas while trying to spread the message of ECK?*

Whenever I encountered limiting attitudes in the past, I worked around them. Since someone, somewhere, is always learning life's lessons and some of those lessons may be left lying in my path, I learned to find a way around them.

In the singular sense, all we learn, no matter whom we encounter or what they try to do to us, is we are Soul and expanding in consciousness. We always walk holy ground.

So I put out ECK books, wrote letters, put out bookmarks, and gave certain ECK books to the library, hospitals, and old folks' home. You'll notice that all these things can be done independently, without anyone's approval—or disapproval.

I always moved ahead in my own God Worlds and never let anyone trip me, for it's true that Soul's resources will always find a way.

## Following the Golden Heart

*A chela in our area was causing a disturbance at the ECK Center, and I took steps to remove him as an Arahata. Afterward, I doubted my action a little. What kind of waves will this create among chelas? As RESA, was I following the Golden Heart?*

Your decision to remove him was the correct one. Vanity gives some people such a vaunted opinion of themselves that they turn into channels for the Kal. A way to see this is by the disruptions they cause. It is very difficult to be a RESA and make decisions about a person and his spiritual path. The decision is all the harder when the individual is blind to the trouble and fear he is causing others.

Vain people and angry gossips can make all sorts of problems where there's no need for any. These two kinds of people team up and give support to each other. Meanwhile, they cause a number of ECK initiates to stumble and fall on the path of ECK. They want absolute power over others and quickly accuse those who call them to task for their spiritual misbehavior as being power mongers. They see themselves all too clearly but don't know it.

Keep on listening to the Mahanta's voice to give you the step-by-step guidance you want. You're doing well. You are certainly in a position that stretches you.

## Just Chant HU

*The lack of leadership from many of the High Initiates concerns me. They are dragging their heels, uncomfortable with ECKANKAR and the RESA structure, or visibly absent from ECK activities.*

*H.I. leadership would make a world of difference in the Vahana program in our state. What can we do to help in the healing and growth of the H.I. consciousness?*

There is a simple answer from Africa.

RESA Phil Morimitsu of Japan asked the ECK leaders in Africa what accounted for the phenomenal growth of ECK there. They said, "Just get together

252

with one or two chelas who share the same vision as you, and do a HU Chant once a week."

That's it!

## Broader Arena

*Among the local ECKists, there are a few who have difficulty with the term* religion. *I'd like to understand more of ECKANKAR's place in the world as a religion. What is its future?*

ECKANKAR *is* the Ancient Science of Soul Travel. That is our *secret* teaching. As the outer form it is the Religion of the Light and Sound of God. While some longtime ECK initiates are put off by this fact, any group that speaks of God, the Holy Spirit, and spiritual freedom—and devotes itself as a group, and individually, to unfoldment by means of spiritual aid to reach God-Realization—is a religion.

Some, it is true, will be put off by the word *religion.* They will have met the latest test of survival in ECK and have failed, in a sense. But only to the extent that they must realize the real ECK teachings are the secret, inner ones. The outer teachings and structure change all the time, because the consciousness of people who are ready to receive ECK is always changing.

We've been somewhat of a selfish group in the past, too ready to make unimportant distinctions between other Souls and ourselves. My mission is moving into a broader arena again. Let all who can, follow.

## How to Serve

*I'm a new Higher Initiate. What's the best way for ECK leaders to serve?*

I greatly appreciate your recent letter asking advice on how to serve as an initiate in service to ECK. It is an art learning how to work with people.

The basis of how the ECK message is presented in the community is done through the RESA structure. As needed, the RESA or person appointed by the RESA will call a meeting of all the ECKists who wish to help set up plans and projects.

As a Higher Initiate, your role is to make sure that the plans stay in keeping with any of the guidelines available to you. For instance, Arahatas must follow the guidelines in the *ECK Arahata Book*. If this is not being done, I wish you would call the errant ones' attention to the page in question. If they will not listen and you feel that your suggestion relates to keeping local practices in line with the guidelines from ECKANKAR, then call up the RESA and ask for insight into the problem that will give you an idea how to approach it.

Respect the ideas of those who are at all levels of unfoldment. Do bear in mind, though, that you stand as the guardian of the ECK truths and how they are taught in purity on earth. Speak up in a spirit of goodwill when things are not being done according to the ECK guidelines.

As a High Initiate you will find yourself glowing with greater self-confidence which will also serve you well in your personal life.

I always appreciate what you do for ECK. Doing such things for others is actually doing it for SUGMAD, but some unfortunate people don't know that and try to keep it all for themselves. You're different. The Mahanta is your drummer, and that's what counts.

# How to Be Clear

*I have never felt adequate to be an ECK Spiritual Aide. From the beginning I wondered why I had been given the responsibility. The first ESA session I did, I felt such a failure.*

You'd be surprised how often a new ESA is insecure about how to be a clear channel for ECK. Treat it like an initiation insofar as cleaning up your body and mind beforehand. Then, mostly, listen. Rather than trying to be the grand Wizard of Oz who knows all and sees all, gently ask the one who comes to you what he or she sees as a possible solution. Be a sounding board rather than the answer person.

I'm not going to try to lay out a format that will fit every situation that comes up, because it's not necessary. One caution, however, is to keep your emotions apart from the person who brings the problem. Your function as an ESA actually continues outside the formal session until the ECK can bring a balance to the situation. If the future ESA sessions begin to get sticky, turn the person over to a different ESA, one who you feel is right.

It is such a blessing to serve as an ESA. The Mahanta will broaden your insight with each session. Of course, the ESA speaks to no one of what takes place, unless it is to the Living ECK Master.

## Inquire Within

*How can I best answer the questions of new chelas in Satsang class? I often feel inadequate.*

No one has all the answers, for there is always one more step to unfoldment. We can use the creative imagination to get an answer within, however.

Ask the class members to research the question in the ECK books and bring their findings to the next class for discussion.

## ECK Vahanas

*My wife and I are planning to travel together to help bring the ECK teachings to places in our country where there is little ECK activity. Is there anything we should know?*

Follow whatever guidance is given on the inner side. You let people help and grow wherever you go, so the place you wish to go is wholly your own choice.

You'd find it interesting to see how the people of different countries think of themselves in regard to ECK. The majority of people in some countries like to order things and people about; in other places, the initiates get the same amount of work done by working with people.

All depends on whether the leaders go by love or power, but even those leaders who operate mainly from the love principle find that they must make firm decisions in some matters if they expect everything to get done on time.

You love the ECK with a pure heart and serve It with a single-minded purpose. The return It gives is a greater state of awareness into life around us. The most dear thing anywhere is love, so love each other and Soul and ECK and SUGMAD.

## Spiritual Law

*As of late, I have heard numerous complaints from some Higher Initiates who directly criticize ECKANKAR under your leadership. I challenged them with love in my heart. By challenging ECKANKAR critics am I breaking spiritual law or upholding it?*

Many Higher Initiates do understand the ECK principles, but unfortunately, there are always some who do not. It is the people in this latter group who do so much to harm the spiritual unfoldment of others.

In the early years of ECKANKAR, there were many initiates like you, who understood the privilege of finding the ECK teachings. And they loved the teachings. They understood the spiritual law, which requires that one find the true Master to help him find the way home to God again.

This ECK principle includes the need for the Inner and Outer Master. But some, who neglect the Spiritual Exercises of ECK, have no experiences with the many aspects of the Sound and Light. So they feel others must be as barren spiritually as they themselves are. They are to be pitied. Having found the love of ECK, they so carelessly toss it aside, thinking, in their vanity, that they can rewrite the laws of ECK. No one can. Not even me.

I'm already taking steps to reduce the abuse of power by people such as the ones you mentioned in your letter—the people who try to destroy the ECK faith of others. But this action will be quiet and hardly noticed. Look back in a year.

## Bringing Others to ECK

*Is it all right for ECK initiates to join other groups then talk about these groups with other chelas, to the extent that the other chelas get drawn into the groups?*

This is in regard to your concern about ECK initiates who join other groups but then actively recruit other ECKists to join these groups. As you correctly feel, my intention in opening the teachings of ECKANKAR to the public is not to give ECK leaders free license to draw newer ECK initiates away from the path of ECK. This is a willful distortion of the ECK missionary program.

Those who engage in such a practice are actually servants of the Kal. What else can I say? They are being missionaries to draw people away from the ECK teachings.

My intent in opening the path of ECK is just the reverse—to make the teachings of ECK available to the public. So if someone draws chelas away from ECKANKAR by using his influence as an ECK leader, ask him, "Do you think the Mahanta wants you to draw people *away* from ECK, as you are likely to do because they look up to you as an ECK leader?" Then ask, "Why don't you make the same effort to find those people who are ready for the teachings of the Light and Sound and bring them *to* ECKANKAR?"

There really is no law on earth that says one can follow only a single path at a time. I would expect that to be the case for the ECK leaders, however. The lessons of life themselves will tell them when the time is right to drop membership in the other religious path. They may want to drop ECKANKAR instead.

*Some of the Higher Initiates in our area pass books to new initiates that are no longer in ECKANKAR's inventory. They also interfere with the RESA's actions in a neighboring country. I don't understand this. Why are they leading people away from ECK?*

In your country there are Higher Initiates whom I love dearly. This is why I am so slow to act in removing them from ECK, a path to which they give lip service and which they do not understand. They think they are clever and that I do not watch them in their spiritual treachery.

So many are ready to conquer the world by conversion to ECK, but they have lost the battle to the Kal Niranjan in their own worlds. All their converts and teachings are tainted, because they do not have love— only power.

The RESA position is one of great spiritual honor. It is subject to an annual review. The RESA is given an area in which to give his outpouring of love for the SUGMAD, the ECK, and the Mahanta. He is an ECK Spiritual Aide for a region. He is like a noble of his country and does his work for ECK there, no matter how great or humble that may be. He would never think of trespassing into another's area, because this is the psychic invasion of a Brother's space. Isn't it?

When we serve the ECK with love and honor, it is not by the use of force—no matter how subtly done. The ECK knows all. We make plans to foster the ECK teachings in our home area, being wise enough to keep our presentations within the customs, laws, and expectations of our neighbors; and we respect our civil government.

When two initiates meet each other on the street, their faces should light with joy.

## Letting Go of Guilt

*A friend said something that made me feel bad about missing an opportunity to speak at an ECK seminar. I had family obligations and felt I shouldn't go. Was staying home the right thing to do? And if so, why do I feel so guilty?*

It's not necessary to attend every ECK meeting. I don't want ECKANKAR to become a spiritual organization where people attend meetings because they're afraid not to.

In my early days in ECK I once cut a talk at a seminar and ended up in an elevator with Paul Twitchell. You should have seen my feelings of guilt—that was like missing church at home on Sunday. Of course, the feelings of guilt were my own problem and had nothing at all to do with Paul. I was seeing him through the eyes of my Christian conditioning.

I got over that, but you'd be surprised how many people in ECK haven't. So I don't feel guilty about any guilt they haven't let go of yet.

Please say no whenever you are asked to speak and you feel you shouldn't. Your spiritual strength will grow, not weaken, because of it.


*A High Initiate meeting ran late; two of our friends are great talkers. Some people were depending on me for a ride home, and I felt my responsibility quite keenly. I tried to get the facilitator's eye to let him know I was leaving, but in the end I just had to slip out. I felt badly about this.*

You are certainly welcome to leave any meeting because of a responsibility to others who are depending on you.

It really is amazing to me how, when the ECK opens the hearts of the initiates, there is always one more thing for someone to say. After an hour and a quarter, I generally let them know that the hour is late and individuals are free to leave. It may be necessary to curtail the meetings, because the ECK keeps flowing when there are important issues to resolve.

## Law of Noninterference

*I am bothered by the actions of a fellow Higher Initiate. They do not seem appropriate for someone of this initiation level. In contemplation I was told that someone else's business is his business, and that I have enough to tend to in my own space.*

Even though the individual you mention feels her activities are both right and unknown to the Outer and Inner Master, be assured that all is known. Indeed, the mill wheels of God do grind slowly, but exceedingly fine.

You have seen the problem in perspective, however. Whatever others do is between them and the Mahanta. I sincerely wish that all ECK initiates understood this. It doesn't mean to shut our eyes to trouble, but to deal with it in a matter-of-fact way—so our own journey to God may continue.

*I need an explanation on the Law of Noninterference. In the ECK works, even in* The Wind of Change, *I read about letting people have their karma. Does this mean you don't help someone in trouble?*

I can understand your concern for how so many people twist the Law of Noninterference. My point in *The Wind of Change* was to allow others their freedom. That consideration is often forgotten as people intrude into the lives of acquaintances by giving unwanted and unasked-for advice.

Yes, when someone cries to us for help, we may go to give aid. I think you'd get a fuller, more rounded view of how one should act if you read "No Greater Love," chapter 24 in *Stranger by the River* by Paul Twitchell. It's about a low-caste Hindu who gave his life to save a drowning child in the river and the reward it earned him.

In other words, we recognize that this world is a hard, sometimes cruel place, but we can do something about it.

*What's the best way to help a friend who needs to know about a spiritual law he is breaking but doesn't ask?*

It is not possible to give a person help unless he asks for it himself. The best way to work with him is to meet and talk with him when he gets in contact with you. This might sound like a fine distinction to make, but it is the clean way that the ECK works.

You can then give him whatever help he needs to make the contact with the Inner Master.

## Protecting Oneself

*Some ECKists have reported that a person is attacking them on the inner as well as affecting their physical lives. I can talk to them about protection techniques and strengthening themselves, but I feel I must do what I can to protect them too. What may I do and not break spiritual laws?*

The inner is the inner, and the outer is the outer.

In the day-to-day world, I seldom act upon complaints of how other people think or believe. But I do step in when harmful ideas and beliefs become acts that do physical harm to others.

You can safely lend an ear to ECK initiates who feel they are victims of psychic attack. Continue to give them protection techniques. Remind them to fill their hearts and minds with love, then have them turn the matter over to the Mahanta. There are indeed psychic delinquents loose in society, but often the psychic disturbance is within the supposed victim, who is unaware of his own karmic burn-off.

So deal only with the destructive behavior on the outer in the ECK community. Let the Mahanta take care of the inner side.


## ECK Basics

*What would you say to a person who is interested in becoming a member of ECK; how would you advise him on the steps through the first years?*

When someone joins ECKANKAR, he can study the discourses privately or in a Satsang class, if one is available in his area. It's important to go slowly in the study of ECK, for each will find Its reality in his own way. Reading too much in the spiritual works causes spiritual indigestion and actually slows one up in his goal of Self- and God-Realization.

The First Initiation comes in the dream state and is given by the Dream Master. Some individuals are aware of it, while others are not. The lower emotional and intellectual centers come into contact with the higher ones.

The Second Initiation comes after the person has completed two years of study with the ECK discourses. I want him to make a thorough study of the ECK writings before he makes a decision whether or not the path of ECKANKAR fits his spiritual needs. No one path fits all people. This is part of the freedom of the spiritual works.

Above all, tell him to take time with the study of ECK, to use common sense and keep up with daily responsibilities to himself and his family.

## Living ECK

*I long to have a spiritual experience that I may work better with the other ECKists here. I want to feel I can give them help as they need it, but I have trouble with my own inner experiences. Would you please give me the experience of meeting you on the inner and talking to you?*

Since you're not able to see me on the inner planes, let's have you back off from trying so hard. Live your life with joy and serve the Mahanta in ways that please you. Then it is a gift of love.

Continue with the spiritual exercises. Sing HU during them. Create new melodies that are pleasant, but always go back to the regular chanting of HU, which is in a long, drawn-out breath.

Some Higher Initiates rarely have conscious experiences with the Sound and Light, or even with the Mahanta. They live the spiritual experience every day in their service of love to God.

If you can do that, you will be ahead of 99.99 percent of the human race in your understanding of ECK and Its love.

Paul brought out the ECK teachings. The seed of those ideas is planted and must bring forth the mighty oak from the acorn, for that is the destiny of ECKANKAR.

# 11

# ECK in the World

*Why did the ECKANKAR Spiritual Center move to Minnesota? What is your intention for ECKANKAR in the future?*

Somebody once had the idea that ECKANKAR was moving to Minnesota because I wanted to be close to my Wisconsin birthplace. That's kind of foolish, because if I had aimed for Wisconsin, I would have hit it. No reason to settle for a near miss. This is the place for ECK to put down roots, but like the Mormons, we may have to scrap for our little corner of God's earth.

With the dream a reality, there comes the bigger job of taking the ECK teachings out ever more into the world. This long-range job will take careful planning.

There's a list of point-scoring principles in a frame by my desk here. One of the items says, "Concentrate on long-term, permanent solutions rather than stopgap measures." Solid. Another: "Don't waste time telling people what you're doing or what you're going to do. Results have a way of informing the world." Solid too. Also: "When the ball is on the one-yard line, don't risk a fumble; *carry it over yourself.*" Solid.

As the foundations of ECK expand, more of the higher responsibilities of leadership will go to people who want to get the full benefit out of life's experiences. ECK is for the active individual, one who is not discouraged by a multiple set of no's. If he knows inside that something must be done, he will find the way to do it—and overcome any number of obstacles that would have buried a lesser person long ago.

The ECK initiate must expect life to put a shoulder to his stomach when he is running with the ball. But what matters is how he responds after the first hit. Does he roll off the blocker and go on, or quit?

Finally, in the words of the wise old chart of point-scoring principles that watches over me here at the keyboard: "To accomplish your objective, first begin. Second, concentrate exclusively on the project at hand. Third, *don't stop.*"

## Inner and Outer

*How can you appear as the Living ECK Master to thousands of people at the same time?*

The Outer Master, the Living ECK Master, accepts the responsibility to provide the seeker with the ECK writings, books, and discourses. In studying these, the individual begins to practice the Spiritual Exercises of ECK. Their purpose is to gradually open the Spiritual Eye, so one comes in contact with the Sound and Light of ECK, the twin manifestations of Divine Spirit.

After a period of time, the sincere inquirer discovers the presence of Spirit. The Inner Master is the matrix that Divine Spirit chooses to act as the spiritual guide in the dream state or during contemplation.

Since the ECK is life and sustains all life, It is present everywhere at the same time. It establishes a direct linkup with each individual, whether one person seeks, or a thousand. You'll find this out for yourself in time, if you want to.

## True Destiny

*What stands in the way of the ECK teachings fulfilling their true destiny?*

So many fundamental stages must be accomplished before the ECK teachings are established firmly here. The administration of the ECKANKAR Spiritual Center is the number one priority. Until the staff can serve the needs of the chelas in a competent and predictable way, it is impossible to go further with the ECK message than we've gone to date.

When I see the destiny that the ECK teachings are to realize during this cycle and look to where we are today, all I see is a ragtag band. There's no point in throwing up one's hands in despair either. A step at a time in the direction of the distant goal is the way it must be done.

Above all, there must be a way for many individuals to express and use their talents at all levels in ECKANKAR. Their abilities must be recognized, the people and the right jobs be fitted together.

Things have a way of working out when good people are faced with challenges that are within their grasp.

Paul brought out the ECK teachings. The seed of those ideas is planted and must bring forth the mighty oak from the acorn, for that is the destiny of ECKANKAR. But it will take time to grow and mature. The Arahatas and parents are the key roles to watch during this movement into maturity. The Arahatas teach the discussion and ECK Satsang classes, the parents teach their children the ECK works.

The strength of the Satsang lies in the wide variety of chelas who work together for a common cause.

With the Seat of Power established, we're here to stay. But it will take a lot of earnest endeavor by the ECK pioneers to make this dream come true.

If it were up to us alone, the ECK teachings would never have gained the attraction they presently hold. But it's the ECK which stimulates all who love It, and this makes for miracles of a kind that the average person would never recognize.

## Seat of Power

*What is the spiritual Seat of Power?*

The Seat of Power is the center from which the ECK teachings reach the people of the world.

This center is the Temple of ECK in Chanhassen, Minnesota. It became the Seat of Power at a special dedication ceremony on October 22, 1990.

Many thousands of new people will find the Sound and Light of God now that we have located the Seat of Power here.

## Mahanta's Gift

*Can one reach the Kingdom of God without being a member of ECKANKAR, but simply by tuning in to the Mahanta through dreams and daily contemplations, and maintaining a grateful attitude?*

Of course, there is an exception to every rule. However, ECKANKAR serves as an excellent road map to the worlds of ECK, for it is the Mahanta's gift to Souls who want to reach the true heavens in the most direct way.

# Speedup

*Has there been a speedup in time? I find myself asking my wife, "Did we do this yesterday or did we do it last year?"*

The karma in the world situation has speeded up, but when you get into a certain state of consciousness, the past and future have no meaning. But the moment does. At times you won't know if something you saw was on the inner or the outer. You're not able to make a distinction anymore between the walls that separate the physical from the dream state or the present from the past or future. You're living in Soul awareness.

You'd go away for a weekend, and you were washing the dishes before you left and your whole mind is filled with catching the plane and what will happen at the meeting. You go through the whole weekend, and Monday morning you find yourself back at the sink again, washing dishes. And it seems as if you've been washing dishes forever. Because that moment when you are washing dishes takes in all eternity and transcends the borders of time. You are living in the moment, in a spiritual consciousness.

## Working with the Times

*Why don't you go out into the streets and preach the message of ECK as they did in days of old?*

Each period of history has its own special way to preach the message of ECK.

Malati, the Living ECK Master among the people in Polara, simply showed them how to plant and harvest the fruits of the earth. Primitive man was too busy looking over his shoulder for wild beasts and other

271

enemies to have much time for contemplation. Malati could thus give a few of the outer ECK teachings to Polarian man, but he did so in the dream state.

It would be foolish to talk openly about ECK today in China or in countries where Islam is the state religion.

I like ECK initiates who love SUGMAD as I do. The public has its many gods and is happy with them. It further believes that the Light and Sound of ECK are merely stories made up by ECKists with fertile imaginations.

Sometimes I play Ping-Pong at a city recreation center. Hardly any of the high-school students there know that I am in ECK, but they respect my game. Someday they'll put two and two together, and think to themselves, "Anybody who plays Ping-Pong like that can't be all bad!" In the meantime, I get both exercise and fine company.

This is being a silent channel for the ECK, where actions speak louder than words. And I love it!

## Silent Channels

*In my country of Israel, ECKANKAR has been called a cult. A government committee was established recently to investigate the activities of various cults here because of the fear that they negatively influence the youth. So we spread the message of ECK through personal contact rather than as we used to, by advertising events in the local newspaper. We do have a weekly HU Chant which is wonderful.*

Thank you most sincerely for your letter. Please express my appreciation to the others who come to the HU Chant for their willingness to be the instruments of the ECK.

I endorse your sensitive approach to the government's fear of cultic groups' influence upon the youth. Be discreet, and do not feel compelled to make a great commotion in your promotion of the ECK works. This will only lead to problems for all of you, which is not necessary for you to experience. The ECK works through you in the majesty of Its will.

People from other countries might point a finger at the government of your country and mistakenly say that their suppression of so-called cults is the same discrimination that has so unfortunately been heaped upon your countrymen in countries where they live as guests. Now the same practice of intolerance is coming to your own doorstep. But the war climate dictates higher caution than is possible during peacetime.

The political and military leaders are justly concerned with factions that might pose a threat to the safety of the nation. Therefore, understand the special circumstances in which you all find yourselves. If there is ever a way to win the support of people higher in the government who will insure that you do not become victims of prejudice in your own country, work with them.

We support the governments of our native lands, and know there is never an advantage to causing such disturbances. Contemplate in private, hold your HU Chants as long as they do not cause any of you to be put in jeopardy with your police.

Remember, the love and protection of the Mahanta is always with you. Perhaps some day I will be able to visit your country when the political structure has become more stable. The ECK flows through each of you, touching all you meet — though none are likely aware of a change because of your nearness.

## Inner Message

*I have a question about the Los Angeles earthquake in early 1994—the ground is proving to be very unstable. Should people leave?*

Not even public officials dare sound a general alarm, because it would disrupt the lives of millions of people. If they could be sure about a knockout punch, maybe they'd say something. But if wrong? Where would those millions of people move to—Arizona, Nevada, Oregon, where? There are just too many people to warn.

Some ECKists will stay around to help in the event of a disaster. Those who should leave the state will get a message on the inner planes.

## Unwinding Karma

*I live in a country which is undergoing great political upheaval. As an ECKist, can I help in this cycle of my country as a vehicle for the will of ECK?*

Though all the outer things we love are put to the trial, the Master is with us at all times. Please know that your concerns are in the hands of the ECK, which is always working in behalf of your greatest good.

The karma of your nation is being burned off to a large degree now and some of that will pass through the ECK initiates, who act as filters for the Mahanta. This is not the old savior idea of somebody who suffers or dies for the sins of many. But there is a parallel.

When the karma of a nation or group, of which one is a part, begins to unwind, then all who are at the top of spirituality in that nation or group will feel the side effects of that burn-off. You may ask that some of this load be lifted from you if at any time it becomes too much to carry.

Here's a spiritual exercise that may help you open up to the Mahanta. It is a simple one. Every morning upon awakening, say to the Master, "I am a child of ECK and move and have my being in the arms of Its love." Then go about your day with sweet confidence, for the presence of the Master will be with you everywhere, in the most troubling of times.

You will be the shining light to all who need help, for you are then a clear and open channel for the Sound and Light of God. It will gently reach through you to bring comfort or healing of spirit to those near you who need it.

## Defending the Path

*I recently wrote a letter to the editor of our local newspaper protesting an article about ECKANKAR which I thought was an example of yellow journalism. How long will we have to defend the teachings of ECK in this way?*

Thank you for your words in defense of ECKANKAR.

It is noteworthy that the newspaper did not check facts about the alleged criminal and find that her claims of being an ECKist were untrue. Thank you for challenging the blind prejudice of this newspaper, whose main interest is not so much the correct news as it is in selling copy.

These challenges will be made against ECKANKAR by the most "respected" people. Recently an ECK couple wrote to me of prejudice they were suffering in a Quaker community. You'd think that the Quakers of all people would have learned tolerance from their own persecutions by other Christians, but it is not so.

As long as the human consciousness stays in its

present state, there will be the anguish caused by one person upon another in the name of his religion. The ECK initiate is the channel by which the ECK brings enlightenment to the hearts of men.

I am gratified that Higher Initiates like you use your gifts of communication for ECK when the need is there.

## ECK Is All

*A friend of mine is interested in ECKANKAR, but something is holding her back. Her inner guide, which she calls Spirit, told her that another religion is the true path. She wants to know, if ECK is truth, did Spirit lie to her?*

Divine Spirit, or the ECK, doesn't lie. Remember that ECK encompasses all religions, all people, all life. It merely said to her that she must first learn the truths from this other religion before she is ready for the teachings of ECK. When she is ready, the Mahanta will appear. Then she will know ECK is the most direct path to God.

## Origins of ECK

*Is there a particular reason for using words of Eastern origin in* The Shariyat-Ki-Sugmad *and in ECKANKAR terminology?*

People in the East are traditionally ahead of the West in understanding the facts of spiritual life. Eastern languages can make fine distinctions about things that are unknown to Western man.

Karma is a good example. It takes reincarnation for granted. Christianity, however, does not accept past lives. The ECK Masters, in trying to reach people from a Christian background, had to either borrow Eastern words or coin new ones. It was simpler to borrow them. Eastern words were already known to many people around the world.

Anyone who tries to speak of ECK and use only words of Western origin is at somewhat of a disadvantage.

## Shariyat and ECK

*What is the difference between the Shariyat-Ki-Sugmad and the ECK?*

The Shariyat is a repository of wisdom that rises from the Sound and Light. The ECK is the Sound and Light.

## Being Happy

*Are there people on earth from other planets?*

There certainly are. Plenty of books in the library talk of this.

I sometimes wonder, though, if people who are very interested in space beings are happy. It sounds as if they are reaching for a star, to escape from their own lives. To others, the question of whether there are space people is just one that is interesting to them.

There are space people working on missions to help one of the spiritual orders that answer to the Vairagi Adepts. Most people who meet these visitors never recognize them, any more than they do the ECK Masters in disguise. These visitors move in their own orbits, intent upon their duties to God, just as each ECKist works with his own problems.

I recommend you find good things to do in your life and do them. Count the blessings of health as being without equal. Be thankful that you earned the right to come to ECK in this lifetime, for life without ECK is a living hell.

## Creation Question

*How did God make man, and who was the first being?*

Our scientists run all over the globe in a search for the oldest human fossils. They want to know the age of humans. Once they learn that, they hope to tackle the big question: How did the first human come to be?

The answer would shake the main religions to the core.

Way back, there was no earth, no creation. But SUGMAD wanted a place to educate Souls, so the ECK (the Word of God) began to create things. It did so by changing the vibrations of Light and Sound in a certain region. That area became the lower worlds.

First was the Light and Sound of God. Then, at a lower step of vibration, came the gases. Eons of time later, liquids and solid matter began to form: the building blocks of lower creation. The Etheric Plane was the first plane to appear, then the Mental Plane. Much later came this Physical Plane.

Galaxies and planets were the first to form on each plane, and then the ECK began to experiment with life-forms. On earth, they included the dinosaurs.

In the meantime, the ECK had evolved higher life-forms, like humans, on the Etheric Plane. They began to seed the planets there by establishing colonies of mind travelers, who could move from place to place without slow, clumsy spacecraft.

Those people pushed back the frontiers of space, even as our astronauts do today. With colonies all throughout the Etheric Plane, the early ECK Masters began to open a new frontier: travel between the Etheric and Mental dimensions. So the seeding of colonies now began on the Mental Plane.

Visitors from space seeded Earth with the first colonies. There was no first man or woman. A spaceship brought a small group of people here to start a colony. Then somewhere down the line came you.

Someday, and not too far off, this seeding of the planets will be common knowledge among people of higher spiritual awareness.

## Real Detachment

*Sometimes, as in the recent war in the Persian Gulf in which people were killed and physical destruction took place, it seems a cop-out to say, "Well, it's just their karma."*

*I know that we should not get caught up in the illusions of this physical world, but where is the middle ground of compassion and true understanding? What is the spiritual reality of some of the situations of upheaval and change which are being experienced on the planet today?*

You must first know what it really means to be detached from the world. It is a spiritual point of view that a person can adopt: to see through the eyes of Soul. In no way does it suggest a cold heart, as so many imagine.

What does it mean to be detached? It simply means to know that life does have a purpose, even when you can't see it in a given situation. Just be a channel for

ECK, which is Love Itself. Then you'll find there is all kinds of room in this world for compassion and true understanding.

Why the upheaval in the world today? It is nothing new. Please begin your own study of history; then very little of what you hear about people will ever surprise you again. Earth is often a kettle of boiling water, but it's still the best place for Soul to find the purity of being.

## Blessings

*When I first got my Second Initiation in ECK, I mistakenly went down Main Street blessing every unfortunate-appearing human in sight. Now I am wondering how to do it right.*

A blessing is merely passing along the love of ECK in such a way that the person can accept or reject the gift. The safest course is simply to say, "May the blessings be" or "Baraka Bashad." And release the entire outcome to Divine Spirit, without directing it in any way.

## Accepting Change

*What is the absolutely hardest thing you have to do?*

Helping adults accept a change for something spiritually better. Doing new things is quite natural for young people. They're always growing out of clothes, so they get used to buying new things in a larger size.

Adults normally have fewer changes. They've stopped growing years ago. In fact, some adults tend to hang on to an image of themselves as youths. But the 1920s, and even the 1970s, are gone.

Most people can accept new developments of science like TV, the calculator, and the personal computer. These products can help them to become unstuck from their old ways of thinking. Science has transformed the way we do things.

Yet now, people are too busy with scientific gadgets to bother about learning Soul Travel. But some individuals in the crowd will always desire truth more than anything else. It is for them that the Living ECK Master agrees to serve mankind.

## Personal Choice

*I'd like to participate in a local weight-loss program that follows twelve spiritually oriented steps. Would this conflict with ECK?*

How one chooses to bring health to the body or to earn a living must always be a personal choice for those who follow the way of ECK.

A possible objection would be when someone brings his personal business in contact with people at the ECK Center or an ECK function. Another objection would be if an ECK leader pushes his product or service upon another ECKist for personal profit. But I know you do not intend to mix Spirit with business. Complete freedom exists for you to make a decision about the weight-loss group.

## Life-forms

*Do plants have Souls? Assuming that they do, do animals get the same karma for killing plants that a person would get for harming another human being?*

Just for a minute, shut your eyes and look at life here on earth in a different way. Think of the trees, people, animals, buildings, and every other thing as fields of energy instead of objects you can touch. All these trillion balls of energy weave and blend into one big ball of energy: earth.

Now think of the Law of Karma. What is it? It is only the ECK giving a balance to each ball of energy within its sphere of influence in these lower worlds. Then what is karma for? It is to spiritually uplift each Soul. And the Law of Karma only appears to be more exact for people than for animals or plants, because we are looking at karma with a special interest in our own case.

So how karma works depends then upon where each Soul (in human, animal, plant, insect, or even a smaller form) is at the moment spiritually. In general, though, we can say that karma is the same for all. Every act returns to the sender like a letter with postage due.

## Who Is Christ?

*Who or what is Christ? Paul Twitchell often wrote about Christ similar to the way he wrote about the ECK Masters. Was he referring to Jesus the person or a consciousness? If the latter, what kind of consciousness? I have many Christian friends, so I would be grateful for an answer.*

Yours is an important question, so I will answer you like this:

Jesus in fact was the person, and Christ was the consciousness in him. In telling of Christ's mission, John the Baptist said: "As many as received him, to them gave he power to become the sons of God" (John 1:12). Jesus thus came to show people the way to the Christ state within them.

In speaking of "the kingdom of God," Jesus means the Christ Consciousness. He promised his disciples that some of them would enter it before death. "There be some standing here, which shall not taste of death, till they see the kingdom of God" (Luke 9:27).

Christ was very direct about the location of the spiritual kingdom. To Pilate, he said, "My kingdom is not of this world" (John 18:36). To the Pharisees, "The kingdom of God is within you" (Luke 17:21). Yet too many Christians still expect the kingdom—or Christ state—to appear in the sky.

Today, thousands continue to search for the lost key to spiritual consciousness. Many discover it in the ECK teachings.

This short answer can't begin to cover your question, but it may help your Christian friends to find the Christ Consciousness within themselves. A few will go on to the ECKshar state of consciousness.

## Truth in All Beliefs

*Since there is a grain of truth in all beliefs, what is true about the Greek and Roman myths?*

The Greek and Roman myths are legends of space visitors who came to earth in ancient times.

Science now feels that the human race developed in Africa, but few scientists can agree on where the first people came from. What began the rise of civilization? Science doesn't know.

Back in the 1930s, the Dogon people of West Africa jolted many astronomers by the facts they had about Sirius B, a distant star. The star is so faint that photos weren't made of it until 1970. Then how did the Dogon learn so much about a star they could not even see with the naked eye? They insist that space visitors told them long ago.

For now, the people of Earth have their hands full just trying to get along with each other.

## Serving in Other Religions

*Can an ECK initiate serve the ECK as a priest, minister, or rabbi of another religion?*

The future will continue to see ECKists who fill roles as leaders for other religions. One of Paul Twitchell's chelas was a minister. In Africa, one initiate is chieftain of his people, which requires him to conduct religious services. Such service to the Mahanta reflects the universality of ECK, for It is not bound to any creed or religion. Rather, It supersedes them all, for It is the unifying force of life.

## Too Pushy?

*A friend got interested in ECKANKAR through our conversations and went to an introductory talk. She was then pestered for weeks by a chela who kept calling to see if she had questions or wanted more information.*

*Overall, I feel there is not enough sensitivity to other people's space.*

Some ECKists still don't understand about the sacred ground that all people walk on, besides themselves. You don't like to be pushed and neither do I.

People are people no matter which path they take. Be bigger than those who are holding themselves back spiritually by pushing their narrow beliefs upon others. Presenting the ECK message is one thing, bothering people is another.

Please tell the offender about his behavior in a decent way, but don't let this get you down.

## Personal Discrimination

*What kind of a reply would you suggest an ECKist make when invited by others to attend their church out of concern for his spiritual well-being? I do not wish to offend those who appear to have only my best interest at heart. Neither do I want them to think I am immoral. I would like to tell these people about ECKANKAR, but I feel it would cause worse problems than letting them think I am only a lazy backslider.*

You're in a tough spot. There is a no-holds-barred battle between the ECK and Kal forces. Such people may say they have a sincere concern for your spiritual welfare, but they are channels for the Kal.

Nothing you say will stop them from trying for your conversion. You may reply to them along these lines: God has given us many ways to return to the Kingdom of Heaven. I have a personal relationship with God that I do not talk about.

Then change the subject with a smile or leave politely. Tell them you have to be someplace for an appointment and have one set up in advance if you suspect a confrontation.

There is no reason to parade the ECK teachings in front of people who are on a mission against you. Chant HU silently, obey the Law of Silence, and excuse yourself the first chance you get.

## Those Who Love God

*Your article on church and religion in the* Mystic World *was most welcome. Some others are not as happy about the changes in ECK. A friend told me he was finished with ECKANKAR, and I saw the light leave his eyes. How do you keep going amid this kind of resistance?*

I am aware that some initiates don't know why *church.* We must avail ourselves of all our constitutional rights if we expect to survive as a spiritual teaching of any longevity.

Why *rules?* Everything is governed by rules or laws. As a baby grows, its rules in the home take on new shape. They're not better or worse than the old rules, but they fit this age of the growing child. Don't we know that the laws of the spiritual planes also change as we move up in consciousness? A molecule obeys certain laws of nature, or it would cease to exist.

The mutterings you've heard and told me of are natural. There really are strong, important changes occurring in ECKANKAR. The resistance is only the natural inclination to resist a change from the status quo. People aren't happy where they are, yet complain when the ECK tries to move them on to greater things.

It would all be a discouraging mission if it were not for the relatively few initiates who love the ECK first, last, and always. They simply want God-Realization. They know they're not in competition with the crowd, so the values of the crowd don't matter to them. They know they must climb the Mountain of God at their own pace or hurt themselves. So they listen to the advice of their guide, the Mahanta, the Living ECK Master.

What keeps me going are the humble people who love the SUGMAD, the ECK, and the Mahanta. They have their own experiences with the Sound and Light, and are grateful for the blessing. I love them, for theirs shall be the Kingdom of God.

You may go with me too.

# Earth's Initiations

*I heard an ECK initiate refer to earth getting its overdue Third Initiation. Could you shed light on this and related subjects, such as planet karma and the Temple of ECK?*

For now, earth remains at the Second Initiation. Its group consciousness is largely grappling with its emotions. However, a growing vanguard of people is nearing the Third, or Causal, Initiation.

It's too soon to tell about planet karma. The group consciousness of earth has free will: It can decide whether to progress spiritually or not. If it does, then you'll see the concern over pollutants and individual freedom continue to grow. Otherwise, nations will go back to large-scale or pocket warfare to settle differences.

The Temple of ECK marks the dividing line between the Second and Third levels of mankind's group consciousness. The Vairagi Adepts want the Temple because mankind must soon move forward spiritually.

So the ECK Temple is here to help uplift the human race.

The Temple of ECK is spiritually important, because it will help many people find the Sound and Light of God. It will help other people understand that ECK initiates love God too.


# Cookies and Dreams

*Some ECKists want to provide a stepping-stone to ECKANKAR by giving a public class on the ECK view of dreams. They would not speak about ECKANKAR except to answer a direct query. Other than that, the class is not an ECKANKAR event.*

*Does this approach fit the Vahana mission? And is it in harmony with the Mahanta's vision for ECKANKAR?*

A class like that is certainly worth a try.

The question then arises whether the RESA and ECKists in an area may sponsor an event, like a dream class, that does not speak of ECK.

Yes, as long as they do not use ECK resources, such as the ECK Center or ECK funds.

A class on dreams that does not mention ECK or ECKANKAR is no different from a class on baking cookies. Each event that uses ECK resources must have a *direct* link with the ECK teachings. A class in an ECK Center on how to bake Christmas cookies would be in poor taste (pun intended). So also would a dream class that doesn't mention ECK or ECKANKAR be out of place in an ECK Center.

## Golden Age

*How can ECK help the average person, compared to other religions?*

An initiate gave a workshop on ECK for families with a spouse who was not in ECK. She gave a lot of help and common sense to people with concerns about the place of ECK in a family of mixed religious beliefs. This is how we can be leaders among the religious systems.

We are sensible people who have to face all the problems of other groups, but we have less baggage in the mind to prevent a straightforward decision.

These are exciting times. Something simply has to be done to get people to start looking out for their own interests, and not rely on the state to do it all the time.

It will take gradual change to go from the dependency state to one of independence. Otherwise, one's whole world would be turned upside down for no good reason at all.

These changes will come, because they are part of the Golden Age that can be ours again, if there are enough good initiates to help bring this about.

## Household Words

*Would it be better to change the name of ECKANKAR—since it is not a familiar word—to help the Vahana movement?*

There are many unusual names in the world today. A name is nothing by itself, but only in how well it identifies something of value.

How do people find out about it?

Unless those with something of value make the effort to tell a lot of other people about the benefits of their service or product, who would ever hear of it? For example, we were not born with the knowledge of Big Mac hamburgers. Somebody had to tell us about them. In fact, millions of people got along very well for thousands of years before the first McDonald's restaurant opened to the public. Now many people feel they couldn't live without a Big Mac hamburger. It may once have sounded like a weird name to some people, but today few ever pause to think twice about it.

The name ECKANKAR isn't the problem. Instead, it is with ECK initiates who are ashamed of the ECK teachings. So they refuse to tell others about them— afraid of a reaction by society, of what people might say.

Those who are faint of heart do not win missionary or military campaigns. In fact, the spiritual force that urges an ECK missionary onward is the same one that drives any true seeker of God: a bold and adventurous spirit.

How will *ECK* and *ECKANKAR* become household words? Only by our efforts. It will not happen on its own.

## Nothing Less than God

*I have had many experiences that have shown me the changes occurring in the ECK organization. I know now more than ever that I must work as a God-Realized individual and nothing less, because that is what is needed now.*

You are indeed fortunate to be able to go to the Inner Master to understand what's happening out here in the outer organization. That ability is the heart and core of the ECK teachings.

Several directions are possible at this point, but the best one over the long haul is to see how we can build for the future. Leave the past alone unless it presses upon us to resolve a matter that just won't be still. It is possible to waste a lot of precious time chewing over what appears to be something or not. When this lifetime is over, can we look back over the decades with a clear mind and say, "I've done in this life those things I set out to do before I came into the body"? Whatever pulls us from our ultimate goal of God-Realization is wrong.

I have put together a comprehensive program that is going into motion step-by-step. There is much detailed planning involved. A complete change was necessary on all fronts, but the overall theme is still to bring the message of ECK to all who want to hear it.

What a lot of initiates don't know is that the secret way into the royal kingdom is through service to God — a service that is all-consuming, because it is done for the love of ECK. Yet plans must be made, a direction chosen, and then the steps taken that will bring this into being.

There eventually has to be a place for everyone to serve the ECK, young or old, healthy or homebound. This is what's happening now with ECKANKAR. It's becoming a channel of service to the ECK. The giver and receiver are both blessed. That's the nature of ECK.

It's a long, slow pull at times, but our planning is for a solid future, when the ECK message will be commonly accepted by people in all nations. So much time is needed to lay a solid basis for the field organization, but it must all start at the top and work on down. That's going on now.

If the ECK teachings are to endure, there must be the training of both staff and initiates. But we must do one thing at a time or all is lost. You'd be surprised how many people try to get us from level one to level five by a broad jump that misses the in-betweens.

## Changing Times

*In recent times, I have seen some people leaving ECKANKAR to start their own organizations or write their own books, which, in turn, lead others away from ECKANKAR.*

*At the same time, the Temple of ECK has been built in America, and many other changes are taking place. All of this has caused me to wonder whether or not ECKANKAR is going to become an orthodox religious institution, like Christianity. There are many parallels between the history of Christianity and what is taking place in ECKANKAR today, and I fear that the true teachings of ECK will end up being suppressed in order to maintain the outer organized structure.*

*Could you please help me end this fear by explaining what is going to happen? I don't want to lose ECKANKAR.*

Thank you for your concern. The Living ECK Master of the times always sets the direction for the teachings of ECK and ECKANKAR. In his day, Paul Twitchell knew that ECKANKAR would need a Seat of Power one day. Altar, cathedral, temple, or what? Get an audiocassette or videocassette from the dedication of the ECK Temple to hear what he himself said.

History can be a good teacher. But only if one studies enough of it. For example, people have not left ECK only "in recent times," but also in Paul's day. It is as natural for people to come and go as it is for the seasons to change. That's how life is.

Few understand what the Living ECK Master does. Still, he has a mandate from the SUGMAD to carry out plan after plan, to bring the teachings of Light and Sound to people. Everything is in its right time and order.

Inner experiences are important, but love and service to God stand above any inner experience. Service demonstrates love.

# 12

# Being a Vehicle for God

*There's a paradox I've found about serving God. We say to Divine Spirit, "Do with me what you will," but at the same time aren't we movers and directors of Spirit as vehicles?*

We don't really direct Divine Spirit; we don't say, "I want to learn to use ECK in my life." Our real question should be How can I open myself as a clear vehicle for the ECK's use?

You go through your life and the knowingness of what must be done presents itself as you carry out the will of the SUGMAD.

A lot of times I will get inner direction and know what I would like to do. I start in that direction, then the ECK steps in. It may come through another person who tells me, "The computer can't do that." So I try something else.

The ECK might choose a way that I feel isn't as direct, but considering the people involved in the program, it is the best way for everyone to grow. So I stand back and say, "All right."

Divine Spirit gives each Soul a direction and something to do. You do the best you can. But if all of a sudden it doesn't work, then open yourself to Its guidance. Say to Spirit, "I know there's a way to do this, but how do I accomplish it?" And someone will walk in and say, "I've got a solution." It may not be the complete solution. It may not be enough of a solution to even put your plan into motion, but it'll lead to the next idea.

## Harmony in a Community

*I live in a fairly isolated rural area where my husband and I farm. There are no ECKists nearby. I often feel pretty lonely and confused about how to be a good ECKist here, especially when my neighbor tells me I should go to church and read the Bible to be a better person.*

It can be very difficult being an ECKist in a rural community. Nearly everyone goes to church because it is one of the main social centers where people can get together.

After two years in ECKANKAR, I felt very out of place in church. But I kept going for another half year or so because of my family. Finally, the inner direction from the ECK told me to find people who believed and felt as I did.

The first painful step was to leave my country church. It was one of the hardest things I had ever done, but I couldn't force myself inside that church any longer. Family and neighbors pulled at me from every direction to return to the fold. How could they understand that I no longer belonged there? That doesn't mean I thought I was better than they were—I just didn't belong anymore.

If you'd feel more comfortable to go to church

occasionally or read the Bible, feel free to do so. You will develop a growing confidence to choose what you want to do. After all, it is your God-given right.

Never let anyone tell you that you count for less than other people. Didn't Christ say, "Love your neighbor as yourself"? You must first love yourself, a child of God, before you can love your neighbor.

You do not need to listen to hours of ECK audio-cassettes to be a good ECKist. Nor do you have to read the ECK books nonstop, or watch only ECK videocassettes. You work hard on the farm. Sometimes you just need to relax in front of the TV after a hard day and watch *Roseanne*. It can also be good for the family to do things together.

Let me say that everyone who does any searching at all in life is constantly having to weigh one idea against another. That's life. Nobody has all the answers. What is important is that you learn because you want to. That alone makes you different from 95 percent of the people you know. And no amount of forcing yourself to go to church will change that.

You're not better than your neighbors, but you certainly are different. Your interests prove that. But understand, in most places it's considered a sin to be different, so don't expect people to like you. That's their problem, not yours.

Life on earth is community living. Do what you can to live peacefully among your neighbors, because farm living often means you must depend upon each other. That doesn't give others the right to tell you how to live your life, though.

It is good you are working to serve the SUGMAD, because everything that's done for God is done for ourselves.

## Making ECK Real for People

*What is the key to keeping the teachings of ECK around for a long time? How can we make ECK real for people?*

The ECK purifies Soul bit by bit, until Soul is fit to become one with the ECK. In the meantime, one must keep steadfastly to the self-disciplines, such as the spiritual exercises and monthly initiate reports (whether or not the initiate feels they must actually be mailed).

The scope of the ECK is life itself. It is a wonderful service that many initiates perform when they go out into their own communities and bring the Light and Sound to others through their profession, whether it is as an employee or an employer. All that matters is that they learn to open themselves as a vehicle for Divine Spirit to work through.

ECK leadership is finding ways to successfully reach spiritual seekers. Leadership, in accord with the Spiritual Exercises of ECK, brings inner growth. By leadership, I mean getting the ECK message out to the public.

If someone would do a study of religious paths that have succeeded or failed, they would find that in most cases—not all—a religious teaching proved successful because of a strong central leadership in the community.

This is why the Mahdis are so important as the right arm of the Mahanta. You are able to carry out the message of ECK to those who would not be reached in any other way.

## What Is Success?

*I want to earn a lot of money so I can be a greater channel for ECK. Recently, I started a construction business, but no matter how hard I work, most of my money seems to go for taxes. Are these taxes a violation of spiritual law? What can I do to become a success?*

Let's take your concerns one by one. It doesn't take a lot of money to be a greater channel for ECK. But you already know that. Yet it's in the cards (karma) for some individuals to have wealth and learn to deal with it, either in a spiritual or selfish way.

Taxes are taxes, neither good nor bad.

Of all the people who face the tax problem, each has a somewhat unique situation. Rich people, poor people—some pay too much, while others don't pay at all. You need either to become an expert on the changing tax laws or else find a good tax consultant (CPA or tax attorney) for expert help.

But that's beyond the scope of my advice.

Every country taxes its people to pay the cost of government. Some taxes are fair, while others burden the people, robbing them of the chance for a life of freedom and personal choice. Again, that's a social or political issue beyond the scope of my advice. People who make and enforce tax laws, and all other laws, may violate the spiritual law, but the Lords of Karma will deal with them in good time.

How can you become a success? What is success? It is happiness, and that does not depend upon wealth. There are miserable rich people as well as happy poor people, and vice versa, so don't fall for the illusion that wealth makes for bliss. Nor does it mean a greater ability to serve ECK.

All real success is about love. Love the breath of air, for it's a gift of life. Love your work: It will expand your God-given powers of creation. And love and serve your dear ones. Above all, do everything in the name of the Mahanta.

A final word: Obey the two laws Maybury gives in *Whatever Happened to Justice?* Again, "Do all you have agreed to do," and "Do not encroach on other persons or their property."

Success is hard to come by, but love can make it happen.

By the way, I commend you on your enterprise.

## Negative Ties

*Our small community is very clanlike and against ECKANKAR. At first we only suspected we were being unfairly treated and that my husband had lost job opportunities, but some outspoken people confirmed it last night. I love ECKANKAR, but I'm not sure how to be a vehicle for it in this town.*

Be discreet in your outer ECK activities since the community has turned on you. Get along with them as well as possible. When the ECK has finished doing what It must do through you as channels in that community, the opportunity will come for you to move to a better place.

You are only being sensible in keeping quiet about your feelings toward ECK. Hatred is not the easiest thing to soften once it is let out. Those who direct it at the innocent—especially those who are chelas of the Mahanta, the Living ECK Master—will suddenly find things going very wrong for them. This may not show outwardly to the neighbors, but those with hatred will surely find themselves going downhill in things they have taken for granted, such as health.

What is important here is your faith in ECK, which must be strong and unshakable all day long. If you will put a mental picture of me, as the Inner Master, in your Spiritual Eye and chant HU silently, you will be able to endure the hatred from any encounter.

This is a karmic situation where people you've been with in previous lives, in their religion, see your presence as a threat to their beliefs. In the past you were one of them; but now you are the outsiders, for you are there as the silent channels of the ECK to speed up the karma of the group. Their hatred against you will certainly hurry along their karmic obligations for payment. But all this is needed for the Souls in the community to someday break free of the negative ties that keep them from the realization of spiritual liberation.

## We Are Always Protected

*How can I know for sure that I am protected as I grow, in becoming a greater channel for the ECK? I have a real struggle being a Vahana for ECK in my country.*

When troubles come to us, they are easier to understand and endure if we see they are Divine Spirit's way of letting us gain perfection. See if you can hear what I'm saying: There is always a way to live the spiritual life no matter how much others try to stop us.

Your inner life is under my care. There is nothing to worry about. You will find good ways to serve the ECK in quiet ways that everybody else has overlooked. We must give out service in return for the love that ECK gives us, or we burn up.

Look humbly and simply—sweetly—to the Inner Master. Let the Mahanta be your friend when the world hurts you. Walk away from those who trouble and harm you. Be a silent carrier of the message of ECK.

You will never get credit for the help you give, but you are building rewards in heaven. Remember that my love and protection are always with you. You have only to ask.

## Preserving Freedom

*I recently sent a letter to the editor of a large newspaper about my concern with prayer in schools. I quoted the Bible and found passages where it preserves our freedom to pray as we wish. I am also the local contact for the public to learn about ECK in our small town. I hope this helps you and your mission.*

Your letter to the editor is a good one. In fact, I am putting together an article on prayer that quotes Matthew 6:5–6. I greatly appreciate your help in preserving the individual freedoms that stand in danger from our own government.

Thank you for being available for the people in your community who want to know about ECK. The best response to the spiritual exercises is serving others out of love, as you are doing as the ECK contact for the public. Inner experiences are important, but love and service to God stand above any inner experience. Service demonstrates love.

The point often missed by a seeker is that he must return the love of ECK that comes to him. This comes through service of some sort, a way to balance the physical with the spiritual things.

## Your Everyday Experiences

*What exactly is meant by the phrase "the living Shariyat"?*

The Shariyat is the holy book of the Vairagi Adepts. It is a record of spiritual evolution on every plane of God.

The living Shariyat refers to the action of the ECK as it occurs in creation, before it is recorded in a book. For us, it means the dynamic influence of ECK in our daily lives.

On a second level, the Shariyat is the Sound and Light of ECK. When the spiritual energies of life have been condensed into the written form, we call it a book: *The Shariyat-Ki-Sugmad.* This is the history of ECK in the lower worlds. From the Soul Plane on up, the Mahanta may teach one by direct experience with the Sound and Light. That is also the living Shariyat.

In short, the living Shariyat is every experience in your life that teaches something of SUGMAD's love for Soul—and Soul's love for IT.

## More of an ECKist

*My ninety-seven-year-old mother likes me to take her to church on Sundays. I enjoy the service, even if I don't participate. Am I being less of an ECKist by doing this?*

I think it's wonderful you can take your mother to church on Sunday. Our life is service: And if it's not for us, it is for others—their spiritual and emotional needs. Your mother needs your warm love because it is what makes living worthwhile for her.

Thank you for letting the ECK use you as Its instrument. It knows best.

## Expanding Awareness

*Why did Soul have to come into the lower worlds?*

*Did it do something bad in heaven and have to be punished?*

Thank you for your thoughtful question about Soul and Its arrival in the lower worlds. These Souls did nothing so *bad* as to have to be sent here, except that they needed to move to the next phase in SUGMAD's purpose for creating them. Please understand that the true spiritual worlds above the Fifth Plane do not come under the laws of logic from the Mental Plane. You may or may not have trouble understanding this.

SUGMAD created Souls so that IT could come into an expanding awareness of ITSELF through their experiences of *love and mercy* toward others. See?

The Souls at play in the spiritual worlds fulfilled a part of SUGMAD's self-discovery (if we can even use that word). After watching Souls at play for a while (again, time and space have no relevance in the spiritual worlds. They are merely a convenience for us when trying to communicate in human languages— all still from the Mental Plane), SUGMAD was ready for a whole new level of an expanding awareness of ITSELF. Soul exists because God loves It.

This element of SUGMAD—expanding awareness—also underlies the "plus element" of the ECK teachings. That is, there is always one more heaven. Always one more state of consciousness above the last.

## Reaching People

*A truly neurotic person attempted to take over a discussion group about a week ago. He was the sort of person who thrives on ridiculing others. After several fierce attacks on the people there, I abruptly told him the meeting was over. We all just stood up and left him*

304

*without any audience. Afterward, I admit to some serious soul-searching. Did I do the right thing?*

The ECK has Its own schedules and made sure you were at the discussion class to handle the disrupter. It's interesting how quickly the man was able to make the ECKists cower. And no wonder, when anger is unleashed in such a storm upon unsuspecting people who expected a quiet evening in ECK.

To me, such an attack says a lot. It means that the current wave of ECK presentations is catching the public's eye. The reaction is normal for these times and will be roughly as strong on the one hand as the ECK is on the other: for balance.

## Swings

*I really enjoyed attending the last seminar and seeing you physically. But I noticed that the talks are geared more to what the ECK can do for us rather than Self-Realization and God-Realization. Is this the right direction for our goals as ECKists?*

There are swings in the ECK programs, alternating between the "classical" high spirituality of Sound and Light presentations, to those about attributes of the enlightenment. An ultraconservative approach would be to have just private contemplations and study of the ECK discourses. Some would feel comfortable with that.

Others would prefer more of the social gatherings like Satsang classes and ECK seminars. Of this latter group, some would favor a main program of talks and no creative arts. Others like to know what ECK will do in their lives. These people are not Self- or God-Realized and so must be taught according to their needs and interests.

Thank you for your comments about the ECK seminar programs. They are well taken, and will be passed along to the seminar department.

## Law of Surrender

*How can we help get the message of ECK out? And how does this relate to learning about ourselves as Co-workers?*

The whole key behind getting out the message of ECK is set in the Law of Surrender: to give without any thought of receiving. ECK is love, says *The Shariyat*. To get love, we must give love. That summarizes the mission of Soul: to be a Co-worker with God.

I have people who ask for a Soul Travel experience so they can know that ECKANKAR is real. Few are willing to serve the ECK without expecting a reward. Those who do, see the miracles. They are not able, in words, to tell the spiritually blind how to get the same vision for themselves. The reason is that the glories of God are not given to one just because he asks for them. They must be earned in a sweet, childlike way.

I can only give the pure truth to a few. The rest of the people demand answers to material needs like more money. To each is given according to his service and faith in ECK. Some don't get much. Such are the different states of consciousness that the Vairagi ECK Masters deal with each day.

## Soothe Troubled Waters

*There are times when life gets extremely hard. Work gets stressful, and my health worsens.*

*I noticed this at the beginning of the Persian Gulf War and just before the dissolution of the Soviet Union. My impression was that ECKists were helping on the inner as these karmic events were set in motion.*

*Am I just having personal illness and stress, or is the ECK consciousness really part of the unfolding of world events?*

Your feelings are right, of course. As an ECKist, you are a channel for the divine Light and Sound to help soothe troubled waters.

Be careful, though, as an ECK leader not to let the added spiritual load become an excuse to treat others thoughtlessly. You will need to exercise more love, patience, and understanding with others.

Choose one or two of the initiates who you know are spiritually sound to help you do some of the ECK work. Your health, your family, and your job are equally as important as the ECK service. I don't want you to harm your health or lose touch with your family. We need the love and support of those dear to us.

*My country is going through great political upheaval. Can I as a vehicle of the Light and Sound help this situation?*

I know the great difficulties your country is facing in the opinion of the world. This could cause problems of instability in the political area soon, more than in the past.

The ECK chelas can blunt much of this destructiveness as they go about as conscious channels for the ECK. How? By not being preachy about their beliefs and practices but simply walking among people while being actively aware of the grace of God that walks with them.

Anytime one sets out on a mission for the Mahanta, every possible attempt is made to defeat him. The resistance gets much greater as one enters the high worlds of ECK, but so does one's spiritual strength.

*A neighboring country is having problems in presenting the message of ECK. I have traveled there with love and humor to assist in any way the RESA sees fit. Sometimes, I guess, we can get caught in personality traps and do not see the ECK at work. Is there anything I can do?*

Thank you most kindly for taking a trip there. The ECK comes through those who love It, giving others the spiritual help they need. You act with proper detachment, even when the ECK uses you as a vehicle to accomplish a spiritual good that you may not be aware of for some time.

As you well know, lighting the Light of ECK in any place takes enormous amounts of patience and love. Only continued diligence to the task has any hope of long-term success. Our mere presence allows the divine ECK to work miracles in our daily life without our ever having to say anything to anyone, if that is how we are most comfortable.

## Families and God

*When I attend ECK meetings, it causes a lot of conflict in my family because my husband is not an ECKist. What's the best way to handle conflict like this?*

If you find a conflict between your family and attending ECK meetings, give more time to your family and go to fewer meetings. We are trying to create a life that is as balanced as possible, and our families come first.

You do have the Sound of the Holy Spirit as a part of your spiritual life, so this means things are going well for you.

*Please elaborate on the priorities you set in your life.*

First, God. Not so that we become so attached to the idea of God—because then we lose IT—but the first relationship to have is with the Divine, the Ocean of Love and Mercy.

Secondly, we take care of those responsibilities closest to us, including family. We get this squared away. We're then working from a position of power and love when we work in the ECK organization. We're in a position of strength, not scattered, not rushing.

Third is ECKANKAR. But take care of your responsibilities first.

## Law of Love

*I quarreled with a friend who had told me something in confidence. He believed I betrayed his trust. Later he left ECK. I don't know if he left because of our quarrel, but I feel so bad.*

You did not give away the secret of your friend, who had confided in at least one other person and who knows how many others besides you?

The Law of Love is above the Law of Silence. Do not ruin your happiness, thinking that you did some horrible deed that caused your friend to leave ECK.

One cannot ever leave ECK, because It is life. He did what was best for him.

And don't feel responsible because he introduced

you to ECKANKAR. Often, a person gains much spiritually by introducing another to the way of Sound and Light. That may be the very reason he came into this life.

You are too willing to blame yourself when things go wrong, and perhaps your friend is too quick to accuse another of being the cause of his problems.

What did happen, however, is that you had a chance to love someone with your whole heart. Not many people are able to achieve such a state of selflessness. Whatever others do with pure love is up to them, whether they accept the gift or turn from it.

There is no spiritual reason to continue to hold yourself responsible for the direction your friend is taking with his life. Love as you have before, and the joy of living will again be yours.

## Community Service

*How does community service fit in with ECK? I am a volunteer with the Red Cross and in our local hospital.*

I am very happy about your volunteer work with the Red Cross and in the hospital. This service will do more to diminish any barriers that might exist between you and ECK than I can think of.

The heart of the ECK path is love, love for the divine principle of being. Your loving service to the ECK is well regarded in the spiritual circles of the ECK Brotherhood.

Each culture, and the different levels in it, must be approached in a unique way. Perhaps you already do it, but a helpful practice that opens the spiritual eyesight and perception at a moment's notice is declaring oneself a vehicle for God.

This can be done in a most simple way, for instance: "I declare myself a vehicle for the SUGMAD, the ECK, and the Mahanta." This can be done when you wake up; and there is more effect if you can say it aloud—in the privacy of the bathroom or bedroom so as not to disturb family members. It is also effective if done silently at special times during the day when you wish to be opened more completely to Divine Spirit. An example is before an ECK talk at a seminar, or if you are present at someone's translation, where it can be done silently.

## A Silent Channel

*In the past I have been a member of the Freemasons, and now I am a High Initiate in ECKANKAR. Is there any way I can be a silent Vahana among other Freemasons without conflicting with ECK?*

You know the quiet ways that someone may choose to work in the cause for Divine Spirit, and you should enjoy that right. Your membership in the Freemasons, however, could stand in the way of your leadership in outer ECK activities. This is because someone would always talk about it, and it might upset those new to the path of ECK. But if you have no objection to working quietly in the background as a Higher Initiate among Freemasons, I have no objection. I know that your loyalty and love are founded in the Light and Sound of God.

You may be the silent doorway for certain Freemasons to find ECKANKAR.

## ECK Explorers

*I've had strong inner guidance that's becoming increasingly difficult to ignore. It's been pushing me to explore the possibility of becoming an interfaith minister. I would take a class and become ordained. Have any other ECKists done this? Can you help me resolve this conflict so that I can move on in my training?*

I think your wish to become an interfaith minister is an excellent one. Everyday life is a harbor full of vessels of every size, whose passengers all have special cargoes and destinations. You're learning to become a harbormaster, one who makes sense out of the apparent chaos on the waterway.

Paul once spoke of ECKists who would go out into all parts of life to tell people of the Light and Sound of God. Some of the ECK Vahanas would also become interfaith ministers.

About 1890, the U.S. census bureau made the announcement: There is no more frontier. The need for mountain men and explorers had long before come to an end. But we had only ended a very necessary but elementary chapter in U.S. history: of *geographic* conquest and exploration. The adventurers still lived on, except now they went on new quests: in medicine, in science, and in religious and political freedoms. Since then, we've gone to the moon, into far outer space, to the ocean's bottom, and into the smallest part of the cell structure. Life is more interesting than ever.

As I see it, the time of greatest challenge and adventure for ECK initiates is just beginning. The Golden Age begins now. Please let me know what you learn, should you decide to enter the interfaith ministry. It's a very important link between the ECK teachings and orthodox religions.

## What Is the Main Focus of ECK?

*At recent seminars, you have talked about abortion, AIDS, and homosexuality. I find these topics very important today. Why aren't these issues formally addressed in workshops at seminars?*

They are social issues. The main purpose of the ECK teachings is to help people find their way back home to God, no matter what their circumstances in life.

People have all sorts of problems in life, simply because that is the way of things on earth. There are those who have to deal with heart disease, cancer, mental and emotional problems, old age, deafness, war in their homeland, crime on the streets, and even the effects of accidents.

The teachings of ECK are about spiritual freedom. The main focus in ECK is not on relationships, an abused childhood, or on any of the other social conditions that result from karma that people bring from the past. We look at these problems from the top. How can people gain in spiritual freedom and not do in the future more of what has brought on their problems of today?

Yes, we must deal with the issues of daily life. However, we also must watch our emotions and not let them trap us into tunnel vision.

This would only bring on more lifetimes in spiritual darkness.

## Being Divine Love

*I have been in ECK for twenty years and have never heard the Sound or seen the Light or your inner presence. I've only had patience and hope that I could someday know the reason why I lack these experiences. How can I be a Co-worker if I can't accomplish your spiritual direction to have the Light and Sound?*

The difficulty of teaching people about ECK is that each person is unique, which means that the general spiritual guidelines in the ECK works do not *seem* to work for some. But they do.

While I like to see everyone in ECK have a conscious experience with the Sound and Light or the inner part of myself, the overall objective is to show them how to love. After all, the Light and Sound are only divine love in motion. The same principle applies to the Mahanta, the inner guide. They are all aspects of divine love.

The lessons of earth are to show one how to gain the good in life. At first, in early incarnations, Soul looks to power and ambition. Then It seeks phenomena and the religious life. But all these pass away. Then, in the end, there's only love and service to God.

You are a down-to-earth and practical person. Look for quiet ways to give love to others. Your lesson now is the fullness of love as the fountain of life.

## Kal's Job

*Would you please explain to me why the Kal, the negative power, is in this physical world causing confusion for people?*

It's his job.

People will find life confusing until they can open the Spiritual Eye, which sees through the play of illusion the Kal throws over them like a hood. ECKists who are further ahead spiritually don't go around in a state of confusion from him anymore.

You can learn to see life clearly too. Do the Spiritual Exercises of ECK. So many people cannot let go of their personalities and egos when trying to serve God and others. No wonder they botch things up.

## Going Forward

*My life is changing a lot as I grow spiritually. Sometimes I feel very lonely. How can I keep my head above water and still serve God?*

Sometimes people on the path of ECK struggle with life for a while, and just when they're starting to make headway then they throw up their hands and say, "What's the use?" Maybe they're right that there's no point for them with these teachings; they're looking to become healthy, wealthy, and wise. I have no objection to that, but Divine Spirit isn't at all concerned with those things. Spirit drags us along to our eventual destiny.

Nobody will know your sacrifices and disciplines. Nor will you always believe that they are really necessary or worth the trouble. I never looked back and not too far ahead—both are fearsome because the mind begins playing with the awesome possibilities.

Keep listening to ECK. It has brought you farther than most people will realize in several lifetimes. The way gets lonely, but life works in cycles. This cycle will dissolve when all is learned. It has to, because that is the Law of Spirit.

## Symbols of Light

*Can you tell me the purpose for the ⵣ symbol and the six-pointed blue star of ECK?*

The ECK symbol ⵣ stands for the Holy Spirit. We wear it to show our respect for ECK, our name for the Holy Spirit. Those who put their minds on a holy emblem of their religion often receive divine protection when they're in trouble. The ECK symbol also helps ECKists know who are ECKists among strangers.

315

The six-pointed star is an ECK emblem that stands for the Light of God. It is the same star that is said to have shone over Bethlehem at the birth of Christ. Although people of the Jewish religion have the emblem of a six-pointed star, too, it was originally linked very directly to the Light of God. Most people have forgotten that original meaning and have today attached lesser meaning to the six-pointed star.

In ECKANKAR, some members have seen it as a blue light, while others speak mainly of white or a high yellow. Wise men saw the star two thousand years ago, and those people with a pure, loving heart still see it today while doing the Spiritual Exercises of ECK, our way of praying.


## A Common Language

*What's the best way to present ECK to people? Should we think about how we present ECK or just do it? As a writer, I wonder how to tell others about this spiritual path, but I'm concerned that if I work too hard on how I say things, I will lose the spirit of ECK.*

The spiritual works of ECK give a real advantage to someone who is looking for truth.

Material about ECK can be well written without tricking people, without violating spiritual laws. A novice wants purity sometimes at the expense of common sense, and it is our job to find the balance where we tell the inquirer about the ECK services in a clear, friendly, and attractive manner.

There is no point in ignoring the development of writing and communication skills today. If we know that short sentences are easier for today's reader to understand—because the poor educational system has left him that way—use the simple way. It is not a crime. Do not use a 1930s writing style in a mistaken belief that the stilted and incomprehensible is somehow more spiritual.

Find exactly where the consciousness of today's people is at, and then address it right where it is, in a language it can understand.

If we can find the formula that tells people about ECK in a way they can understand and appreciate—and still give them complete freedom—we will have created a masterpiece. The major goal all initiates have is to establish the ECK teachings around the world in a way the people at home can understand and love.

## How to Love God

*How can I love God more and serve IT more?*

The essential purpose for being in ECK is for spiritual enrichment. It is greater than can be expressed in words, for it is the experience of God that we seek.

I went into a store tonight. A woman checker in her early fifties checked out my purchases. She said she preferred the job of checker rather than stocking the aisles. "I don't want to hide from people," she said. "Up here at the check stand it's always fresh because of the different people I serve."

The ECK puts Soul through this kind of work in order for It to learn to be a Co-worker with God. The most effective way to teach the principles of ECK to others is to demonstrate them. How you live your everyday life tells others more about the ECK ideals than any sermon ever could.

Some days the going gets easier, and other days you just keep your head down. The fact is, the higher you go, you find there are greater things thrown up to try and stop you. But you also find you have more resources to figure your way out of the paper bag.

Quietly living ECK is the hardest thing one can do if he tries to force it. Otherwise, if one's actions are guided by love and understanding, it is the easiest and most natural thing one could imagine.

The ECK is always opening doors for us to go through if we are advancing spiritually. It means that Divine Spirit is giving us the opportunity to move into a greater life if we have the awareness to see what is being offered us. We also have to personally take whatever steps are necessary to walk through that door which leads to a more abundant life.

You have the opportunity to move into a greater state of consciousness. Watch for openings.

# Glossary

Words set in SMALL CAPS are defined elsewhere in this glossary.

ARAHATA. An experienced and qualified teacher for ECKANKAR classes.

CHELA. A spiritual student.

ECK. The Life Force, the Holy Spirit, or Audible Life Current which sustains all life.

ECKANKAR. Religion of the Light and Sound of God. Also known as the Ancient Science of SOUL TRAVEL. A truly spiritual religion for the individual in modern times, known as the secret path to God via dreams and SOUL TRAVEL. The teachings provide a framework for anyone to explore their own spiritual experiences. Established by Paul Twitchell, the modern-day founder, in 1965.

ECK MASTERS. Spiritual Masters who can assist and protect people in their spiritual studies and travels. The ECK Masters are from a long line of God-Realized SOULS who know the responsibility that goes with spiritual freedom.

HU. The most ancient, secret name for God. The singing of the word HU, pronounced like the word *hue,* is considered a love song to God. It is sung in the ECK Worship Service.

INITIATION. Earned by the ECK member through spiritual unfoldment and service to God. The initiation is a private ceremony in which the individual is linked to the Sound and Light of God.

LIVING ECK MASTER. The title of the spiritual leader of ECKANKAR. His duty is to lead SOULS back to God. The Living ECK Master can assist spiritual students physically as the

319

Outer Master, in the dream state as the Dream Master, and in the spiritual worlds as the Inner Master. Sri Harold Klemp became the Living ECK Master in 1981.

MAHANTA. A title to describe the highest state of God Consciousness on earth, often embodied in the LIVING ECK MASTER. He is the Living Word.

PLANES. The levels of heaven, such as the Astral, Causal, Mental, Etheric, and Soul planes.

SATSANG. A class in which students of ECK study a monthly lesson from ECKANKAR.

THE SHARIYAT-KI-SUGMAD. The sacred scriptures of ECKANKAR. The scriptures are comprised of twelve volumes in the spiritual worlds. The first two were transcribed from the inner PLANES by Paul Twitchell, modern-day founder of ECKANKAR.

SOUL. The True Self. The inner, most sacred part of each person. Soul exists before birth and lives on after the death of the physical body. As a spark of God, Soul can see, know, and perceive all things. It is the creative center of Its own world.

SOUL TRAVEL. The expansion of consciousness. The ability of SOUL to transcend the physical body and travel into the spiritual worlds of God. Soul Travel is taught only by the LIVING ECK MASTER. It helps people unfold spiritually and can provide proof of the existence of God and life after death.

SOUND AND LIGHT OF ECK. The Holy Spirit. The two aspects through which God appears in the lower worlds. People can experience them by looking and listening within themselves and through SOUL TRAVEL.

SPIRITUAL EXERCISES OF ECK. The daily practice of certain techniques to get us in touch with the Light and Sound of God.

SUGMAD. A sacred name for God. SUGMAD is neither masculine nor feminine; IT is the source of all life.

WAH Z. The spiritual name of Sri Harold Klemp. It means the Secret Doctrine. It is his name in the spiritual worlds.

# How to Take the Next Step on Your Spiritual Journey

Find your own answers to questions about your past, present, and future through the ancient wisdom of ECKANKAR. Take the next bold step on your spiritual journey.

ECKANKAR can show you why special attention from God is neither random nor only for a few saints. It is for anyone who opens his heart to Divine Spirit, the Light and Sound of God.

Are you looking for the secrets of life and the afterlife? Sri Harold Klemp, today's spiritual leader of ECKANKAR, and Paul Twitchell, its modern-day founder, have written a series of monthly discourses that give unique Spiritual Exercises of ECK. They can lead you in a direct way to God. Those who join ECKANKAR, Religion of the Light and Sound of God, can receive these monthly discourses.

## As a Member of ECKANKAR You'll Discover . . .

1. The most direct route home to God through the ECK teachings on the Light and Sound. Plus the opportunity to gain wisdom, charity, and spiritual freedom in this lifetime through the ECK initiations.

2. The spiritual meaning of dreams, Soul Travel techniques, and ways to establish a personal relationship with Divine Spirit through study of monthly discourses. These discourses are for the entire family. You may study them alone at home or in a class with others.

3. Secrets of self-mastery in a Wisdom Note and articles by the Living ECK Master in the *Mystic World,* a quarterly newsletter. In it are also letters and articles from ECK members around the world.

4. Upcoming ECK seminars and other activities worldwide, new study materials from ECKANKAR, and more, in special mailings. Join the excitement. Have the fulfilling experience of attending major ECK seminars!

5. The joy of the ECK Satsang (discourse study) experience in classes and book discussions. Share spiritual experiences and find answers to your questions about the ECK teachings.

## How to Find Out More

To request membership in ECKANKAR using your credit card (or for a free booklet on membership) call (612) 544-0066, weekdays, between 8:00 a.m. and 5:00 p.m., central time. Or write to: ECKANKAR, Att: Information, P.O. Box 27300, Minneapolis, MN 55427 U.S.A.

# Introductory Books on ECKANKAR

### We Come as Eagles
Harold Klemp

Harold Klemp, spiritual leader of ECKANKAR, discusses how: to discover our greatness as Soul; the power of divine love can bring spiritual healing; to travel by thought, stop nightmares, and recognize when God is speaking to us.

### ECKANKAR—Ancient Wisdom for Today

Are you one of the millions who have heard God speak to you through a profound spiritual experience? This introductory book will show you how dreams, Soul Travel, and experiences with past lives are ways God speaks to you. An entertaining, easy-to-read approach to ECKANKAR. Reading this little book can give you new perspectives on your spiritual life.

### The Spiritual Exercises of ECK
Harold Klemp

This book is a staircase with 131 steps. It's a special staircase, because you don't have to climb all the steps to get to the top. Each step is a spiritual exercise, a way to help you explore your inner worlds. And what awaits you at the top? The doorway to spiritual freedom, self-mastery, wisdom, and love.

### HU: A Love Song to God
(Audiocassette)

Learn how to sing an ancient name for God, HU (pronounced like the word *hue*). A wonderful introduction to ECKANKAR, this two-tape set is designed to help listeners of any religious or philosophical background benefit from the gifts of the Holy Spirit. It includes an explanation of the HU, stories about how Divine Spirit works in daily life, and exercises to uplift you spiritually.

**For fastest service, phone (612) 544-0066** weekdays between 8 a.m. and 5 p.m., central time, to request books using your credit card, or look under **ECKANKAR** in your phone book for an ECKANKAR Center near you. Or write: **ECKANKAR, Att: Information, P.O. Box 27300, Minneapolis, MN 55427 U.S.A.**

# There May Be an
# ECKANKAR Study Group near You

ECKANKAR offers a variety of local and international activities for the spiritual seeker. With hundreds of study groups worldwide, ECKANKAR is near you! Many areas have ECKANKAR Centers where you can browse through the books in a quiet, unpressured environment, talk with others who share an interest in this ancient teaching, and attend beginning discussion classes on how to gain the attributes of Soul: wisdom, power, love, and freedom.

Around the world, ECKANKAR study groups offer special one-day or weekend seminars on the basic teachings of ECKANKAR. Check your phone book under **ECKANKAR**, or call **(612) 544-0066** for membership information and the location of the ECKANKAR Center or study group nearest you. Or write **ECKANKAR, Att: Information, P.O. Box 27300, Minneapolis, MN 55427 U.S.A.**

☐ Please send me information on the nearest ECKANKAR discussion or study group in my area.

☐ Please send me more information about membership in ECKANKAR, which includes a twelve-month spiritual study.

Please type or print clearly                                    810

Name _____

Street_____ Apt. # _____

City _____ State/Prov. _____

ZIP/Postal Code _____ Country _____